Creating Community:

A Roundtable on Canadian Aboriginal Literature

Creating Community:

A Roundtable on Canadian Aboriginal Literature

Edited by Renate Eigenbrod
and Jo-Ann Episkenew

National Library of Canada Cataloguing in Publication Data

Main entry under title:

Creating community
ISBN 1-894778-08-1

1. Canadian literature (English) – Indian authors – History and criticism.* 2. Indian literature – Canada – History and criticism. 3. Native peoples in literature.* I. Eigenbrod, Renate, 1944- II. Episkenew, Jo-Ann.

PS8089.5.16C73 2002 C810.9'897 C2002-910483-1
PR9188.2.15C73 2002

Editorial: Anneliese Baerg, Samuel W. Corrigan
Digital photography: Ken Frazer, Frazer Studio of Photography
Design: Jan Brancewicz
Typesetting/Composition: Cynthia F. Peech

THEYTUS
BOOKS
Green Mountain Road, Lot 45
RR #2, Site 50, Comp. 8
Penticton, BC
Canada V2A 6J7

BEARPAW
PUBLISHING
Brandon University
270 18th Street
Brandon, Manitoba
Canada R7A 6A9

The publisher acknowledges the support of the Canada Council for the Arts, the Department of Canadian Heritage and the British Columbia Arts Council in the publication of this book.

Canada Council for the Arts Conseil des Arts du Canada

Canada

TABLE OF CONTENTS

Introduction

Renate Eigenbrod
Jo-Ann Episkenew

A work is defined as literature when it is primarily aesthetic in structure and significance, because it conveys a particular confluence of meanings in ways that are particular to literary discourse. The imagination, the community of experience, the major emotions, the aesthetics of personal experience that give it communal significance, that render the personal in ways that make it part of the universal, that move the personal from the isolation of the private to the communion of the communitary – these are the distinguishing characteristics of literary work, and when and how truly […] a given narrative accomplishes these tasks determines its literary – that is communal – worth.

Paula Gunn Allen. *Spider Woman's Granddaughters,* 7-8

This book builds on three other anthologies of critical writing on Aboriginal literatures which have been published in Canada – *Native North America: Critical and Cultural Perspectives,* edited by Renée Hulan,[1] *Looking at the Words of Our People,* edited by Jeannette Armstrong and *(Ad)dressing Our Words,* edited by Armand Ruffo. While those three anthologies stress a North American and/or international focus, the present work is Canadian in the sense that it emphasizes Canadian Aboriginal literatures and that its contributors live in Canada. Many readers might question this limitation stating that the border between Canada and the United States has been imposed as a colonial structure. We agree. However, the imposition of the border has had far-reaching consequences, not the least of which have been the different patterns of colonization, which affect the literature produced by Indigenous people on either side of the border. As Emma LaRocque says in her contribution to this book: "There is an Aboriginal experience unique to the Canadian context."[2] Also, this anthology came about as the result of a roundtable discussion on Aboriginal Literature that took place at the Canadian Association for Commonwealth Literature and Language Studies (CACLALS) Conference held at the University of Alberta on May 26th, 2000, as part of the Canadian Social Sciences and Humanities Congress. Although defining/confining in some ways, national boundaries do provide the context for our teaching and researching of Aboriginal literatures in this country and hence need to be acknowledged.[3]

We are pleased that the scholarly articles and creative non-fiction contained in this anthology evoke the spirit and the sharing that manifested itself at the roundtable and therefore want to talk briefly about the ideas, events and people behind it.

It started at an earlier CACLALS Conference, in 1999 at Bishop's University. Following a panel on Aboriginal literature whose format was a conventional one—three read papers followed by a few minutes of discussion—a number of students and scholars reconvened in the dining hall where they expressed their frustration with this format. It was in the informal setting around a big table that the most productive interactions occurred and where the participants expressed their need for sharing beyond a few minutes question period. Followed by another long conversation between Jo-Ann and Renate late into the night, the idea of a roundtable was born. Over the winter of 1999/2000 in discussions between Renate and her Anishnabe graduate student Peter Rasevych at Lakehead University and with input from CACLALS President Wendy Robbins, a clearer idea developed and eventually a "call for participants" was sent out which read as follows:

> Call For Participants In A Roundtable Discussion on Aboriginal Literature: Pedagogical, Epistemological And Canonical Concerns.
> CACLALS at COSSH: May 26, 2000
>
> Those of you who plan to attend the 2000 Congress in Edmonton, consider your participation in a roundtable (or talking circle?) on Aboriginal (or Native or First Nations?) literature. Those of you who (want to) teach or research or study Aboriginal literature(s) may have concerns or questions that fall under the above heading, like: Is a text-based approach sufficient? Where to place it within the (English) curriculum – Canadian, Postcolonial/Commonwealth, Women Studies contexts or "a stream" of its own, cross-listed with Indigenous Learning/Native Studies? Any selection of texts that "should" be taught? Which literary theory to use? How does one gain access to cultural contexts? Which cultural knowledge can be transplanted into an academic setting? Who is qualified to teach traditional stories? Should the knowledge of an Indigenous language be a prerequisite for teaching and studying Aboriginal literature? And many other questions … Those of you who want to experience a different format than a series of read papers, join us in our circle. As Jo-Ann Thom (SIFC) put it: "Leave your papers at home and bring your brains." All we are asking for is your commitment to attend and make a contribution with a brief informal statement. We will list your names in the conference program, but the session is open to everybody.

Twelve people of Aboriginal and non-Aboriginal background expressed their interest; nine were able to come to Edmonton. No one knew what would happen because roundtable discussions are not common at conferences on English literature. As a result, everyone was surprised and pleased to see forty people crowded into the small room at the University of Alberta campus to join in the discussion on May 26th. Clearly, there was a need for such a forum.

As the participants included academics and students, creative writers and community people, the roundtable took on dimensions that were not anticipated. Although Renate and Peter did not want to call it a "talking circle," as had been suggested initially, because they did not think that it was appropriate to adopt a cultural ceremony in this venue, the discussion did take place in a circle. By its very nature this brought a spiritual dimension leading to community building rather than emphasizing divisions. The circle subverted the conventional format of the showcased experts situated at the front of the room addressing an audience with their prepared papers. Considering that the notion of ("outsider") expertise "has been and continues to be problematic for indigenous communities" (Smith 139) this visual arrangement of a gathering of Aboriginal and non-Aboriginal people was in itself important. It bestowed equal value on every person's contribution while at the same time illustrating the limited view of each position. Saulteaux/Cree playwright Margo Kane commenting on critical reviews of her play *Moonlodge* questions the judging "from a place of omniscience" since "I do not sit where the other sits and my view of life is different." (28) Participants noted that the study of Aboriginal literature compels readers, critics, and teachers to examine their own subject positions extending beyond racial and ethnic identification. Hence, eschewing false expert positions, our sharing of ideas, suggestions and experiences became personal and tentative emphasizing search rather than solutions.

Inherent in the use of the personal voice in the examination of Aboriginal literature is accountability, both to self and to the communities linked to the literature. This accountability demands that we rethink categorizations, labels, and assumptions, which are often distorted and sometimes entirely false. Participants believed that misinterpretations are indicative of the gap between increasing academic interest in Aboriginal literature and the persistent ignorance about Aboriginal communities, but noted that there is no simple solution to closing this gap. Dialoguing with Aboriginal communities and individuals is definitely needed for an understanding of culture-specific contexts of the literary works. A non-Aboriginal scholar who is also an activist may gain the most creditability among Aboriginal people yet is often not given credit for his or her work outside academia by the university employers. As Creek scholar Craig Womack notes about qualifications for "Native lit scholars": "he or she must go to MLA for job interviews and to present papers, or to other conferences equally removed from Indian communities, to remain credible in his or her department and to get tenure if the scholar works, or ever wants to work, in an English department." (7-8)

The emphasis on cultural specificity was often reiterated during the roundtable discussion (and made us choose the plural word of literature for the title of the book) as it ties in with many concerns about stereotypical, homogenizing approaches to "Native lit" frequently taught in one overview course or in a selection of "representative" texts. Also, beyond their specific cultural heritage "Native writers" bring to their literary creations individual preferences for themes and styles like any other writers, but such variations tend to be overlooked by scholars of "ethnic literature" who often approach a text with preconceived ideas about cultural background. In the case of Aboriginal literature, it is, for example, the expectation of humour—as Anishnabe poet Armand Garnet Ruffo emphasized—or, on the other hand, of the theme of oppression (a point made by Anna Marie Sewell). Although both may shape the literary work of an Aboriginal author, preconceived criteria like these easily become the basis for inclusion or exclusion in the publishing industry as well as in canons and curricula of educational institutions.

The rich debate of the roundtable may not have "revolutionized" the teaching of Aboriginal literatures as Aruna Srivastava cautions, but it showed everybody involved that we need to keep talking in order to stay truthful. While compiling this book, we remembered Annharte's lines from her poem "One Way to keep Track of Who is Talking":

> Frozen Indians and frozen conversations predominate.
> We mourn the ones at Wounded Knee. Our traditions
> buried in one grave. Our frozen circles of silence

do no honour to them. We talk to keep our
conversations from getting too dead.

Although it may seem that the procedure of transforming a roundtable *talk* into a roundtable *book* creates quite literally "frozen conversations," the editors believe that the spirit of the roundtable is still recognizable in the variety of voice and perspective. Also, the editors asked each contributor to preface his or her own paper with a quotation or an image by another writer or artist. This gesture towards another voice is meant to illustrate, as Jeannette Armstrong says, that "[c]reative acts are continuance links" (Cardinal and Armstrong 82), not isolated individual expressions but communal.

Anna Marie Sewell's "collection of thoughts, not necessarily in formal essay format" ("Natives on Native Literature: What do We Rightly Write? Or: Shot Headlong from the Cannon") was an obvious choice for the opening of a written version of a roundtable discussion. As an artist of Métis ancestry Sewell is not only concerned about being "herded into a *reservation* of ideas" (emphasis added) but proves her point that her writing is "from stronger stuff" than catering to assumptions about "Authentic Native Literature" in a playful, yet thought-provoking piece created by the moose/muse of inspiration. Still with the approach of a creative writer, **David Brundage's** "confessions" ("Confluence: Confessions of a White Writer Who Reads Native Lit") appreciate and celebrate Aboriginal writing but eschew judgments and definitions. He tries to explain how and why Native literature became influential in his life and in his own artistic career. Illustrating how in a country like Canada it is inevitable that "the intertwining of cultural experience and perspective" leads to "finding and adapting oneself through others," his "confessions" make us wonder how much of this "braiding" is largely unacknowledged in influences of Aboriginal outlook on Canadian non-Aboriginal writers and artists.

After the opening essays which cross multiple borders and eschew definitions, the book continues with two contributions by the editors themselves which, although written independently, emphasize concerns and boundaries. **Jo-Ann Episkenew** pleads for a "socially responsible" criticism of Aboriginal literatures, i.e. a criticism which examines the text not "without examining the context from which it is written" so that Aboriginal people do NOT "become abstractions, metaphors that signify whatever the critic is able to prove they signify" ("Socially Responsible Criticism: Aboriginal Literature, Ideology, and the Literary Canon"). Referring to a passage from Lee Maracle's short story "Polka Partners, Uptown Indians and White Folks" she points out the "risks attached to leaving the ivory tower to investigate the context of the literature." It is this departure from the conventional space a critic often prefers to reside in which **Renate Eigenbrod** pursues further in "Not Just a Text: 'Indigenizing" the Study of Indigenous Literatures." Drawing on an analysis of the theme of the artist character in recent Aboriginal novels, she argues in favour of a reading of Aboriginal texts which reflects their emphasis on community and "communitism" (Jace Weaver) and urges critics to replace the "Western" art/reality dualism for an inclusive understanding which respects the power of all creation.

During the roundtable discussions the point was made that while writers and artists create chaos, critics look for patterns, or as Doug Cardinal explains in one of his reflections on the creative process: "Knowledge is definite. It is definable.... Once something is created, it comes into the definable realm of things." (64) As critics we engage in debates which assess the appropriateness of definitions and patterns seen in certain texts, like postcolonial theories in relation to Aboriginal literatures. **Debra Dudek** in "Begin with the Text: Aboriginal Literatures and Postcolonial Theories" pursues this particular critical approach by illustrating the validity of postcolonial theorizing while at the same time "complicating postcolonial discussions" through an analysis of Louise Halfe's poetry. In another close reading of a text by an Aboriginal woman author, **Karen E. Macfarlane** employs in "Storying the Borderlands: Liminal Spaces and Narrative Strategies in Lee Maracle's *Ravensong*" Maracle's own "theory" of story and storytelling. Macfarlane shows how the "community of voices is an important element in reading notions of 'storying' (as an active, progressive, provisional process) in *Ravensong*" and how it counterbalances the border discourse of the novel. The latter is the more obvious characteristic of the narrative and tends to be considered the main one, especially by students. **Renée Hulan and Linda Warley** exemplify in an analysis of their teaching of Thomas King's novel *Medicine River* the difficulties of weaning students from a consumerist approach of easy responses to Canadian Aboriginal writing (which is often misleadingly simple) to understanding complexities. In "Comic Relief: Pedagogical Issues Around Thomas King's *Medicine River*", the two scholars explain the paradoxical reception of the novel. "Compared to *Green Grass Running Water*, King's *Medicine River* has received relatively little critical attention," but on the other hand it "has been enthusiastically reviewed" and "gratefully consumed" by students. Through their reading of the novel, Hulan and Warley demonstrate that easy consumption of Aboriginal literature has more to do with "cultural *illiteracy*" than with the presumed simplicity of the text.

Hulan and Warley's contribution is the first one in this collection, if read linearly, which incorporates pedagogical issues around Aboriginal literatures. The three subsequent papers further foreground pedagogy as well as the institutionalization of this literary field (which, of course, impacts on teaching methods). Again drawing on teaching experience, **Jennifer Kelly** ("'You Can't Get Angry with a Person's Life': Negotiating Aboriginal Women's Writing, Whiteness, and Multicultural Nationalism in a University Classroom") addresses the "complex, undertheorized, heavily charged, typically frightening, and often-exhilarating space commonly known as the 'University Aboriginal Literatures Classroom'." She utilizes class discussions on Beth Brant's *Writing as Witness*, Beatrice Culleton's *In Search of April Raintree* and Marie Campbell's *Half-breed* in order to illustrate her points about the challenges of "anti-racist pedagogical practices." While Kelly taught and wrote her paper from her position of a "white Canadian feminist," the main thrust of the article by **Sharron Proulx and Aruna Srivastava** ("A moose in the corridor": Teaching English, Aboriginal Pedagogies, and Institutional Resistance") lies with the experience of teaching from the position of women scholars of colour. They emphasize that in order to teach Aboriginal literatures respectfully we "must pay attention to the how, the process and pedagogy and not the what, the curriculum, the texts, the course outline." Tellingly, it was the process and the pedagogy which Sharron Proulx, a Métis educator, employed in her designing of an Aboriginal literature course at Mount Royal College, which caused her dismissal from the college. As this paper shows, the fight against institutional racism continues and, as Métis scholar **Emma LaRocque** testifies looking back at "two decades of teaching Canadian Native Literature ... in a large mid-Canadian, middle-class mainstream university," has always been a component in academia. In her paper "Teaching Aboriginal Literatures: The Discourse of Margins and Mainstreams", she questions existing canonical and institutional contexts by re-viewing qualifications of a Native literature scholar and by defining an Aboriginal, or more specifically Métis, epistemology. Her notion of "resistance scholarship" is based on her colonial experience as well as her Indigenous worldview as "a Cree-Métis of Red River roots." A cultural perspective linked to land and language is also important in the discussion of epistemological complexities by **Kristina Fagan**, a scholar from a different Métis background. Just starting out as a professor of Aboriginal literature, she calls for "openness and self-awareness" in a paper which she titled: "'What about you?': Approaching the Study of Native Literature." Her suggestions, which emphasize culture-specific approaches, are encouraging and inspiring in so far as she "tried to model" in the paper itself the methodology she considers appropriate.

Fagan's vision of the future of Native Literature studies concludes a series of articles in this collection which discusses the rightfulness of pedagogical and analytical approaches and the problems of institutional contexts. However, we decided to add another ending which emphasizes very clearly the importance of the sheer existence of Aboriginal literatures on a personal and a societal level. **Jonathan R. Dewar** ("Fringes, Imposture, and Connections: Armand Ruffo's *Grey Owl: The Mystery of Archie Belaney* and 'Communitist' Literature.") reads Ruffo's auto/biographical collage not just as the work of a Native author about a non-Native imposter, or merely as aesthetic journeys into the exploration of themes of identity and authenticity, but also as part of his "legitimate attempts to learn as much about his heritage as possible" and hence to "explore the boundaries of community." As a person of mixed blood heritage he wrote himself into an analysis of Ruffo's text and thus realized that "Native literature" is a tool that teaches." In the case of Dewar's choice of literature, the work "teaches" about the complexity of insider/outsider discourses, while the literature discussed by the last contributor, **Deanna Reder**, "teaches" about destruction and renewal in the lives of Aboriginal people, including her own life ("Stories of Destruction and Renewal: Images of Fireweed in Autobiographical Fiction by Shirley Sterling and Tomson Highway"). In the metaphor of thc fireweed (visually emphasized throughout this anthology) Reder captures not only a central image in two works of Native autobiographical fiction, but also a descriptor for Native autobiographies and Native literature in general since fireweed is "the textual equivalent of the relentlessly enduring perennial that is first to reappear in earth scarred by fire, ironically spreading 'like wildfire'." By using this image as a central concept in her analysis, Reder asserts the important role which Aboriginal literature plays in processes of decolonization and healing.

Because of its potential as a powerful "tool" Aboriginal literatures need more roundtables, verbally and in writing. We therefore hope that for our readers this book may become, in Sewell's words, "a launching pad for their ideas, discussions and conclusions." In our own conclusions of an introduction to a book celebrating community we want to point toward the epigraph for the first essay which reminds all of us of "the greatness of creation" in which we are "small and vulnerable" but which also makes us "relatives" as "[t]he winds are common to us all." (Cuthand 105)

Notes

1. We want to thank Renée Hulan for her encouragement and help at the initial stage of this publication.
2. Two recent comparative studies (without the inclusion of literature) illuminate some differences:
Nichols, Roger L. *Indians in the United States and Canada: A Comparative History*. Lincoln and London: University of Nebraska Press, 1998.
St. Germain, Jill. *Indian Treaty-Making Policy in the United States and Canada. 1867-1877*. Toronto: University of Toronto Press, 2001.
3. The different approaches in two recent single author studies on Canadian Aboriginal literatures may illustrate the conflicting views on this issue. While Helen Hoy in *How Should I Read These?* indicates a national context in the subtitle *Native Women Writers in Canada* and further explains in her introduction the importance of Canadian-specific legislation for the literature, Dee Horne chooses the (misleading) title *Contemporary American Indian Writing* meant to devalidate the border, as she explains, for a book which focuses exclusively on Aboriginal literature written in Canada.

Works Cited

Annharte. *Being On The Moon*. Winlaw, BC: Polestar Press Ltd. 1990.

Cardinal, Douglas and Jeannette Armstrong. *The Native Creative Process*. Penticton, BC: Theytus Books, 1991.

Cuthand, Beth. "Feast of Four Winds." *Crisp Blue Edges: Indigenous Creative Non-Fiction*. Ed. Rasunah Marsden. Penticton, BC: Theytus Books, 2000. 103-17.

Kane, Margo. "From the Centre of the Circle the Story Emerges." *Canadian Theatre Review* 68 (Fall 1991): 26-29.

Smith, Linda Tuhiwai. *Decolonizing Methodologies: Research and Indigenous Peoples*. London and New York: Zed Books Ltd., 1999.

Womack, Craig. *Red on Red: Native American Literary Separatism*. Minneapolis: University of Minnesota Press, 1999.

Natives on Native Literature: What do We Rightly Write? Or: Shot Headfirst from the Canon

Anna Marie Sewell

a collection of thoughts, not necessarily in a formal essay format

"The old man told me to tell the people what to expect during the ceremony and I began to speak like this,
'My relatives. We are here today to honour the Four Winds. Who ever hears the winds can attest to their words. They know that we are small and weak in the force of the greatness of creation. They know we are nothing without the land. They see that we come from every direction and that we are small and vulnerable before them.'"

Beth Cuthand "Feast for the Four Winds" in *Crisp Blue Edges: Indigenous Creative Non-Fiction*. Edited by Rasunah Marsden.

When i consider Native Literature, one thing is readily apparent to me: the existence of Native Literature as a genre is based on bigotry.

This should not, on the one hand, be too surprising. After all, Canada is a country founded in large part on treaties between First Nations and the crown of England. These treaties, from the beginning, have been ambiguous and subject to misinterpretation and downright abuse, for the purpose of making way for the Empire by solving Our Indian Problem. Part of the solution has involved marginalizing treaties and indigenous history, and promoting the idea of a Vanishing Race. Canada is young, runs this idea, but the treaties and the indigenous people's part in our history, that was over long ago.

However, Canadians today are still going through the treaty-making process. The demographics, the players, the power structures have evolved, but the process remains; and injustices remain. It has taken a long time for Native writers to gain access to mainstream publication, so that we could talk about our reality; and those who led the way brought with them uncomfortable truths. Does the fact that we now can discuss "Native Literature" mean that those truths are being heard? I'd like to think so.

However, i really wonder if this is so, because if one is a Native and a writer, one is then assumed to belong under the heading "Native Literature" and then runs the risk of being herded into a reservation of ideas. i have heard Natives hold forth the opinion that the only authentically Native life there is is the life On the Reservation, as if reservations were our natural choice of design for sustainable, healthy communities, and not the result of a colonial policy aimed at solving Our Indian Problem via isolation, forced assimilation and/or genocide.

In the same way, somehow, although this is probably not anybody's conscious intent, Native Literature seems sometimes to have taken on the character of the worst kind of reserve, where the options for meaningful employment within a healthy community are crushed into a cycle of hopelessness, helplessness and violation. Real Indians live on the Rez. In parallel, the things "we" write about are: Our oppression, Our experiences as drunks and druggies and prostitutes, how we miraculously Found Our Culture and got healed, and Eagles and/or Bears and/or Wolves.

And if one doesn't write about these things? One hears that their work is not Native enough. This one has heard that, and can only respond: Why should i accept that only certain of my experiences are valid and useful and Native? Did "we"—Aboriginal people—decide that there were only a few valid patterns for our lives as Natives? And that these patterns must involve a quota of particular kinds of suffering? And that, now that we haven't lived up to our billing as a Vanishing Race, our new role is as a culturally bereft remainder, pleading to be given back our dignity?

Must we always go on about how we're doing carrying the Whiteman's Burden? – because if that's the case, i'm out of it. And i'll stay out. And this is not because i don't know the weight of it. It is because something good might happen for us if we just put it down for a moment, that burden. We could poke a hole in it, and let the air out of a tired old sack of an idea that has had its day.

My life is real, and i'd like to honour the reality of this life, which is a gift which my family struggled hard to give to me. It's not cut from a racist pattern that says i must experience and write about only certain ideas, in order to be part of the Canon of Native Literature. For whom are we writing when we have a limited range of topics which are considered Authentic Native Literature? Surely i am no less Native when i consider the global implications of the Free Trade Area of the Americas, or the beauty of a Japanese temple, than i am should i spend my energy writing to seek acceptance for the relative worth of my personal stumble down the prescribed Aboriginal Via Dolorosa. i have been told that there is an audience for my pain, so long as that pain is part of the accepted glossary of Native suffering. It's not that i don't know about some of the darkness that colonial Canadian practices feed. For the sake of healing, though, i'm trying to weave my life, and my writing, from stronger stuff.

the moose of inspiration and the horse of whimsy

When i was a child, i had no idea there was such a thing as targeting an audience. I thought writers just wrote, and anyone who liked what they wrote could read it. Myself, i wrote about whatever moved my heart. A lot of my earliest compositions were about horses.

Horse songs, horse poems, horse mysteries, i wrote 'em all; without regard for the lines between disciplines. I also drew, painted, sculpted and danced horses. Foreshadowing my studies in theatre, or perhaps in homage to shamanic ancestors, i *became* horses. In fact, one of my earliest memories is of the Catholic church at Rio Grand, Alberta, where, at the age of two, the spirit overcame me one Sunday, and i became a horse during Mass. With a child's purity of purpose, the horse who was me somehow sprang onto the elbow ledge on the back of the pew, and trotted unerringly to the first available bale of hay, which i began to devour.

I came only to find my mortified mother had snatched the rolled up weekly missal from my jaws and was trying to silence my equine outrage at my stolen dinner, before the wrath of God and the community could smite us down. My father, who had always known my instinctive soul, lifted me up and carried me out into the foyer of the church. There, we strolled along a gallery of pictures depicting the stations of the cross, and he gently explained that while it was very good indeed to be a horse, sometimes a person just had to keep it to their own self. It seemed to me, looking around from my vantage point high in his arms, that the painted people on the walls were nodding at his matter of fact wisdom.

'Dad,' i asked, 'are they ever horses like you and me?'

'Sometimes, my girl, i'm sure they are.'

Sometimes, it's good to be descended from animist folk.
It's always good to be understood.

So now, when i write, i try to hold that same spirit of calm and love - sometimes i picture my dad and the serene people in the church-foyer pictures, and the robin's-egg blue that surrounds them all. Can i write beauty? Can i reach that part of every reader who chances along, that part that knows what it is to be overcome by the playful pull of horsekind? We are all like that, sometimes, aren't we? And i know we have to keep it to our ownselves sometimes, because there's another kind of praying going on; but here, on this page, shall we not prance together?

Oh, we don't have to do horses in particular, by the way. Just so long as we breathe freely and accept between us that we are moving in a mystery. Which reminds me of my first year university art professor, Mary Grayson, who used to speak of the Moose of Inspiration – of course she meant the Muse, but it amused her to say Moose, and i'm a better person because she did. How much richer life is when you can picture a big-nosed ungulant hovering just above your shoulder, ready for your breathing to sink to the same level, so you can rise on the divine and moosely breath into the realms of inspiration. This is art. This is magic. This is healing. This is just plain silly, too, but talk to the Moose, if it bugs you.

When in Rome –

I like to amuse myself with thoughts of Pocahontas. Inaccurate thoughts, to be exact. So sad, her life, if you are an Aboriginal woman yourself, and her life can be read as a pattern for our fate: Lauded for what some say was a real mistake –saving some foreigner from a spot of pre-emptive foreign policy; married off in a political deal, and sent to a foreign land to become an exotic parlour oddity, at the same time as her community at home was being ravaged; probably often lonesome for the language, the customs, the food and the land she called her own; and then, dead of some dreaded European disease in draughty olde England, at far too tender an age, and her bones left to feed strange dirt. Then again, says the Moose, Elvis is reputed to be 'of the blood,' a 'breed' descended of some southern-fried tribe. Follow me now – not only are there legends about his Choctaw hair, but there are also legends about how he's not really dead. He just faked it so he could be free of his now-unwanted fame, and live as a person again. He keeps turning up in burger joints, and garages, and small obscure human places all around the nation that adored, and devoured, him. He could've just been stricken by this solution as a brand new plan. Then again, he could have been following in some dainty moccasin prints. See, reminded of Elvis, i get to thinking, maybe our gal Pokey gets to thinking, 'i'm tired of this media circus, Indian princess, friend of the white man, exotic lovely on parade gig – think i'll die, so as to gain some breathing space.' Ah, yeah, says the Moose. Ah, i say, but how does she figure out how to survive in white England, given that she's brown? Italians, replies the Moose. Or she could try to pass for Spanish, or maybe French.

But most intriguingly, say she decides to remake herself as an Italian. And you know she had to be a pretty sharp cookie, princess and all, and she's probably gone and educated herself in her travels, too. At least, she'll have been told about the Church. And if she is researching Italian ways and disguises, what if she learned the tale of Pope Joan? What if she thought, 'it might be fun …' that's when i put it all together, and the Moose starts giggling, because we've both pictured it, a poster for a feature film i'm sure i'll never make, about an adventurous brown Gidget/Erin Brockowitz/Mary Tyler Moore of a gal, free of her identity, striking a secret blow for her endangered people back home. This movie is called 'Pope-ahantas,' and the tag-line for the trailer is, "When in Rome, Take Over."

Trickster goes to Skoool, or "Hi there! I'm your Indian Problem."

My late sister Cathy once showed me a paper she was about to hand in. Well, okay, this happened more than once, but this one particular time it was a paper about the experience of being Aboriginal at university, and she had compiled a catalogue of typical attitudes and encounters. I laughed a lot, reading it, because she hit the nail repeatedly on the head - this, too, had been my lot as a student. One entry into her list was particularly poignant to me, as a gal who passes the colour bar. You see, i'm not particularly slow to learn. In fact, i do okay academically, if the wind is right and my life is balanced and the topic turns me on.

For example, i did really well in South East Asian History. I achieved excellent grades, and earned enough respect from my prof that he was happy to write me a letter of reference for a summer writing job. When he retired, and he and his wife were getting ready to move out to the country, i was honoured to be one of the chosen few students who were allowed to help.

It was the end of an era, i thought, shifting boxes down the hall. Here, sealed in discreet wrapping tape, was all the evidence of a life of scholarly dedication - a slight smell of hard work, an aura of honing, the weight of holding a life together and carrying the burden of moral precision. He liked trains, and they had both survived the Second World War.

His wife, a dainty and distinctly silver lady, gave me a box of champagne glasses, by way of thanks. Every time i used those glasses, i thought of her, so thin, fine, kindly and upright, out there in the semi-wilderness of another province, loyal to her husband's choice of retirement home. For her, i hoped for waterbirds and a small garden space where she could sit, peacefully watching the seasons ebb and flow.

And what does this have to do with what Aboriginal writers write about? Just this: He also wrote me a letter of reference for the Japan Exchange and Teaching (JET) Program. When they left town, i was proud to be able to say that i had been accepted, and was set to join this prestigious program - i was a JET! Well, said my prof, good for you. You must stay in touch, and you must of course go to Singapore if you can (Singapore had figured largely in our studies together). And by the way, he had a son—i hadn't known—who had a Masters in history and would be perfect for JET, so could i send him information on how to apply for the program. Now JET recruits through universities, and most any Canadian university can fairly easily provide information—there are certainly more direct ways to get the goods than to ask me—but i was touched to be asked. I was also leaving on a five week jaunt down to my ancestral homeland on the east coast—my first Canada Council grant ever!—to learn about my Mi'gmaq relatives and write some poetry. I'd get back just in time to go to Japan. It was my year. It was also a bit hectic. So i didn't manage to go rustle up JET info for the mysterious son before i left to go writing. I found myself in Montreal, taking a few days to visit a friend en route; and so i contacted the Japanese Consulate there, and asked that they forward the information to my friend for his son. I remember quite clearly the novelty of a snooty Quebecois voice ridiculing me for asking this information - why did i not do this in BC? Look, just send it, thank you kindly, i replied. And went on my merry way. My prof had asked my help, and i had done my bit. I was a university graduate, a real writer, and a JET.

The next spring, i wrote to him from the famous bar in the Raffles Hotel; there i was, peanut shells scattered at my feet, big fans drifting round overhead, one hand on my Singapore Sling, and i was in love with my life. My dreams had come true, and the poor half-breed girl was really a writer, a teacher, an explorer. I was on vacation from Japan, seeing one of the cities of my dreams. And i had turned down the offer of another year of this fabulous life, because i wanted to work in the Aboriginal community. I wanted to bring back glimpses of Kyoto and of the Andaman Sea, and show them to other poor half-breed kids, the way my dad showed me pictures he kept in a suitcase, pictures of the world he had seen. I also wanted to work for change and balance in my own land, because the issues were the same here, i had found; knowing that, i had to work where i had the most at stake, and do what i could at home before i started trying to tell the Asians what to do. And i had to tell my mentor how this sojourn in the farthest places had strengthened my love for where i came from and my resolve to apply myself to the health of my home. And by the way, i wrote, it was a real hoot being an Indigenous person sitting in Raffles Bar, like a spy right in the heart of the colonial image. And by the way, i wrote, did your son ever end up applying to JET?

His letter was waiting when i returned to Japan. No, he never received any information from me, and so his son had not the chance to be a JET, and was stuck with a job beneath his worth. But this was not the main thrust of his letter; rather, he took to task all those in Canada who had recently arisen as part of a "cult of whiners" seeking amends for any kind of slight they could think of, which was preposterous in such a prosperous land as Canada. No, he thought, if these people had lived through the War, they would know what hardship was and would certainly not complain.

I had always admired him for his tough debating style, and was pleased that he still felt me a worthy adversary. Ah, the old academic thrust and parry, i thought, and set to work on my reply, including a few stories of journeys i'd taken with my father as a teenager, to the homes of the fourth world, to people who considered *us* rich. i recounted my father's advocacy in one case in particular, where some 34 people were forced to live in a trailer in the winter, with their supposed water supply a long walk away in a government shack under lock and key. My father brought in the media, and incited an article headlined with a comparison to the Black Hole of Calcutta, right here in our own back yard. My father had been to war, too, and could recognize injustice in various guises. You would've liked my father's style, i thought, sending out what would be my last letter to my mentor.

It was his wife who wrote back. That tough little silver lady had typed the letter with such force that words dented the page, nearly biting it through in spots. Her husband, she wrote, had no more time nor respect for the likes of me. He joined her in commiserating with me, because i could never know that any thing i had in life was not given to me as a sop, out of political correctness and the grotesque practices of bleeding heart liberals. Had he known, she confided, that i was *Aboriginal*, he would never have given me high marks, nor written me letters of reference, for he abhorred the thought of being mistaken for one of those who supported Affirmative Action and the like. Her outrage stunned me. I could not fathom this sudden hate. I had never hidden my ethnicity. I was shocked that their bigotry had been hidden from me. So i walked with that letter around my wee home in Japan. i walked to the local shrine, and talked to the kami (those Shinto folks believe like we do, that every part of the world is inhabited by spirit). And then i burned that letter. *This is my life, my adventure, my tribute to the faith of my ancestors that we are as human as anyone and we, too, belong to the beauty of the whole world, and you cannot take it from me.* And i began to laugh; but i never quite knew why i was laughing, until i read Number Five in my sister's essay on those top ten challenges to Aboriginal students:

> People saying they're surprised to find out that you're Native because you don't talk with an accent and you're not an alcoholic and you got the highest mark in the course.
>
> … Not only have I had people act surprised, I've had people become hostile when they "discover" that I'm Aboriginal —almost as if they're angry at me for "putting something over on them."… Perhaps I should forget everything I've learned … and incorporate a few more "Ugh"s into my discourse style …[1]

And then again, perhaps not. Perhaps the important thing is to cherish my adventure, which was after all, very fine. And in my mind, when i need to, i return to the shrine in my Japanese home town, and sit by the water. The fish drop down deeper and the pool becomes still, and look – there in the water, you can see the whole round sky.

Reflections on Elders, or Re-visioning, or steering clear

Speaking of reflections, i'm not the first person to point out that as soon as you see mirrored shades on a suspected 'Elder' you ought to suspect ego, too. And i'm not the first to write about the sad fact that abuses happen to young seekers who misplace their trust, and Indigenous gurus are as guilty as any others. And i understand that criticizing 'our spiritual leaders' is dangerous: one could become a target for vengeful medicine on the one hand, and on the other, one could find oneself unwittingly, and erroneously, allied with right-wing, 'neo-Christian' (or is that neo-Nazi?) defenders of 'Heritage.' So i generally keep my mouth shut, as a writer, about this stuff.

After all, i'm a half-breed, and i understand that i am suspect to both sides – the neo-traditionalists, who tend to start out harbouring resentment that i even exist, because i'm dirtying the bloodpool; and the neo-heritagers, for pretty much the same reason, as well as because they can't tell i'm one of the tribe, and might slip up and say actionable stuff in my presence. Yup, i keep my writerly mouth shut. i am not into battling either side. I'd rather just write some happy wee poems and songs and stories, and leave the "Neo"s of both colours to strut up and down like roosters, squaring off against each other, without me in the middle.

Far be it from me to point out to the born-again "Traditional People" that as soon as you start separating things up into 'sacred' and 'not sacred' you too are colonized; when you drive up in your handsome gas-burning conveyance, take a pull from your styrofoam container of refreshment, and open your mouth to run me down, you are revealed as human, flawed, vulnerable and frail, and we are alike in this.

Far be it from me to even comment that any time i hear a person (and i have) tell me in a superior tone that they are a 'traditional person' i want to point out the obvious; that phrase applies to any human being – we've pretty much been made like this (bodies, hearts, minds, souls and prejudices) for as long as any tradition cares to call us 'persons.' Of course, if i did, they would likely get mad, and go off to waste their energy poking medicine at me to teach me a lesson, when they could be using that energy for much more healing work.

Or they might get all noble and explain to my ignorant face (it's gotta be ignorant, cause it's too pale to know anything) that they mean 'traditional' in the Native sense, in terms of their spirituality. And then i'll have to ask them if they mean 'person' then applies to all beings, which are all held to be sacred relatives with wisdom and grace, even magpies and stray cats and humans of mixed blood? And then we might have a fist fight.

Too risky, i say – even though we might also come to an understanding if we both get over it, and end up making more grace and space in our little corner of the sacred world. Ditto the question of whether or not i am a spiritual person (they don't inquire about my physical reality, oddly enough).

Nope, you won't catch me writing on these topics. No way. That's sacred stuff, and oughtn't to be talked about. Besides which, it's best not to waste my time attempting to educate neo-heritagers of any colour.

the ground my wee feet adore

If i didn't have all this trash about identity and colonialism and post-colonial restitution clogging up my pen, i'd certainly write about how we could do a lot for ourselves and the world if we cared to. I'd write about being alive here now, and how what it is possible for me to do with being alive is what being alive is worth.

I'm worth turning my attention to world problems. I'm worth spending my time and effort in the field of finding solutions to human problems of how humans relate to our world. I'm worth total dedication to changing my own small life and the life of my community in life-affirming ways. I'm worth gardening, i'm worth teaching, i'm worth singing, i'm worth parenthood, i'm worth engaged intellectual discussion, i'm worth traveling, i'm worth dreaming and praying and dancing and listening. This would be the ground i'd bring to you and we could get down to discussing what we can do, each of us and all of us.

nomad's land

As i mentioned in my introduction, i've encountered Native people who now hold that reservations are the only valid place for real Indians to be. In putting forth this view, they are honouring the fact that people on the reservations preserved what they could of their culture. For their sacrifices and their strength, those people do deserve honour and our sincere thanks. However, i do not think it would honour them if i went "back to the rez." I wasn't born there. Many, many of us weren't. Many of us 'mixed bloods;' many of us 'urban Indians;' and also many, many of us before the treaty process. Our deep traditions, did they not include travel, trade, exploration? Oh, the records of it are scanty, but i have heard that my folks liked to ramble. So who am i not to honour their lives? i ramble. And in that rambling, i find the Earth to be beautiful in every region.

If i could only tell you one thing here, perhaps that would be it – although you may certainly already know this, i am telling you as a writer and as a Native writer, the Earth is beautiful. People, we do unjust, barbaric and plainly sick things with the gifts we have here. i have seen some sad and cruel things. Even so, this world is beautiful. Can that be entered into the Canon?

Say from me, for my part, that the Earth is beautiful, that Life is big, holy and grotesque, and that we do not really own Her, but we can set each other free to enjoy the gift of life. This setting free, by the way, might just take a lot of hard work and arguing and compromise and sacrifice, but what else is really worth doing? In balance to the hard work, there is joy. That's the rumour i hear from those who have dedicated their lives to Life. Like a proper nomad (yes i know we weren't all nomads, Moose, i'm tryin' to make a point here), like a pre-reservation injun, like a human being, i'll be hunting for the truth in that rumour. Maybe that makes what i do Native Literature, maybe not. It is sure to be interesting.

By the way, i am glad that i speak English, because i can share ideas with people from many many cultures, even though English may be their second (or third, fourth, fifth) language. English—their second language—brought my parents together. They taught me English first, because (i asked them why once) the larger world into which i would be moving spoke English. So they believed I'd find it useful, and i do. I also, with all its lumps and scars and evidence of the rise and fall of empires, find English beautiful.

Some might argue that therefore i will never know the truth of my Native heritage, because it depends upon language. With all due respect, i must reply that the best truth, the truest truth, the truth that all my relations belong to, that truth is bigger than any one language.

So i'll never catch that truth in these, or any other words. Still, i'll continue to try to write with truth. Can't help myself. I'm a writer. This here moose on my shoulder snuffles in my ear and i bust out laughing. And i'm gonna tie up this essay right about here, without any particular conclusion.

I'm doing this for three reasons: because the issue under discussion is part of a society undergoing huge changes and i don't feel well enough educated to make conclusions on a process that big (in fifty more years, i hope we see that we have transformed our problems as a bunch of people living together into growing pains, and have let these problems teach us to live more beautifully together); because i hope this essay, in this form, will be engaging enough for readers to use it as a launching pad for their ideas, discussions and conclusions; and because the ungulate on my shoulder says it could be amusing to just stop here.

Note

1 Sewell, Catherine F. "The Top Ten Challenges of Being a Native Student at the University of Alberta:" An Examination of Native Educational Policy Issues and a Reflective Journey through the Hallowed Halls of Academia" Paper for Educational Foundations course at University of Alberta, Edmonton, 1988, unpublished.

Confluence: Confessions of a White Writer Who Reads Native Lit

David Brundage

"There were no Indians and there were no whitemen. There was only life."

Richard Wagamese (Anishnaabe), *A Quality of Light*

The epigraph may suggest some of my hopes and fears on this topic. I'm a little uneasy with boxes of writing, like "Native," "Canadian," and "Women's." Though the fallout from mechanical classification has been all too real, still, we seem more determined than ever to pigeonhole. I like to read *many* kinds of writers, and I put what I consider "good writing" over the trade or academic category it appears in. Furthermore, while I am honoured to contribute to this book and to talk about my own work as a writer, this, too, is intimidating. One of my hopes is to write naturally and instinctively. I share the common fear that exposing the chrysalis can imperil the flower. Still, I owe an enormous debt to the inspiration, guidance, and moral imperative of Native literature, and it seems to me important to acknowledge this connection. Native writing in Canada is surely destined to be afforded the same broader importance as jazz music in the United States, but true to our Canadian pace we have been mostly rather slow to catch on.

The editors suggested I discuss *why* and *how* Native writing has influenced me. The *whys* seem to me a manageable departure point. First has been my time with First Nations literature. Then there are qualities in many Aboriginal writers that touch particular chords in me. These include evocation of nature, oral use of language, attention to the spirit over mechanized life (and certain motifs related to this), and portrayals of how someone of another heritage can help you find and adapt lost dimensions of your own heritage. This last theme sums up the personal value for me of all the elements I have just mentioned: in Native writers I find deeply relevant guidance and affirmation.

How various influences enter into my own work, as I have already suggested, is perhaps too much for this short paper – or for my finite abilities. However, various examples of influence abound throughout my plays, fiction, and songs. I will conclude by looking at one such example, from a recent song.

When I speak of my *time* with Aboriginal literature, I mean that when I was old enough to read, my mother and I began visiting the library and taking out books on "the Indians" – oral stories, ways of life, spiritual beliefs, and so on. All of this, at the time, was sifted through White viewpoints, but at least I was sensing a glimmer. My mother had a way of suggesting that

Indian beliefs were different from but equal to ours. We were in Montreal, but she was from the country; and there was no doubt to us that Native ways, being more natural, were in some important respects better than our own. One night I went to my mother's room, scared of my first realization that someday I would die. She had me imagine myself drifting down river in a canoe. I associate the Native books with that calming image, but also with something profoundly sad in the history, in the oral stories, with something a little scary, like the feeling of the Bible: it's going to bite your nose if you're naughty. Probably a main reason I remain interested in Aboriginal literature is I associate it, like canoeing, with my mother.

I learned enough from various books and my mother's comments to dislike portrayals of Indians on TV, in colouring books, and - later - in novels such as *The Last of the Mohicans.* (To my sister's understandable chagrin, I read the Classic Comic book rather than the edition she gave me. You can see how I carried the seeds of politically correct protest even then.) As I mentioned, the books my mother and I took out were entirely by White authors. Still, I know she wanted to find accurate, sympathetic material so that I would begin to see the falsehoods and remember the wrongs. From all that early reading, two particular images remain in my mind: one of an Indian boy watching the "Iron Horse" enter his land. The story was from his point of view, and I badly wanted that iron horse to go away. I still do - especially some days when email, phones, the fax, TV, speeding cars, and all the other noises reach their zenith. The other image, from a story about Crazy Horse, was the first graphically brutal image I recall encountering in fiction. It occurs after the central character is killed. His body is chopped into pieces, and these go back to the earth. Perhaps the author knew more about Greek and Egyptian mythology than about First Nations history, but the image resonated for years as an assertion of rebirth.

As time went by, the books were no longer just about Natives, they were *by* Natives. For Christmas one year I got the *The Unjust Society* by Harold Cardinal (Cree) and a collection of Laws and Treaties. Perhaps my mother's influence worked too well, for I was becoming a Johnny Gebbardt, the activist wannabe in *A Quality of Light* by Richard Wagamese. Rather than join barricades, I made do with speaking dismissively of "Whites." My brother, who did not so much care to be thus dismissed, thought I was having a problem seeing my face in the mirror.

My hope is that since I have followed Native writing and issues over my entire reading life, I may be inclined to draw naturally on certain aspects as things lived with. I think the influence has had time to be absorbed into some part of how I see things rather than stick out as an unduly visible or derivative element. I suspect this is the case for a good many White Canadian writers – the debt is little recognized or understood.

I spoke of the appealing way that nature appears in various works by Native authors. I am especially moved by nature in novels such as *Honour the Sun* by Ruby Slipperjack (Anishnaabe) or *Keeper 'n' Me* by Richard Wagamese, and in many poems. Having spent summers and occasional winters in the Eastern woodlands, I find that nature in these novels feels like the real thing. I hasten to add that I find the same real, honest treatment in Margaret Laurence, Margaret Atwood, and a great many other White writers. For those who know it well, nature becomes a major character: multifaceted, unsentimentalized. It is close-at-hand. *Honour the Sun* offers the fictional diary of an Anishnaabe girl (the "Owl") coming of age in the 1960s (my coming-of-age era as well). She grows up in Northern Ontario in a small Native community along the CNR line, isolated and disenfranchised. There is much drinking and general abuse in the community, but during the girl's younger years, her sole support, her mother Delia, is a beacon. Living the traditional life of fishing, gathering, and storytelling, Delia teaches the girl independence, self-reliance, and love of life. "Honour the Sun, child," she says to Owl. "Just as it comes over the horizon, honour the Sun, that it may bless you, come another day...." Among my favorite novels, this book draws deeply upon its portrait of Delia, a portrait in equal parts ordinary, tragic, and heroic. Owl's mother embodies the sense of someone connected for centuries with the land. There is a stillness in Sipperjack's evocation that allows us to listen.

Such books bring me back to the nature I remember from childhood summers, a world I used to wish I could inhabit year round. Since I didn't experience the woodlands year round, I wouldn't attempt this sort of "nature writing," but it is, for lack of a better word, sacred. It is one reason I enjoy much Native literature. If a little of that fictional nature has crept into my system, as perhaps actual nature has, it couldn't hurt. From the time my English professors began to challenge me to think about theories of art, I leaned toward a belief that writing, however stylized or abstract, should be natural. It should arise from the earth and reach for the sky, strive toward some sort of peace with the relations therein.

All "naturalness" in writing depends, of course, on language. Margaret Atwood puts it simply and clearly in a recent essay: "... the examination of 'language' is something every good writer is engaged in by virtue of vocation." (32) I'm particularly interested in what Jeanette Armstrong has said and written on this subject. Her observation that she uses English in a unique way because it is a version of the language filtered through her own tongue speaks to the revitalization of literature and life.[1] As a former Montrealer, I have grown up hearing Englishes filtered through French and Yiddish. I sometimes missed these familiar accents while lodged in the "pure" English of the classic authors I was exposed to at university. *Coyote City* by Daniel Moses (Delaware) makes engaging use of the contrasting Englishes Native characters between Eastern and Western Canada sometimes find themselves speaking. I find these accents and patterns of language celebrated and deftly applied by Native writers across the country. In contrast, think of a writer like John Updike who, I understand, used to labour at great pains to make his sentences less literary and seemingly contrived. There is a freshness of voice in much Native writing that by its very sound and character invites us to see ourselves anew. This use of written language rests, of course, on the oral tradition of literatures, described so beautifully by Robert Bringhurst as "parts of the old-growth forest of the human mind." (17) As his metaphor suggests, nature, orality, and spirit are virtually inseparable.

In her essay "White Breast Flats," Emma Lee Warrior (Peigan) remembers, as a little girl, fearing a water spirit in the rushing Old Man River. Rudolf Steiner, expounding his ideas of spiritual awareness, speaks of nature as an ideal setting to interact with the spiritual.[2] Not just works by Native writers, but any works with convincing worlds of nature help us re-establish those connections. To say that Native writing has the patent on Spirit is like saying black music has soul; a racial stereotype. Nevertheless I find in much Native writing remarkable attention to the natural links between the human and the spiritual. Not to dismiss Wordsworth, Whitman, and numerous others, but this feature is simply not as prominent in most non-Native writers. Even trapped in the city, the Native voice of a poem such as "Falling Song" by Daniel David Moses asserts nature in central terms.

There was the sweet but reedy
honking of geese coming down
this morning with rain over
rush hour streets, coming
through like bells that celebrate.

I got right up, pushing up
close to the sooty window
pane. I peered out and up through
the weather, imagining
that that line of winged dots would

be shifting as if waves moved
easily through them, as if
waves floated them south. I wanted
to catch them riding, spots
on the wind, marking

the certain direction of
their migration. but I got
no satisfaction. Mist kept
them mysterious, quickly
dampening their call. Leaning
over the sill, I gaped at
a window shade dull sky, at
a hollow city, and felt
like I'd missed a parade I
would have wanted to follow.

From 1976 to 1978 I lived in New York City, supporting my writing habit on under-the-table jobs that included a good measure of house-cleaning. Every week the soot I had rubbed away from the homes of various clients was back again, redoubled, it seemed. Yet everywhere – from the Hudson River crawling past my tiny 13th floor window to the new shoots poking through cracks in the concrete of Times Square – were reminders that long after the urban experiment has passed away nature will prevail. All of this comes through for me in the images and rhythms of "Falling Song." Separation, confusion, and regret mark our time, but they are not ubiquitous or eternal. The bells of divine assurance continue; waves of endless breath, invoked by the poet's repetitions and line breaks, rise and circle.

In hand with honouring nature, the Native writing I enjoy invariably includes critiques, such as "Falling Song," from good natured to infuriated, of the mechanized nightmare we have brought to these shores.

The nightmare splits everything into pieces, so that art goes into a frame, the frame goes into a museum, and God goes into a Church on Sunday. The Spirits dry up, replaced, now, by virtual reality. Why listen for a Spirit when you can search the web for Britney Spears (the most visited web site, I'm told). A recent book by animal specialist Rupert Sheldrake contains some apt reflections on the Split resulting from our mechanistic/empirical world view. I quote from *Dogs that know when their owners are coming home and other unexplained powers of animals*:

> "[There are] split attitudes to animals expressed in our society as a whole. During working hours we commit ourselves to economic progress fueled by science and technology and based on the mechanistic view of life. This view, dating back to the scientific revolution of the seventeenth century, derives from René Descartes's theory of the universe as a machine. [3] Though the metaphors have changed (from the brain as hydraulic machine in Descartes's time, to a telephone exchange a generation ago, to a computer today), life is still thought of in terms of machinery. Animals and plants are seen as genetically programmed automata, and the exploitation of animals is taken for granted.

> Meanwhile, back at home, we have our pets. Pets are in a different category from other animals. Pet-keeping is confined to the private, or subjective realm. Experiences with pets have to be kept out of the real, or objective world. There is a huge gulf between companion animals, treated as members of our families, and animals in factory farms and research laboratories. Our relationships with our pets are based on … I-thou relationships rather than the I-it approach encouraged by science." (2)

Another view of this great divide is nicely expressed by Robert Bringhurst:

> "The Old World and the New are not two regions marked reliably on maps. The Old World is wherever indigenous traditions are permitted to exist and acknowledged to have meaning. The New World is wherever such traditions are denied and a vision of human triumph is allowed to take their place. The Old World is the self-sustaining world—worldwide—to which we all owe our existence. The New World is the synthetic, self-absorbed and unsustainable one—now also worldwide—that we create." (17)

The Delaware poet in the heart of the great Canadian city nevertheless hears and affirms the Old World. Though his relationship to the geese is hardly one of owner and pet, the connection remains "I-thou." The hidden power, still with nature, is not entirely lost. Native writers generally resist the dualistic, divisive way of thinking. The relationships have to be I-thou. Though the resistance may be passive, it is strong. When I read Maria Campbell (Métis) remembering her Cheechum saying that every thought and action is a prayer, I am reading my own belief, even if too often I fail to embody it. The Split comes about when God cannot be reconciled with science. Einstein seems benign to us, for example, because he was Spirit-respecting, even if his insights were turned to the familiar empirical outcome of mass destruction.

There are various motifs in Native writing which, I think, offer resistance to the Split and impetus toward healing. One is the use of four. Four was my favorite number from childhood. I remember a playmate who always chose three in our games, and there was definitely a sense of rivalry. Each thought his number was "better," and I know we thought this because of meanings contained within, meanings we could not articulate. Since reading G.I. Gurdjieff in the late 1970s,[4] I have been fascinated by his presentations of the Enneagram, a mystical pattern (and mandella) combining his law of three and the western musical scale of eight steps (divisible, of course, as four). In various ways, I find my work combining three and four. We think these numbers are opposed, but as William Blake so wisely observed, "All religions are one." Three and four belong together. Reading Native literature, I gain a surer connection with my own roots in four, and move toward reconciliation.

Another motif of major interest to me is the Thunderbird. When I returned to Canada from New York City in 1978 it was to Vancouver where I spent some time with members of the Squamish band. Their Band Manager Percy Paul gave me a gift of a carved Thunderbird attached to a leather thong as a necklace. To my consternation, one day the amulet went missing. I eventually concluded I must not have been worthy of such a token, and I assume when I am, it will return. Partly with this personal regret in mind, I wrote a song with the refrain

> Thunderbird, how many lifetimes have you ruled the world
> I don't believe it has been truly heard you are gonna come again
> Across the sky the drumbeat of your mighty wings will cry
> I never could determine why we betrayed you Thunderbird

"Thunderbird" is my song of contrition and prayer for healing. It sounds more cosmic than the story of a lost personal gift, but voila: the distorting imagination. My musical partner James Kwong and I were recently at a China exhibition. There were ancient drawings of Serpents – Serpents with great spread wings – looking and sounding to me a lot like Thunderbird ... Healing may start one person at a time, one culture at a time, but until all the parts are back together again, we won't be healed.

Other motifs that speak strongly to me in Native literature are related agents of healing: the red road, water (blood of the mother), earth, smoke, and braiding/intertwining. I admit to drawing on some of these images in my work, especially my songs, and I can only hope that readers will feel all right with such direct uses. If there were room in this short paper, I would elaborate, as well, on the prominence of children and women in Native writing, handled, for the most part, in natural, sensitive terms. Much of my writing, especially my early work, took or invoked a child's point of view. Perhaps one reason readers often find a naïve quality in my writing is that the child's view may not have left.

I mentioned braiding separate strands as an important idea. Since the seminal work *Halfbreed* by Maria Campbell, to which I have previously referred, I have been struck by the number of Native works dealing with how to reconcile mixed heritages. For me this is part of the healing after the Split, as well as a personally relevant subject since I, too, in less dramatic terms than a Native of mixed blood, am a cultural mix. My mother's father was French, and something of the heritage came down to us, just as living in Montreal, even in its Anglo corners, imbued us with a certain Gallic mood. I was interested in a recent comment by actor and talk show host Julie Snyder (now working in France): "As a Quebecer, I have a very Anglo-Saxon side ... When you live in Quebec, you have both cultures." (Gagnon 38) The parallels between people are stronger and deeper than we sometimes bother to notice. I particularly like the use Thomas King (Cherokee) makes of cultural parallels throughout *Medicine River* to show such things as abuse, poverty, shame, deception, and so on, existing throughout the human condition. All literature appeals to me for its universal reminders. Stories such as *Keeper 'n' Me* and *A Quality of Light* by Richard Wagamese, or "Turtle Gal" by Beth Brant (Mohawk), particularly engage me by dealing with the universality across cultures, the sense of one family, however troubled and unresolved, learning from its different members.

A few years ago I received a phone call from a former student. We hadn't seen each other in ages. He wanted to know if I knew the Robert Frost poem "Acquainted with the Night." I told him when we had a poem to choose for analysis in first year English class, that was the one I picked. My former student said he had been thinking a lot about this poem, which he related to personal ordeals in overcoming addiction. He understood the "luminary clock" to be the moon. His interpretations from the viewpoint of an elder raised on a Western Canadian reserve renewed my involvement with the poem. When we were done talking, I found a copy of the poem and began setting it to a melody and chords. This small personal experience illustrates, I think, the endlessly inspiring dialogue that can occur when subjects are viewed from different perspectives. In this case, a "Native" reading of a White American text enabled a musical response by a White Canadian. Something in the Native response brought meaning that I suspect would not have appeared for me in any scholarly analysis from a Yale or Harvard professor. My former student's analysis helped bring the work home.

Years ago as an undergrad at Carleton University, I enjoyed hearing a Mohawk classmate describe her ideas about the works of Shakespeare. She helped me to see things in him I would not have seen otherwise, though perhaps it took years for me to realize this. I needed to understand more about her experiences and obstacles growing up in Canada before I could sense how these related to new meanings in the texts of England

This brings me to the example I alluded to earlier - an example of direct connections in my writing between my life and its confluence with Aboriginal life.

> "I sit there and watch that sun go down and then I sit there and watch the night take over the sky. Me I call it my magic time. There's a moment just before the dark really takes over that still gives me a thrill when I see it. See, there's a shade of blue in that night sky that there's really no name for it in our language or any other that I ever heard. It's hard to explain that color, it's so magical. Deep and dark and light and metallic and silver and purple all at the same time. It's a blue that seeps inside you and makes you wanna cry and laugh and smile and dream. It's right on the edge of that line between dark and light. It's there in the winter and it's there in the summer except it might be even more powerful on those long summer evenings alone on that lake. I sit there and wait and wait and wait and when it finally slides into view there's a part of me inside that just goes, Mmmmmmmmm. A peaceful silent blue. The only word I ever heard that comes close to explaining how that blue feels inside me is "eternal." Eternal

> blue. My favorite color and my favorite feeling. There's an Ojibway phrase that comes close. Goes, Wass-co-nah-shpee-ming. Light in the sky. That eternal blue's the big light in my sky and my world these days on accounta it reminds me of where I want to be mosta the time. Peaceful, silent, alive inside.
>
> So I go out on that lake to get some of that blue inside."
>
> Richard Wagamese, *Keeper 'n Me*, 146

This passage is spoken by the character/narrator Garnet Raven, a young Ojibway (Anishnaabe) man who was removed from his family at age three. Garnet bounced from White foster home to White foster home until he ran away to Toronto, encountered a family of sympathetic Blacks, and, for a time, adopted the identity of a street Black. Moving some drugs for his new friends landed Garnet in jail. While doing his time, he received a letter from someone professing to be his brother. Released from jail, Garnet reluctantly boarded a bus to the northern White Dog reserve. Still decked out as a hip Soul Brother, complete with Afro, Garnet met his real family; presently, adapting more to the style of the reserve, Garnet has begun to learn Ojibway wisdom from an old former acolyte of his deceased grandfather - a recovered alcoholic named Keeper (Keeper of the sacred drum).

From Keeper, Garnet learns the importance of balancing male and female within oneself. Keeper, who also narrates sections of the novel, tells the reader of a time when he set out alone into the forest, seeking a vision, just as Garnet is doing at this point in the story. Keeper was visited throughout his retreat by two eagles. His teacher—Garnet's grandfather—explained that the two eagles were a sign of living in balance with the mother's gifts and the father's. "Sacred union inside me." (165) When Garnet returns from his own vision quest to the old cabin of his grandfather, he has had a dream. Coincidentally, in Garnet's dream he was in a canoe when he noticed two eagles. "I watched them watching me for a long time ... " (174) The eagles fly down to the ground and turn into an old man and woman, dancers in ceremonial costumes. Then they leap into the sky and become birds again. So, without knowing of Keeper's experience with eagles, Garnet has virtually the same vision.

Adding to the impact for me of this material is Garnet's insistence on the canoe. During many summers of camping and canoe tripping north of Montreal, the canoe had become one of the most important beings in my life. Quite rightly, Garnet connects the canoe with flying:

> "If you ever wanna get the idea of how it feels to fly, all you really gotta do is paddle a canoe alone across a northern lake when it's calm. When there's no wind and no waves it's like moving through glass. You look over the sides and it's like you're suspended above everything. Water so clear you float over the rocks and boulders and logs on the bottom like an eagle over land ..." (159)

Recently James and I were in the recording studio and the engineer commented that one of the pieces being sung for us was very introspective. He was referring to a song I had recently written called "Twilight Wind," and indeed much of its introspection flows from the style of Garnet Raven's narration in *Keeper 'n Me.* I had been especially inspired by the passage on page 146, which I have reproduced above; the use of two eagles, the experience of flying, and the need to make sense of the past with all its crazy attractions and separations were significantly at play.

The song did not begin as a literary derivation, however. I was remembering the Mohawk classmate, whose relationship with me for a good time had been more than that of classmates. We separated not because of an Indian-White divide but rather because she was settled and I was too young to settle down. It was more the usual woman-man divide, whereby the male matures slower. For all of us there are times we sometimes revisit, imaging what might have been and perhaps saddened by what seems to have been lost in the old choices. I suppose one aspect of a possible Indian-White divide was my frenetic energy – especially in those days. "You're always running everywhere," she used to object, "Always rushing and planning and scheming." Sometimes I think she was merely too polite to have added "like Duddy Kravitz." This "hustler" side is nicely captured in Garnet Raven –

in his love of R&B, his desire to be in the fast lane, where "it is happening." Ironically, my fast lane ended in Edmonton, a relative sleepy hollow where at this point of my life I find it quite acceptable to enjoy a slow pace and do some reflecting. It was in a mood of reflection that I felt provoked to write "Twilight Wind," and since memories of a Native friend were primary parts of the subject, the many allusions to *Keeper 'n Me,* that suggested themselves, felt particularly relevant.

Song lyrics don't have the same effect apart from their music, and for those of you who have the chance to hear the music as well, I can say it was every bit as inspired by the world of *Keeper 'n Me* as were the lyrics. Though the push for this song was largely personal nostalgia, perhaps the song's greater meaning is close to that suggested by the Wagamese novel: not just the Native societies but all our societies are desperate for healing, and until we respect and balance the female, in wholeness, we will continue in our dark ways of progress and desolation. Perhaps there is the recognition as well that love and possession are quite separate, indeed, alien forces.

Twilight Wind

willow weep
falling on the twilight watch I keep
eagles on the night
a man and woman fly
a silver purple sky
blue inside of you
no words that could describe
makes you wanna cry

upon the wind
across the fields
on and on
as twilight yields
now changing gears
like a hurricane
reversing years
in the driving rain

long ago I took your hand
but I let it go
I lost control

maybe I was young
caught up in the race to win the gold
those eagles on the night
they just flew on by
too late to contemplate
but if you hear this song
I was only partly wrong
if it brings you peace
if it fills your heart
if it says to you
how I wish I knew
what I do tonight
how I long to ride
the twilight wind
twilight wind
I long to ride to you

- Recording by Judith McKee, Audrey Reynolds, and George Mok at the following web site: http://www.confluencemusic.ca may be sampled.

Truly, the journey to where I am today—wherever that may be as a person and writer—could not have occurred without the gifts and guidance of Native people. I find much of myself in the works of Wagamese and Slipperjack - a vital part that is not in any of the canonical works I was expected to analyze in my English classes. Things are changing in respect of curriculum and outlook, but surely not fast or far enough. Euro-Canadian eyes have yet to see this land, its problems, and its potential to the degree available in the works of our Native authors. "There's those that call us Indians the people of the dream" says Garnet Raven; (175) "we pay a lot of attention to dreams". (79) More dreaming, more visions, more true tolerance, less lipservice to politically correct tolerance, more healing, more willingness to write from the spirit rather than the cash register or the awards podium - all of this is encouraged in the best of our Native writers. Speaking from the inside, I know the value of Native words to an outsider as yet seeking peace with a cold land and its terrifying history. If Canada is to emerge with a literature of world significance, it will do so in large measure on the basis of its Aboriginal voices. May those voices ring in the hearts of us all.

Notes

[1] I'm thinking, in particular, of a paper she gave at Perspectives on Native American Oral Literature, First Nations House of Learning and Green College, UBC, March 6, 1998. Her talk was called "How Narrative is Body Present in Oral Tradition."

[2] See, for example, his *Knowledge of Higher Worlds and Its Attainment*.

[3] For a thorough analysis of the roots and consequences of our mechanistic thinking, see Albert Borgmann's *Crossing the Postmodern Divide*. The University of Chicago Press: Chicago, 1992.

[4] There are many books by and about Gurdjieff, including very opposed interpretations of his motives and contributions. A good introduction to his life and work is Kathleen Riordan Speeth's *Gurdjieff: Seeker of Truth*. It contains a bibliography.

Works Cited

Atwood, Margaret. "If You Can't Say Something Nice, Don't Say Anything At All." *Saturday Night*. January 6 & 13, 2001, 27-33.

Borgman, Albert. *Crossing the Postmodern Divide*. Chicago: University of Chicago 1992.

Brant, Beth. "Turtle Gal," in *All My Relations*, ed. Thomas King. Toronto: McLelland & Stewart, 1990.

Bringhurst, Robert. *A Story as Sharp as a Knife*. Vancouver: Douglas & McIntyre, 1999.

Campbell, Maria. *Halfbreed*. Toronto: McLelland & Stewart, 1973.

Gagnon, Michelle. "le show." *Saturday Night*. December 25 & 30, 2000, 35-39.

King, Thomas. *Medicine River*. Toronto: Penguin, 1989.
Moses, Daniel David. *Coyote City*. Stratford: Williams-Wallace, 1990.
___________. *Delicate Bodies*. Vancouver: Blewointmentpress, 1980.
Sheldrake, Rupert. *Dogs that know when their owners are coming home and other unexplained powers of animals*. New York: Three Rivers Press, 1999.
Slipperjack, Ruby. *Honour the Sun*. Winnipeg: Pemmican, 1987.
Speeth, Kathleen Riordan and Ira Friedlander. *Gurdjieff: Seeker of Truth*. London: Wildwood House, 1980.
Steiner, Rudolf. *Knowledge of the Higher Worlds and Its Attainment*. New York: Anthroposophic Press, 1947.
Wagamese, Richard. *A Quality of Light*. Toronto: Doubleday, 1997
__________________. *Keeper 'n Me*. Toronto: Doubleday, 1994.
Warrior, Emma Lee. "White Breast Flats," in *Gathering of Spirit: Writing and Art by North American Indian Women*, ed. Beth Brant: Sinister Wisdom Books, 1984.

Of Related Interest

Dickason, Olive. *The Native Imprint: the Contribution of First Peoples to Canada's Character*. Athabasca: Athabasca University Educational Enterprises, 1995.
Francis, Daniel. *The Imaginary Indian: the Image of the Indian in Canadian Culture*. Vancouver: Arsenal Pulp Press, 1992.
King, Thomas, Cheryl Carver and Helen Hoy, eds. *The Native in Literature*. Toronto: ECW, 1987.
Monkman, Leslie. *A Native Heritage: Images of the Indian in English Canadian Literature*. Toronto: U of T, 1981.
Taylor, Drew Hayden. *Funny, You Don't Look Like One*. Revised edition. Penticton: Theytus Books, 1998.
Wilson, Colin. *The Outsider*. London: JB Tarcher, 1987 (re-issue, first published 1970).

Socially Responsible Criticism: Aboriginal Literature, Ideology, and the Literary Canon

Jo-Ann Episkenew

During my most cynical moments I believe that the literary canon—that collection of "great" works of literature—is merely a creation of academics looking for teachable works of literature, and publishers looking for the profits that are likely to ensue if their texts are taught in university English classes. Works of literature, then, become incorporated into the cannon when a significant number of academics teach them. At some point in our development, most burgeoning academics deduce—or are told—that we must have a specialization, our "turf" if you will, an area in which we are the experts. Tenure and promotion depend on it. As a result, we look for some area of study that piques our interest and, with luck, has enough room to enable us to carve out an intellectual space for ourselves. If Shakespeare is our passion, our challenge is a large one; after all, it is hard to make a space for one's self in such an occupied area. Clearly it is easier to find a space in an area that is new and unoccupied, one like the area of Canadian Aboriginal Literature. That choice, however, brings with it its own challenges.

Unlike its relatives south of the border, writing by Canadian Aboriginal authors still occupies the literary margins of the canon. While the works of Native American authors, such as Silko, Momaday, and Erdrich, appear in every new anthology of modern American literature, the works of Canadian Aboriginal writers, especially early writers, such as Clutesi, Campbell, and Culleton, are absent. In the U.S., the canonized Native American writers are well-educated in a western sense and are often academics themselves. Although their works include many allusions to Native American epistemology, they are complex in a way with which academics are comfortable. Canadian Aboriginal Literature is not comfortable for many academics for a number of reasons, not the least of which include its apparent lack of academic sophistication and complexities in the conventional sense. We can find a reason for this when we examine the social and political context from which it came into being.

Although governments on both sides of the 49th parallel used education as a weapon of colonization, they wielded this weapon in different manners. Both colonial governments chose to use residential schools as a strategy to assimilate the Indians; however, in the U.S., many Native Americans[1] were encouraged to obtain further education—usually in the trades—after finishing boarding school. Some Native Americans found their way into universities. The government hoped that educated Native Americans would gain employment in the cities and assimilate, thus abandoning the resource-rich reservations or selling their land to mainstream Americans. In Canada, attitudes were much different, and First Nations people were sent back to their reserves when their tenure at residential school was complete. Smaller and rarely rich in natural resources, reserve land was not coveted to the same extent. It was valued more as a place to confine First Nations people. First Nations people were typically discouraged from attempting to gain access to higher education, and Métis people were often denied access to any education at all.[2] In the unlikely event that they did gain access to a university, status Indians could lose their legal status as Indians if they received a university degree.[3] Métis and Non-status Indian's access to education was inconsistent. They were allowed to attend residential schools if there were vacancies, but forced to leave when the schools became full of status Indians.[4] If living near town, they found themselves at the mercy of the white property owners who could deny their children access to school, which they often did, especially if the Métis families did not own property.[5] Canadian Aboriginal literature reflects this history. Most early writers, therefore, were not well-educated and could not be expected to be familiar with the language of academia. Later writers, although more educated, are cognizant that many of their people are not, and so they write in a way that their works are accessible to a variety of educational levels and not solely for an academic audience.

Many academics believe that Canadian Aboriginal Literature is inferior in that it is flawed in its lack of complexity and, therefore, is not "teachable." After all, how does one handle a simple narrative when one has been trained to analyze and deconstruct complexities? Nevertheless, some academics are choosing to teach Canadian Aboriginal Literature as witnessed by the growing number of "Native Lit" sessions at mainstream academic conferences. It is only a matter of time before works of Aboriginal literature begin to appear regularly in anthologies of Canadian literature. Canadian Aboriginal Literature is knocking on the door of the Canadian literary canon, and scholars are already publishing articles about this new area. The challenge that they face is finding something to say about these seemingly uncomplicated works of literature when they have been trained to look for and analyze complexities.

Even before works of Canadian Aboriginal literature begin to make regular appearances in anthologies of Canadian Literature, articles about them have begun to form a canon of interpretations. Although scholars write ostensibly to analyze works of literature to make them better understood, we also write to refute or augment the ideas presented in the critical writings that precede ours. And so, critical works beget more critical works, and often the literary works that are their subjects often become mere examples illustrating the critical thoughts of the academics who create them. I see this happening with Canadian Aboriginal literature, and as an Aboriginal academic it concerns me.

When analyzing literary works, most scholars are very conscious that ideology is embedded in the text; what they often forget is the ideology that they bring to their reading. I use the term "ideology" to refer to those ideas and beliefs that we take so for granted that we do not hold them up for critical examination and consider them to be "just the way it is." Interpretations are grounded in this kind of ideology. It is important to note that almost all of the scholars who create these interpretations are not Aboriginal people. Most are members of the colonizer culture and, therefore, cannot possibly share the same ideology as Aboriginal people, whether they be the authors who create the literature, the people about whom they write, or the few Aboriginal students in their classes. Let me give you an example from my own experience.[6]

As an undergraduate student majoring in English, I registered in a class in literary analysis based on New Criticism. The assigned text was an anthology entitled *Literature: An Introduction to Reading and Writing*, 2nd edition, (1989), which included Leslie Marmon Silko's story "Lullaby." (1981) "Lullaby," was the topic of the first writing assignment the professor gave the class. Although I cannot remember the topic of the assignment, I can remember my grade. I received a D+/C-, which I remember vividly because it hurt my pride. At the end of the essay the professor left a note explaining that my low mark resulted from my not addressing the suicide at the end of the story. I was stunned. I had seen no suicide and asked my professor to explain. My professor, a Montreal anglophone, pointed out that when the central character Ayah, an older Dene (Navajo) old woman wraps herself and her drunken husband, Chato, in a blanket, curls up beside a rock, and prepares to go to sleep she is committing suicide. The text, he said, clearly reveals that the old woman, unable to bear the weight of her tragic life, chooses death for herself and her husband. I suspected that he had heard stories of old Native people who, weary of life, walk out into the wilderness to die. If one is analyzing only the text of "Lullaby," this is a plausible interpretation. What is missing, however, is the context of both text and readers.

It is important to consider the context of "Lullaby," in that both Silko and her characters are Indigenous to the American South-West. The land that seemed so frightening and dangerous to my professor is their home. Ayah and Chato live in a hogan, a structure made out of rocks, earth, and wood, which is as much a part of the land as the cluster of rocks beside which they spent the night. It is not suicidal for them to take shelter beside these rocks and cover with their blankets; indeed, they carry blankets along with them for just such an occasion. They are old people, and despite their tragic lives, they have survived. To an Aboriginal reader, "Lullaby" is not a story of suicide; it is one of survival, albeit filled with references to the suffering that result from a lifetime of colonization and oppression.

As reader, my context differs radically from that of my professor. Although I too spent my early years in a large urban center, I moved to northern Saskatchewan as a teenager. What is a cold winter night in Arizona, would likely be a nice day in late autumn in Saskatchewan. I have lived with trappers who regularly go out on foot to check their trap lines regardless of the weather. Sometimes they sleep out in the bush—albeit by a fire—wrapped in blankets in temperatures falling below -20°C. This is how Aboriginal people who live on the land exist; this is how we have always lived. My husband grew up on a reserve near Fort Qu'Appelle in southern Saskatchewan. He tells a story of how he walked from Fort Qu'Appelle to Muscowepetung Reserve, a distance of about 40 km., one cold winter night. When he found that he was too tired to go on, he made a shelter in a farmer's field by piling bales of hay around himself. He slept there for the night and finished walking to the reserve in the morning. My brother-in-laws found it necessary to do the same thing from time to time. This land is our home, and Aboriginal people have learned to do what they must to survive. I didn't tell this to my professor, however. Somehow, at the time, I felt embarrassed to reveal that I—and my people—still live this way at the end of the 20th Century. Somehow my husband's story smacked of poverty and social problems and all the things that I was sure that my professors associated with Aboriginal people. Even worse, what if I told him and he didn't believe me? What if he accused me of telling or believing tall tales? His was the voice of authority. How could I convince him that my voice contained authority, too? So I silenced my voice, kept my knowledge to myself, and tried to always be cognizant that my professors knew nothing of Aboriginal realities. I followed the rules, tried to anticipate their objections, and wrote "objective" literary analyses that did not reflect my personal context.

Over the last few years, I have become increasingly aware that many interpretations of the works of Canadian Aboriginal Literature lack a fundamental understanding of the ideological context in which the works were written. Worse yet, because the authors of these interpretations are educated people with academic positions at prestigious universities, the general public deems their voices to be ones of authority. However, these interpretations are grounded in the ideology of the colonizer culture, not the ideology of the colonized people who are the authors and subjects of the texts being interpreted. It is important to remember that colonization is not only militaristic, economic, and political; it is also psychological, social, and spiritual.[7] No matter how well-intended, interpretations that lack a fundamental understanding of Aboriginal people as victims of colonization can inadvertently become weapons of colonization themselves because their authors' voices become the voices of authority, authority which could easily overpower the voices of Aboriginal people. That is not to say that only Aboriginal people should be interpreting and critiquing Aboriginal literature. What I am saying is that non-Aboriginal scholars need to be cognizant of the authority that society accords their voices. It is inevitable, then, that their interpretations of Aboriginal literature will have an effect not only on the perceptions that non-Aboriginal people have of Aboriginal society but that Aboriginal people have of themselves. It is important that scholars examine the ideological baggage they bring to their readings and counter it by looking outside the texts into the contexts in which they were written to glean some kind of understanding of the ideology of the people whose works they interpret. It is not acceptable to remain secure in the ivory towers writing objective critical articles because these articles, imbued with the voice of authority, have an effect on the social situation of the Aboriginal people who are their subjects. As I said earlier, choosing Canadian Aboriginal Literature as a field of study has its own challenges, especially when Aboriginal people are able to write back.

To illustrate this point, I will examine an interpretation that is both canonized and flawed in that it is based on deeply ingrained ideology of the colonizer culture and is one that many Métis people in this country find particularly problematic. Inevitably, at some point during discussions of identity and representation in Maria Campbell's *Halfbreed* (1973) and Beatrice Culleton Mosionier's *In Search of April Raintree* (1983, 1992, 1999), the icon of the confused and alienated Halfbreed appears. Even though there is abundant evidence to prove that Métis people are not inherently confused, isolated, and alone, this icon remains in tact. The Métis Nation of Saskatchewan represents 85,000 Métis in this province, and Métis scholars estimate that there are similar numbers in Manitoba and Alberta. Clearly it is not lonely in the middle.[8] Granted, negotiating identity in a purportedly post-colonial society is challenge that all Indigenous people face. However, many academics persist in the belief that it is confusion about their identity—and not the racist oppression that is the legacy of colonialism—that cause mixed-blood characters their difficulties. Persons of European ancestry have been indoctrinated into a belief system that views contact, particularly sexual contact, with "the Other"—the non-Christians and non-Europeans—as a constant threat not only to Christian virtue and cleanliness but to the very heart of "social order and continuity." (Farrell Racette, 4) I contend that it is this ideology that many scholars bring to the texts, not the texts themselves, on which they base their interpretations.

Despite the complex legal issues[9] that profoundly influence the social and political context in which *Halfbreed* arises, Maria's Métis family does not experience the confusion and alienation that scholars take for granted. Campbell begins her narration of *Halfbreed* by telling her readers who her people are and where they come from. Campbell identifies her paternal great-grandmother, Cheechum, as "a native woman", a Hudson's Bay Company code word for Métis (Farrell Racette), and as "a Halfbreed woman, a niece of Gabriel Dumont." (Campbell 9) She explains that Cheechum's mother's people were non-status Indians, who "were never part of a reserve, as they weren't present when the treaty-makers came." (10) Cheechum experiences no confusion regarding her identity as a Métis woman. She is not concerned with reconciling her mixed European and First Nations heritage because she neither desires nor requires reconciliation. Cheechum knows that she is Métis and is intensely patriotic despising the European immigrants who displace her people from their land and imposing their religious beliefs on them:

> Cheechum hated to see the settlers come, and as they settled on what she believed was our land, she ignored them and refused to acknowledge them even when passing on the road. She would not become a Christian, saying firmly that she had married a Christian and if there was such a thing as hell then she had lived there; nothing after death could be worse! Offers of relief from welfare were scorned and so was the old age pension. While she lived alone she hunted and trapped, planted a garden, and was completely self-sufficient. (Campbell 11)

Cheechum bequeaths her language, lifestyle, and most importantly, her pride in their Métis identity to her son, her grandchildren, and her great-grandchildren.

Nevertheless, Cheechum is responsible for the injection of Scots blood into the family gene pool through her marriage to

Great Grandpa Campbell. However, his Scots' parentage does not draw her son closer to his European heritage. On the contrary, the opposite seems to have occurred. Her son chooses to marry a Métis woman, and "[a]fter their marriage, they lived miles out in the bush and never bothered much with anyone." (Campbell 11) Despite the violence that Grandpa Campbell endures at the hands of his father, "he was a kind, gentle man who spent a great deal of time with his [nine] children." (Campbell 12) As more and more white settlers move onto the land, his children's lives become more difficult.

Many Aboriginal women are ambivalent towards feminism, and many reject it altogether, which bewilders feminist scholars who read Campbell's descriptions of drunken Métis men beating frightened wives. They see violence against women as evidence of a deeply ingrained patriarchal culture although violence against women was not traditional in many Aboriginal cultures. However, the Aboriginal women who shun feminism consider their men to be victims of colonization and oppression as are the Métis men of Campbell's father's generation who find themselves existing in an impossible situation that causes them endless shame. With the twisted logic of the oppressed, they believe themselves to blame for circumstances clearly out of their control. Had their parents and grandparents been present when the treaties were signed—like Big John, Qua Chich, Grandpa Dubuque were—things might have been better. Had they taken treaty rather than script,[10] their families might have had land, food, and education. But they have no education, so the only employment for which they would qualify is farm labour, which would put them at the mercy of the white settlers who, unlike the Indians, do not consider the Métis their kin. Their traditional roles of providers and protectors are vulnerable. The Métis men are skilled hunters, but because they do not have Indian status, the law does not allow them to hunt as needed for survival. If they hunt outside of hunting season, they run the risk of prosecution leading to incarceration. With such limited choices Danny Campbell and his brothers choose to ignore the law and do what they have to do to survive: "they trapped, hunted, and sold game and homemade whiskey to the white farmers in the nearby settlements." (Campbell 12) If they obey the law, they doom their families to a life of relief workers, fear, and starvation; if they break the law, they doom their families to a life of police, fear, and shame. Failure meets them at every turn, and the chorus of "The White Judges" resounds in their minds: *"You are not good enough, not good enough, obviously not good enough."* (Dumont 11, 13) Readers should not be surprised when the Métis men, more and more often, seek solace in drink.

Non-Native readers usually focus on the tension that Campbell describes as existing between the Métis and the Indians. They interpret this tension as proof that mixed-blood people are alienated from both parent cultures rather than looking at the complex legal issues that divide them. Unable to acquire homesteads, the Métis are squatters on their traditional lands, condemned to live on the unoccupied Crown lands that border the road lines. Their landless state[11] sets them apart from the Indians:

> We all went to the Indians' Sundances and special gatherings, but somehow we never fitted in. We were always the poor relatives, the *awp-pee-tow-koosons.*[12] They laughed and scorned us. They had land and security, we had nothing.... However, their old people "Mushooms" (grandfathers) and "Kokums" (grandmothers) were good. They were prejudiced, but because we were kin they came to visit and our people treated them with respect. (Campbell 25)

The Elders' acknowledgement of their kinship with the Métis is significant because relationships between relatives are sacred in Cree culture.[13] Grannie Campbell's status-Indian sister, Qua Chich, never forgets her Métis relatives and brings her horses every year to help them ready their gardens for planting. Grannie Dubuque's brother, chief of his reserve, dotes on Maria and treats her as if she were his own daughter. Still at this point in history, at least one generation of status Indians would have attended residential schools where they had been internalized, the racist attitudes that made them ashamed of their identity. No doubt, these students would have felt some sense of relief upon returning home and learning that the white settlers considered their relatives, the Métis, as being worse than the students had been taught to feel. As the Métis come into more and more contact with the white settlers, they too learn shame. It is their proximity to the white settlers, their legal status, and their poverty–not their mixed blood–that erodes the Métis' sense of pride and security in their identity.

Maria's feelings of shame and self-loathing begin with her first visits to town where she contrasts the Métis' demeanour with that of the white settlers. Maria's childhood abounds with "happiness and beauty," (Campbell 2) which begins to erode as she becomes overwhelmed by the relative prosperity of the townspeople lives and the scorn that they mete out to the Métis. Maria says, "I thought they must be the richest and most beautiful [people] on earth. They could buy pretty cloth for dresses, ate apples and oranges, and they had toothbrushes and brushed their teeth every day.... They didn't understand us. They just shook their heads and thanked God they were different." (Campbell 27) To a child, the shameful demeanour of the adults–their inability to hold their heads high or to look a white person in the eye–seems to acknowledge their guilt, and causes Maria to ask "Mama why [they] had to walk as though [they] had done something bad." Her mother can only reply, "'Never mind. You'll understand when you're older'." (Campbell 37) As she grows older, Maria comes to understand that, to the white settlers, their mixed blood is their crime and the foundation of the Métis' guilt, a crime of which she is also guilty. She comes to believe in a logical fallacy that states that they are poor, untrustworthy, and violent because they are mixed-blood people.

Maria's feelings of shame and self-loathing are exacerbated by her experiences in the education system. She first attends school at the Beauval Indian Residential School, a dubious gift from her Grannie Dubuque, herself a status Indian educated in a convent. It is significant to note that, although Maria remembers little of the one year she spends there, she says that Spring River School, the horrors of which she goes on to recount, is "Heaven compared to the Residential School." (Campbell 49) At the Spring River School, "lunch hours were really rough" (Campbell 50) for the Métis children, who contrast their meager lunches with those of the white children and are reminded of their poverty, sure evidence that their parents had failed, that their people had lost. School and time spent in close proximity to white children teach

Maria to hate her mother, father, and all the "no-good Halfbreeds" and teach her that "there was no greater sin in this country than to be poor." (Campbell 50, 61)

Maria is confused but not because of her mixed blood. She is confused because the dominant society has taught her to hate herself and her people. She would like to marry Smoky, but cannot:

> When I thought of him and marriage I saw only shacks, kids, no food, and both of us fighting. I saw myself with my head down and Smoky looking like an old man, laughing only when he was drunk. I loved my people so much and missed them if I couldn't see them often. I felt alive when I went to their parties, and I overflowed with happiness when we would all sit down and share a meal, yet I hated all of it as much as I loved it. (Campbell 117)

It is important to note that the Métis community sustains Maria, and only when she leaves it does she experience true alienation. Yet she has been taught to loathe that very community that is her strength. Sadly, the irony here is that her prediction of a future with Smoky is probably accurate given the racism and oppression under which they would live. It is racism that drives Maria to marry a white man, secure in the belief that only white men—not Métis—have the power to deal with the relief workers and the ability to support a family. And, like all racist beliefs, this one proves false.

Beatrice Culleton Mosionier's *In Search of April Raintree* begins with the Raintree family living in Winnipeg in the same sorry state as Maria does in Vancouver but for different reasons. The Raintree family comes from Norway House, a Cree small community on the shores of Lake Manitoba. Unlike Maria's community of Spring River, Norway House in the early 1950s was completely isolated and could only be accessed by boat and airplane.[14] Its people spoke their language and lived off the land by hunting, trapping, and fishing. When Henry Raintree contracts tuberculosis, the family is forced to move south to Winnipeg, an alien environment.

Because Culleton Mosionier chooses April, then of pre-school age, to narrate the story, readers have no access to Henry and Alice Raintree's inner lives. Nevertheless, readers can infer that, with the father suffering from a life-threatening disease, this would be a traumatic time for the family. We can also infer from April's recollections that the move would have had a distressing, and ultimately shameful, effect on her father:

> I used to hear him talk about TB and how it had caused him to lose everything that he had worked for.... Although we moved from one rundown house to another, I remember only one, on Jarvis Avenue. And of course, we were always on welfare. I knew that from the way my Dad used to talk. Sometimes he would put himself down and sometimes he counted the days till he could walk down to the place where they gave out cheques and food stamps. (Culleton Mosionier 9)

From these few words it becomes clear that in Norway House the family had a better life than the one they have in Winnipeg and that the loss of this life, "of everything that [Henry Raintree] worked for," damages Henry's self-esteem. We also can infer that when he "put[s] himself down" Henry is blaming himself for the family's loss and their impoverished circumstances. Alienated and confused, not because of their mixed blood but because of their poverty and their displacement from their community and way of life, Henry and Alice Raintree self-medicate with alcohol to relieve their pain for short periods of time.

The Raintree family's physical and temporal settings reveal much about the cause of the Raintree family's alienation. At the start of the novel, the family is physically set in a "rundown house" on Jarvis Avenue. Jarvis Avenue has become a metaphor specific to the City of Winnipeg. Situated in the poorest area of the City, Jarvis Avenue has become infamous to the people of Winnipeg, who have come to associate its name with poverty, despair, and shame. The temporal setting at the novel's start is 1955, a bleak time for Aboriginal people. Because the "Pass Laws" still limited their movements, few status Indians lived in the City of Winnipeg. Canada had no Bill of Rights, and Human Rights legislation had not yet been imagined. In Winnipeg, racist attitudes made it almost impossible for Aboriginal people to gain employment, so those Métis people who could, denied their identity and masqueraded as French and Scots to enable themselves to support their families, always hoping not to be found out. Even if Henry's health permitted him to work, the likelihood of him gaining any employment is slight and good employment nonexistent. April tells us that he is visibly Aboriginal being "a little of this, a little of that, and a whole lot of Indian." (Culleton Mosionier 9) In her poem "White Belly," Joanne Arnott describes the soul-destroying experience that Aboriginal men of Henry Raintree's generation face in the city when seeking employment. She writes that when a visibly Aboriginal man went looking for work

> [the white people] saw his black hair and brown eyes and redbrown skin. They saw his fear and his pride and his poor man's clothes, and again and again they made the same decision. I can trust you with my truck. I can trust you with a load of bread, a load of milk, a load of laundry. (Arnott 57)

Henry is not even this fortunate and finds no employment. As his tuberculosis goes into remission, his alcoholism deteriorates, and he becomes a permanent welfare recipient.

Although both April Raintree and Maria Campbell are mixed-blood people, it is important for scholars to understand that April's context differs radically from Maria's. Where Maria grows up surrounded by extended family and community, April's only community is a rag tag collection of Aboriginal people whom she calls "aunties and uncles" (Culleton Mosionier 12), and who live on the margins of Winnipeg society. Unlike Maria, April has no Cheechum to teach her pride in her identity, no Native language, and no sun dances. Even with this secure foundation, Maria eventually begins to feel ashamed of her identity when confronted with the relative affluence of the whites and their never-ending racism and oppressive treatment of Aboriginal people. Throughout her life, April learns to associate white skin with goodness, cleanliness, and prosperity, and brown skin with violence, dirt, and poverty. From the margins of the park near her home, April looks at the white-skinned children, "especially the girls with blond hair and blue eyes" and envies them; she imagines "that they were rich and lived in big beautiful houses." (Culleton Mosionier 16) April, as a naïve, and therefore unreliable, narrator, cannot know how unlikely it would be that Winnipeg's wealthy children would be playing in a park near Jarvis Avenue. Because April can only describe, rather than analyze, the complexities of her personal context, the analysis of context is left to the scholars who teach and write about this text.

Scholars are not unfamiliar with the requirement to provide students with an understanding of the social, political, and cultural context out of which the texts that they teach arise. Indeed, any class on Shakespeare would not be complete without a comprehensive examination of the political and religious situation in Elizabethan England, no doubt comprised of information that the instructor has gathered from books in the library. These scholars need not worry that there just might be an Elizabethan enrolled in his or her class and that Elizabethan student just might dispute the information given in the lecture. However, this might very well occur in a class on contemporary Aboriginal literature. And, to further complicate things, the instructor cannot always count on the information on the context of Aboriginal literature that she or he has found in the library. At best it is likely to be incomplete and at worst inaccurate. Nevertheless, if one examines the *text* of works of Aboriginal literature without examining the *context* from which it is written, Aboriginal people become abstractions, metaphors that signify whatever the critic is able to prove they signify. However, to write in this way shows a lack of social responsibility because it has an effect on the living people who are the subjects of Aboriginal literature. To really understand the context of the literature, then, scholars must leave the ivory tower and talk to Aboriginal people. This must be done with care and respect.

The narrator of Lee Maracle's short story "Polka Partners, Uptown Indians, and White Folks" describes what *many* Aboriginal people have experienced when interacting with *some* white people (even though she is guilty of essentializing "white people" herself):

> "...white people cannot deal with the beauty in some of us and the crass ugliness in others. They can't know why we are silent about serious truth and so noisy about nonsense. Difference among us, and our silence, frightens them. They run around the world collecting us like artifacts. If they manage to find some Native who has escaped all the crap and behaves like

their ancestors, they expect the rest of us to be the same. (Maracle 296)

Maracle's statement reveals that there are risks attached to leaving the ivory tower to investigate the context of the literature. There was a time in the not too distant past when Aboriginal people were the objects of academic discourse rather than the subjects of their own. With Aboriginal people telling and writing their stories, this time has come to an end. By seriously considering Aboriginal literature as an object of academic study, many academics have taken a first step in social responsibility. Now it is time for them to recognize their own limitations and address them by examining context.

Notes

[1] In the U.S.A. "Native Americans" is a commonly used term to describe the Indigenous Peoples of that country. Under *The Constitution of Canada* (1982), the term "Aboriginal" refers to Indians, as defined by *The Indian Act*, Métis, and Inuit. "First Nations" is a term now in common usage referring to members of Canada's First Nations, in other words Indians defined by the *Indian Act*.

[2] Farrell Racette points out that in Saskatchewan Métis children had no legal right to education until 1944 when the provincial government assumed responsibility for Métis education after a decades-long stalemate with the federal government over jurisdiction (26).

[3] Prof. William Asikinack of the Saskatchewan Indian Federated College was stripped of his Indian status and membership to the Walpole Island First Nation in the 1960s after receiving his B.Ed.

[4] Although born on the Cowessess Indian Reserve, my former mother-in-law, Mathilda Lavallie Bunnie, was by law a Non-status Indian, her father having applied for and been granted enfranchisement. In the early 1920s, she attended Marievel Indian Residential School until grade two when all Métis and Non-status students were required to discontinue, which put an end to her aspirations of receiving an education.

[5] Isadore Pelletier, an Elder at the Saskatchewan Indian Federated College, had a similar experience. Also a Non-status Indian, Pelletier lived in Lestock, Saskatchewan, where he attended the town school until grade three. At that time the townspeople decided to expel all Métis and Non-status Indian children from the school on the basis that they were squatters and, therefore, did not pay taxes. Although Pelletier's family owned land, he was expelled along with the others.

[6] I remember and appreciate Terry Goldie's cautions that the inclusion of personal reflections in academic writing has the potential to become "self-indulgent" (Edmonton 2000).

[7] Winona Stevenson in *To Colonize a People the File Hills Indian Farm Colony*. Blue Thunderbird Productions, 2000.

[8] I credit Sherry Farrell Racette with this observation.

[9] Farrell Racette examines these complex legal issues that affect identity:

> [T]he pressure to define 'Métis' legally and politically is directly relational to the legally and politically defined 'Indian.' The often arbitrary freezing of an Indian identity and its subsequent administration through the Indian Act is rarely questioned. First Nations bands were given official legal identities; glosses which obscured the same diversity which makes the Métis so difficult to define. The evolution of the legally defined 'Indian' through changes and additions to the Indian Act, a piece of federal legislation, has had impact on the Métis. (2)

[10] Since Bill C-31, amended *The Indian Act* in 1986, Campbell and her siblings have been eligible to apply for Indian Status. Many of the other Métis families named in this book–Vandals, Arcands, Isbisters, and others–have since become members of the Ahtahkakoop, Muskeg Lake, Big River, and Mistawasis First Nations.

[11] My husband remembers the Métis from Lebret, Saskatchewan, visiting his family on the Standing Buffalo Dakota First Nation. His father always spoke with great sympathy when he referred to the Métis as "people with no home."

[12] Campbell translates this word as meaning "half people" (25). Solomon Ratt, Head of the Department of Indian Languages, Literatures, and Linguistics at the Saskatchewan Indian Federated College, does not agree. Using Standard Roman Orthography, the word is spelled "āpihtawikosisān": "apihtaw" meaning "half" and

"kosisan" being derived from "nikosis" meaning "my brother". The Cree word for Métis, then, would literally translate into "half-brother".

[13] In the Cree kinship system, extended family relationships are more important than blood relationships. All of Maria's mother's sisters, had she had any, would also be considered Maria's mothers; all of Grannie Dubuque's sisters would be Maria's grandmothers, and all of her brothers would be Maria's grandfathers. Relatives are wealth.

[14] My mother worked for the CBC in Winnipeg at that time and remembers people who came from Norway House to Winnipeg for medical treatment. They often came to the CBC's offices to send messages home on the radio program *The Northern News*.

Not Just a Text: "Indigenizing" the Study of Indigenous Literatures

Renate Eigenbrod

"I write because I need to write; because for me writing is ceremony. It is a spiritual practice, a way of connecting with others, a way of contributing back to my community and to all of creation. It is a form of activism, a creative, positive, giving, true way to maintain who we are as indigenous people, as Anishnaabe, and to protest against colonization in its many forms. It is a way to share, to reaffirm kinship, to connect with the sacredness of creation. I write because I believe love is medicine, love is the strongest power in creation, and writing is a way of expressing and experiencing this."

Kateri Akiwenzie-Damm, *"Notes on Authors"* 493

In his seminal article "Always Indigenize! The Radical Humanities in the Postcolonial Canadian Society", Len Findlay argues not only for the inclusion of Indigenous knowledges into the curricula of our post-secondary institutions but also for a "radical" transformation of our academic disciplines. He urges "a new beginning for Englishes as the redrawing of the academic map and redistribution of cultural legitimacy and territoriality under Indigenous educational leadership." (322) It is against the backdrop of his vision of "a thoroughly Indigenized future for all citizens" (316) that I wish to discuss the "response-ability" of literary critics toward Indigenous literatures. The term "response-ability" I want to employ with Anishnaabe scholar Kimberly Blaeser as representing "a kind of world view, a sense of being responsible by being engaged in life processes, of having both the capability and the obligation to live this way." ("Writing Voices" 54 and 66)

By taking Findlay's inclusive view of society as my point of departure, I intend to stress right at the outset of this paper that Indigenous literatures as well as other expressions of Indigenous knowledges are not only for Indigenous people. In a "radical" multicultural society striving to become *post*colonial, power relations are transformed so that "each act of cultural interlocution leaves *both* interlocutors changed." (Shohat and Stem 49, emphasis added) As non-Indigenous scholars of Indigenous literatures we may well be outsiders in our reading, teaching and critiquing of Indigenous texts, but we cannot stay outside of the cultural interlocution. Also, we cannot afford "to abdicate responsibility" (Bell Hooks 47) by remaining outside the processes of decolonization. As Indigenous author Lee Maracle explains in an interview, the onus to "undo" the dilemma caused by colonization is on "the White literary critic" (168), not on the Indigenous writer. However, it needs to be understood by the outsider critic that because the impact of colonization is "a serious thing" (Maracle 168), for the Aboriginal people and for all of society, Aboriginal literature is more than "just" another literature in English. It is here where "Indigenization" of literary criticism has to be anchored.

Jeannette Armstrong from the Okanagan Nation addresses "writers and shapers of philosophical direction" ("The

Disempowerment" 241) from the dominant society to *imagine* the different forms of disempowerment Aboriginal people had and still have to endure. It seems to me that such imagination forms the basis for any response to Aboriginal literature. The recognition that these texts form by definition the literature of survivors of genocide - even if humorously written - demands a reassessment of our conventional reading practices. Discussing "cultures of survival," Homi Bhaba argues that an "affective experience of social marginality - as it emerges in non-canonical cultural forms - *transforms* our critical strategies." (172, emphasis added) It is exactly such *affective* experience that Mohawk author Beth Brant demands from a reader of her stories distinguishing a reading with love, as she explains in the preface to *Food and Spirits*, from an exploitive understanding.

The latter still informs so-called postcolonial literary criticism. Mi'kmaq educator Marie Battiste advocates "[p]ostcolonial Indigenous thought" which "should not be confused with postcolonial theory in literature" as it is "based on our pain and our experiences, and it refuses to allow others to appropriate this pain and these experiences. It rejects the use of any Eurocentric theory or its categories." (xix) I am reminded here of a much earlier scholarly text criticizing non-Indigenous approaches to Indigenous literatures, an article entitled "The Imposition of Western Definitions of Literature on Indian Oral Traditions" by Chippewa scholar George Cornell. Although he speaks specifically about the oral traditions, it would be an expression of "Eurocentric theory" to create a boundary between "traditional oral" and "contemporary written" literature.[1] The continuance of an "oral aesthetics" (Blaeser, "Writing Voices"55) has been frequently argued by Indigenous scholars and is one of the reasons why an Indigenous author like Thomas King disagrees with the label "postcolonial" as a descriptor for Indigenous writing since it devalues a literary history which started long before colonization. ("Godzilla vs. Post-Colonial.") The thrust of Cornell's article lies in his emphasis on the limitations of the English discipline in understanding Indigenous modes of expression. He points out that "indigenous speakers never cultivate and develop words for purely artistic ends; ... Their words exist in nature and serve numerous purposes that can only be partially understood when analysed by academics in the disciplines of English and linguistics." (180) To "Indigenize" literary criticism means in the context of Cornell's argument to cross conventional disciplinary boundaries and to broaden European conceptualizations of aesthetic modes of expression. In the following I want to exemplify a variety of Indigenous perceptions of art and literature by analyzing the role of the artist character in literary texts. My methodology is in itself "Indigenized" in so far as I search for critical theory not in texts classified as such but as "existing within and arising from the literature itself." (Blaeser, "Native Literature" 59)[2]

In the third section of his book *Grey Owl: The Mystery of Archie Belaney*, titled "Journey," Anishnaabe poet Armand Garnet Ruffo includes the following poem:

"Why I write"

So I can live in the past
earn a living
protect the beaver
publicize conservation
attract attention,
sell 35,000 copies in 3 months
give 138 lectures in 88 days,
travel over 4,350 miles,
wear feathers,
wear make-up,
play Indian – no
be Indian,
get to go to pow wows,
get to tour Britain,
meet the King & Queen,
become famous,
become alcoholic,
leave a legacy,
lose a wife,
be lonely.

As this poem is taken from the context of Ruffo's book on Grey Owl, one may assume that the speaker is, of course, Grey Owl who indeed protected the beaver, publicized conservation through his writing, met the King & Queen, lost several wives, and was an alcoholic. However, in Ruffo's work there is no singleness of voice. This is not simply the confession of a wannabe Indian, but as well of the Aboriginal poet Armand Ruffo, an added voice which problematizes the persona of the speaker. Ruffo suggests in his biographical/autobiographical collage that there would have been no Grey Owl without a society desiring a Grey Owl. Therefore, the writer's voice may also be read as a criticism of a society which creates their "Indian writers" by expecting them to re-present a museum's type of culture and an "Indian" message.

I opened my discussion with this poem because it singles out the famous and lonely individual artist, an individual who had no roots in a community but appropriated a community speaking *for* them. In a particularly problematic way Grey Owl illustrates the role of the artist in relation to community. From an Aboriginal perspective, this link is an important one as illustrated in Akiwenzi-Damm's answer to the question "why I write" quoted in the epigraph to this paper. Her interpretation of her writing as a way of connecting with her community and all of creation *and*, because of these connections, as "a form of activism," is echoed in Jace Weaver's concept of "communitism," a term he coined of his "own devising" combining the words "'community'" and "'activism'" or "'activist.'" (37) The Cherokee scholar claims that "[a] feature that cuts across various Native worldviews is the importance of community" (37), and in relation to literature he contends "that the single thing that most defines Indian literatures relates to this sense of community and commitment to it." (43) Similarly, in her introduction to *Spider Woman's Granddaughter*, Paula Gunn Allen goes so far as to equate the "literary" with the "communal" worth of a narrative. (8) If, then, literary critics want to view Indigenous texts within an Indigenous epistemology, they have to read for communal contexts.

Cree author Tomson Highway starts off his novel *Kiss of the Fur Queen* with "A Note on the Trickster" thereby rooting his

English novel, from an Aboriginal perspective considered an "intensely egocentric genre" (Owens 10), in the philosophical and spiritual community of his Cree world. He also acknowledges the community of the storytellers of his people "on whose shoulders ... we, the current and upcoming generation of Native writers, stand" (Acknowledgements). Similarly, his autobiographical character Jeremiah Okimasis, the talented pianist, creates community in a context which celebrates the individual, the genius: he plays the "Preludes" by Russian composer Sergei Rachmaninoff for a prize at a competition, but he also plays "the loon cry, the wolves at nightfall, the aurora borealis in Mistik Lake" (213), of his home in northern Manitoba. In addition, his play connects with his troubled brother, his only family in Winnipeg, who is leaving town in an airplane while he is performing: "he built his crescendo on the runway of Winnipeg International Airport" (213) screaming his anger and despair. His brother Gabriel, deeply disturbed by the sexual abuse he had experienced as a child in residential school, has no use for Rachmaninoff. While Jeremiah is performing, he is leaving for an uncertain future with a lover who controls his life.

Important in the context of the present discussion is the response to the pianist's performance at the competition. The judges recognize his artistic abilities and make him the winner, but they still misinterpret him. "[B]eing from England, they had to be excused their ignorance of facts aboriginal" (212) we are told. They do not bother to find out about his background; Apache, Commanche, Kickapoo – it is all the same to them. What matters is that his "Indian youth" whose father, so they claim, "slaughtered wild animals and drank their blood in appeasement of some ill-tempered pagan deity ... was about to perform Rachmaninoff." (213) Their understanding of community does not go beyond the stereotypical "Indian" context associated with corresponding stereotypes about his "positively animal passion." (213) They are ignorant of those community links which have been severely damaged by the colonial system, but are still existing – "albeit a little the worse for wear and tear" as Highway says about the survival of "the trickster" ("Note on the Trickster"). The incongruity between the pianist's performance and the response of the audience shows in the differing perceptions of the value of the prize: a winner in the eyes of the audience, he knows his losses. Famous, but lonely, he leaves the concert hall for the bar where his brother used to hang out:

> So drunk that only the starch of his tuxedo collar - soiled, punctured by a cigarette - held up his head, Jeremiah stared at his reflection in the trophy. Try as he might to will Gabriel into its smoke-obscured universe, the image remained infuriatingly alone. Beyond it, across the room, drunken Indians as far as the eye could see. He had tried. Tried to change the meaning of his past, the roots of his hair, the colour of his skin, but he was one of them. What was he to do with Chopin? Open a conservatory on Eemanapiteepitat hill? Whip its residents into the Cree Philharmonic Orchestra? (215)

Although one of the Native women in the bar eventually gets somebody to take a picture of her and Jeremiah stating "You make me so proud to be a fuckin' Indian, you know that" (216), her praise cannot distract him from the realization that he has no community for his art. He quits his career as a concert pianist and becomes a social worker instead. Jeannette Armstrong's explanation about the role of the Native artist from her perspective as the director of the En'owkin Centre reads like a commentary on this character's decision:

> [T]hat's one of the things that you'll feel: that in the Native context, what you are gifted with, and what you have been given in terms of skills, doesn't only belong to you. It belongs to the community, and it is there for the benefit of the community, to benefit the community in some way. And the responsibility of the artist is to ensure that, however much the artist is elevated, the community alongside must be elevated as well and must benefit as well. (Isernhagen 162)

Tomson Highway himself gave up Chopin. "I asked myself, what can I do with classical music and the Indian people?" (qtd. in Wigston 8) After working in various Native organizations for several years, he eventually became a playwright and the author of *Kiss of the Fur Queen*. He composed his autobiographical novel like a musical score: Part One - Allegro ma non troppo; Part Two - Andante Cantabile; Part Three - Allegretto grazioso; Part

Four - Molto agitato (contains the above episode); Part Five - Adagio espressivo; Part Six – Presto con fuoco. Reading his script, those of us who are non-Aboriginal scholars are now in the place of the judges, but, as we live in Canada and not in Great Britain, we are not excused for our "ignorance of facts aboriginal." If we want to "Indigenize" our reading of his novel, we need to do better than just give him our prizes and reduce his art to a few stereotypical preconceptions about "Nativeness." If we understand his need for community context as a basis for his art, we need to act upon changing the glaring contradiction between our celebration of Aboriginal arts and our negligence of Aboriginal communities. In short, we should take to heart Drew Hayden Taylor's criticism of a character in his play *alterNatives*, a professor of Native literature: "It's the stories you like, not the reality." (136)

Further describing the scene in the bar after the concert, the narrator in Highway's novel all of a sudden switches from English to Cree: "Oogimow!Oogimow!... Tantee kageegimooteein anima misti-mineeg'wachigan?" (215) (translated in the glossary at the end of the novel as "Chief, where did you steal the big cup?"). The novel character trades the concert hall for the bar to connect with his brother and to find his people and hear his first language; the author of the novel crosses the boundary in the opposite direction: he brings his people's language, usually only heard in ghettoized places of our society, into the elitist literary discourse of a novel. His contrapuntal inclusion of the Cree voice in the musical score of a novel in English obliges us to a cultural listening which "involves a salutary process of dehierarchization" as Heble describes Glen Gould's interpretation of the listening to counterpoint. (29) English is important, yet also limiting. It does not help with the understanding of the opening unglossed phrase of the novel: "igwani igoosi, n'seemis." I asked a Cree-speaking friend for the English translation – "This is for my little brother" – and hence created an oral connection beyond the written text and a link with a community outside academia (my friend needed to consult with other Cree speakers). With Arun Mukherjee, who had similar experiences with teaching the interspersion of an East Indian language in Rohinton Mistry's *Such A Long Journey*, I would argue that

> "[s]uch a hermeneutic, [...], is far more democratic than the expert-dominated literary criticism of the past, where the trained critic spoke as authority. This hermeneutic is built on the premise that knowledge needed to decode the text is dispersed in the social environment the reader lives in and can be had through communicating with friends, colleagues and neighbours." (167)

Aboriginal languages cannot easily be standardized in a dictionary or a grammar book: the best way to learn them is to communicate with the speakers of the respective language. By leaving the opening sentence to his novel unglossed, Tomson Highway points the reader to the community of Cree speakers. One may argue that his dedication of the novel to his brother articulated in Cree could be read synecdochically as an acknowledgement of his primary audience: his people. Those readers who understand this gesture as exclusionary should be reminded that the residential school, featuring so prominently in this novel, forced the English language on Cree speaking students with life-ruining methods. In a society that talks about reconciliation with its Aboriginal peoples it is time that non-Aboriginal readers understand Tomson Highway's gesture not as exclusion but as an invitation to learn about his people *with* his people, to leave the "library fortress" and the "scholarly garrison" (Hoy 35) in order to go out into the communities. In the recent APTN pilot episode of *Story Keepers* on April 24, Maria Campbell explained that one of the effects of her autobiography *Halfbreed* was that (and here I quote from my memory) "it forced people to come inside my kitchen instead of looking through the window." Such views "from the inside" gained through Aboriginal texts should have an impact on our responsibilities as literary critics.

In one of my Native literature classes some years back, an Aboriginal student prefaced her term paper by questioning the role of literary criticism in relation to Aboriginal literature as, according to her, it interferes with the potential for healing which she considered the core of the writing. However, as Constance Rooke reminds us in an article in which she re-assesses the role of theory, we as non-Aboriginal critics do not have to pursue "life-alienating practices" (Bowerbank and Wawia 227); we do not have to practice "criticism as rape" as Rooke puts it (135); we have a choice. We may either choose "membership in a very specialized 'guild' (143)" or we can respond "with love" as Beth Brant demands (and Constance Rooke echoes in her quoting of Rilke) and "hold out a promise of community much larger, more inclusive." (Rooke 143) Although coming from a different perspective, Rooke advocates an approach to literary criticism which I call "Indigenized" in the context of this paper. Similarities in argument may signify a shift in the humanities which does not only relate to the *study of* Indigenous knowledges but is indicative of a larger process of a re-evaluation of scholarship *influenced by* Indigenous thought.

Another recent Aboriginal artist novel, *Whispering in Shadows* by Okanagan author Jeannette Armstrong, points to further complexities of the role and meaning of art. Similar to Tomson Highway, Jeannette Armstrong works in several media; while he went from being a pianist to becoming a playwright and novelist, she turned from being a visual artist to becoming a writer as well. In each case their choices were shaped by their concerns for their people, and particularly in Armstrong's case, the environment. The activist Armstrong who calls herself "a visual artist, primarily" (qtd. In Isernhagen 165) explains that she "can create and write on a plane or on a bus or … wherever" but could not "find a way to do that with the kind of visual arts that [I] she was producing" (qtd. In Isernhagen 165-66), and Tomson Highway could achieve as a writer what was impossible to do as a pianist: combine his "knowledge of Indian reality in this country with classical structure, artistic language." (qtd. in Wigston 8) Each one fictionalized his or her career changes in a novel which reflects their other talent - Tomson Highway by composing his narrative in the structure of a musical score, Jeannette Armstrong by creating "a painting" as Lee Maracle praises her novel (back cover). Other Aboriginal writers share a similar history of working in different media - from visual arts and film making to journalism and writing in different literary genres. Their inclusive understanding of arts and creativity is another reason why Aboriginal literature, categorized as such in non-Aboriginal institutions, calls for interdisciplinary approaches.

There are two episodes in *Whispering in Shadows* which describe the protagonist during a show of her work. In the first one, Penny, a visual arts student from the University of Victoria, displays paintings which were inspired by her participation in an anti-logging protest on Vancouver Island. The last guest of the show, an agent for an art gallery who introduces herself as "artist cum philosopher" (124), asks her why she "decided to work in a purely contemporary format.' (126) Penny's puzzled reaction – "As opposed to what?" – leads the agent to clarify that she was wondering why she did not follow the style of "most Native American artists" who "incorporate or reconstruct symbolism from their heritage in their works." (126) After recollecting herself – "Now what do I say to that? What the heck is she asking?," Penny answers politely:

> Really? I hadn't thought of that. It's my subject, I suppose. My concern has been in the way colour moves. It speaks. It's not something I choose. The imagery is a way to explore meaning within that. But the imagery is secondary. Although at some level the preoccupation I have with the positioning of warm nature against hard science comes from my Indigenous world-view, I suppose. I'm sorry, but I do have a bit of a drive tonight. It's been very nice speaking with you. (127)

As the conclusion of her answer reveals, she is not interested in this viewer of her art. Because of the ghettoization of her work and preconceived notions about "Indian art" (based on societal assumptions that made a Grey Owl possible), she feels "lumped in." (127) Her answer to the agent's query reveals that her art is inspired by several sources, not just by her so-called heritage but also by "the way colour moves." In the words of well-known Ojibway artist Carl Beam, "Indian art that's made as Indian is racially motivated, and I just can't do that. My work is not made for Indian people but for thinking people." (qtd. in Grand 105-106) The novel character Penny prefers the response to her art by a woman from the environmental network because this viewer is a "thinking" person; she does not "exoticize" and "other" her work thereby distancing herself from it but creates a link with her own commitment toward change. Similarly, the author Jeannette Armstrong, the environmental activist, wrote a novel which carries, as Eleanor Sioui says, "the ecological, creative curing power of American Indian poets" (qtd. In Francis and Bruchac 36) and therefore requires a reader response which is "lived, not consumed." (Blaeser, "Writing voices" 63)

The second show of the artist described in the novel evolved out of her trip to Chiapas foregrounding the human more than the non-human community. Her paintings have, as the curator points out to her, an "extreme graphic quality" (202), and although her "sense of colour and composition is … extraordinary" (203), he is still worried that they will not sell because they are too shocking; people "want something that can hang well. Just a teensy titillating and thought provoking." (203) Her paintings may "work as political statement" but "they're so very negative. The eyes in every piece, so haunting, so filled with despair." (202) The artist totally dismisses his viewpoint which judges her art for its market value. "Shock value? Damn right! I want to shock some sense into people. I want them to see it for what it is. There's a fucking outrage happening out there, in case you haven't noticed." (203) Their conversation ends with her realization that, as Beth Brant would say, she "betrayed" the people whose stories she painted because those who visit the gallery and who will be able to afford to buy her paintings will not "love" them, or with Delaware playwright Daniel David Moses: "There is some medicine that non-Natives don't want to swallow." (qtd. in Francis and Bruchac 32) Like the Cree pianist character in Tomson Highway's novel, she misses a community for her art and therefore destroys her paintings and gives up her work as an artist. Eventually, while continuing her commitment to activism, she becomes a writer.

It is shown in both novels that artists need to make a choice between aesthetic and activist values due to the fragmentation, the "atomistic thinking" in our society which Aboriginal scholar Ermine considers "the cornerstone of Western ideology" (103) and which shapes our responses to art and literature. Author Jeanette Armstrong succeeded in overcoming the dilemma of her autobiographical character by creating novels which are written with an "activist aesthetics" as Manina Jones says about her first novel *Slash*. However, as Jones also points out, her writing was not well received initially. *Whispering in Shadows* again challenges critics because of its wide range of styles and tones. Shifting narrative perspectives in loosely connected poems, diary entries, letters, traditional stories and accounts of contemporary events require active reader participation. Their response - ability is comparable to the process of culturally defined listening: "Listeners are drawn into the dilemma and are expected at some point in their lives to actively work themselves out of it." (Maracle "Preface" 12)

Cherokee author Thomas King uses different means than Jeannette Armstrong to draw in his readers. In *Truth and Bright Water*, his most recent novel, the artist character is not constructed as having to make a choice, to sacrifice art for activism or communitism, but as undermining an art/reality dualism by re-validating the transformative power of art. The "restoration artist" Munroe Swimmer makes the church disappear and the buffalo re-appear. His way of painting the church so that it blends into nature has the effect that he "lost track of the church" (218); his installation of buffaloes made of iron wire causes the narrator to comment that "[t]hey sort of look real." (135) In each case the viewer's perception of reality is changed from accepting what is - the presence of the church and the near extinction of the buffalo - toward a desire for what ought to be: spiritual beliefs which are not fixated, neither in a dogma nor in a building, and free roaming buffalo providing the basis for an interconnected lifestyle. After the child narrator comments on the (quasi-)reality of the buffalo made out of wire, "Munroe's face explodes in smiles and tears. 'Yes,' he says. 'Yes,' that's exactly right." (135) Paradoxically then, or paradoxically within a dualistic world view, art takes on an ethical function. The artist's "restoring" of reality makes the viewer (and the reader of the novel) aware of the need for change, an awareness which carries the potential for "real" change. Although Munroe Swimmer is only an artist going "around the world fixing paintings," (129) it is said about him that his brushes are "magic." His special powers are ironically illustrated by his "failure" of fixing a nineteenth century painting: "The new paint wouldn't hold. Almost as soon as I finished, the images began to bleed through again.... There was an Indian village on the lake, slowly coming up through the layers of paint. Clear as day." (130) The "Indian artist" uses his art as "spiritual practice" in the sense in which Akiwenzie-Damm explains her writing as "a form of activism [...] to protest against colonization in its many forms." ("Notes" 493) By connecting with all of creation in a "magic" way he overcomes the art/reality polarity; in fact, he considers magic essential for change: "If you want the herds to return, you have to understand magic.... Realism will only take you so far" (198); his artistic restorations are prerequisites for real change to happen. "By a clever shift of syntax, he [Swimmer] transforms Indians from the subject of removals into agents of their own re-creation. [...] Swimmer knows the efficacy of sacred formulas." (Ridington 93) Although the artist's "magic" may be dismissed as postmodern play and, like King's novel, only seen for its aesthetic effects, there is an "Indian" reality "coming up through the layers" of his art, stories which speak to the responsibility of readers and critics of this novel to take the transformative power of art one step further into the reality outside the text. In the many characterizations in this novel of the merely consuming, exploiting tourists, King seems to make a point about non-desirable reading strategies of "Indian" art, culture and stories - his own included.

Maria Campbell asserted in the aforementioned APTN program (again I am quoting from my memory) that "any single thing that we do as artists and storytellers"—and she considered visual art, film making, writing, etc. interchangeable in this context—"we do to make change." In the second novel by Métis author Culleton Mosionier *In the Shadow of Evil* the transformative power of words is not shown in the genre of magic realism but as a mystery novel. It features two writer characters, a husband and wife team. While he is portrayed as a "serious" writer of novels thinking *about plots* all the time (20), she, the first-person narrator of the novel, does not see much value in her own "inconsequential past as a writer of children's books." (24) This contrast at the outset of the novel develops into an interesting reversal: he will be silenced as he is captured in "a secret compound of white supremacist maniacs" (217), a setting which he had *imagined* for one of his novel plots, while she turns into the "serious" narrator of the *real* story of her childhood, the sexual abuse which she experienced as a three year old, and which affected the rest of her life. What is imagined in the manuscript of the husband's novel, becomes "real"; what is real, a childhood trauma, is first fictionalized, i.e. further repressed, in "wonderful stories for children" (205) but eventually told by the adult narrator who becomes more accepting of herself at the end. In the beginning, "the evil" in this novel is internalized by the victim of the abuse as "my evil secrets." (20) However, as the novel unfolds, the evil is seen as systemic, although personalized in one particular character, as violence against women and Native people. Racism takes on Holocaust dimensions in the compound of the militia with a picture of Hitler and "a poster of a swastika." (296) Revealing for the context of this paper is the role of the male novelist character: he is inspired by the building of the compound, uses it for his imagination, but does not pursue the reality behind it. This reality becomes eventually the way his manuscript gets "published": his writing disappears, but what he wrote is turned into lived experience. It may be significant that in this novel written from an Aboriginal perspective, a non-Aboriginal writer is constructed as successful according to conventional criteria yet is shown as failing when his writing is tested by a reality he chooses to ignore. Not only are his scripts overridden/overwritten by a power he does not care to acknowledge, but they also lack efficacy for real life situations. When his wife is confronted with dangers reminiscent of the imagined murder scenes in his novels, she finds no help trying to apply what she had learnt while playacting for him. (296) On the other hand, the Native woman writer establishes her own voice by re-writing her past in a story which leads from denial and fear to acceptance and healing.

In this paper I tried to demonstrate how the theme of the artist in Indigenous texts suggests ways of "Indigenizing" the study of Indigenous literatures. In each text readers are taken "outside" the text to communal, socio-political and environmental contexts and are reminded of the power of artistic creations written so "that the people might live" as Jace Weaver emphasizes in the title of his book. To "Indigenize" the study of Indigenous literatures means to respect the connectedness that Indigenous artists and writers name as their source of inspiration in approaches which are in themselves connected - with different disciplines, languages and discourses and reaching out into Aboriginal communities.

In conclusion I want to come back to Akiwenzie-Damm who set the tone for this paper and put my words *in relation* to hers. In her poem titled *kegedonce* meaning (as, again, I found out by asking) "little word,"[3] she celebrates the writer not as the lonely Grey Owl but as *in conversation*, making connections. Words are "given" by all of creation, and they give back creating community:

words are my manitouwan my conjurors
with their magic the spider can be set in her web
the old people can live in the memory of generations
people from every direction can be made kin

It is hoped that those who read and "study" these words may continue building community.

Notes

1 As the perspectival approach of this roundtable book de-emphasizes expertise and values an acknowledgement of limitations and *process*, I think it is appropriate to add a brief anecdote here. I learnt about Cornell's article in my early days of studying Aboriginal literatures at a conference in Northwest Ontario. Asked to present my ideas about a course on Aboriginal literature, I gave an outline structured around the very genres Cornell criticizes as "imposition." During a break one of the Anishnaabe organizers of the conference took me aside and showed me a photocopy of Cornell's paper which at that time had not been published. After my initial reaction of shock – why had I not seen this earlier? – I explained that of course I was not dealing with the oral traditions but with contemporary writing in English. However, neither the person accompanying me nor other Native people at the conference to whom I talked later considered this a valid argument. I accepted their criticism of my approach, but it took me years to really understand it.

2 In more detail, Lee Maracle comments on theory in story form in her article "Oratory: Coming to Theory." *Give Back: First Nations*

Perspectives on Cultural Practice. North Vancouver: Gallerie, 1992. 86-93

[3] Anishnaabe students in my class also gave me the translation: "I am talking."

Works Cited

Akiwenzie-Damm, Kateri. "kegedonce." *An Anthology of Canadian Native Literature in English.* Ed. Daniel David Moses & Terry Goldie. Toronto: Oxford University Press, 1998. 458.

- - -. "Notes on Authors." *An Anthology of Canadian Native Literature in English*. 493.

Allen, Paula Gunn. *Spider Woman's Granddaughters: Traditional Tales and Contemporary Writing by Native American Women*. New York: Fawcett Columbine, 1989.

Armstrong, Jeannette. "The Disempowerment of First North American Native Peoples and Empowerment Through Their Writing." *An Anthology of Canadian Native Literature in English.* Ed. Daniel David Moses and Terry Goldie. Toronto: Oxford University Press, 1998. 239-42.

- - -. *Whispering in Shadows*. Penticton: Theytus Books Ltd., 2000.

Battiste, Marie, ed. *Reclaiming Indigenous Voice and Vision*. Vancouver: UBC Press, 2000.

Bhaba, Homi K. *The Location of Culture*. London and New York: Routledge, 1994.

Blaeser, Kimberly M. "Native Literature: Seeking a Critical Center." *Looking at the Words of our People*. Ed. Jeannette Armstrong. Penticton: Theytus, 1993. 51-62.

- - -. "Writing Voices Speaking: Native authors and an oral aesthetic." *Talking on the page: editing aboriginal oral texts*. Ed. Laura J. Murray and Karen Rice. Toronto: University of Toronto Press, 1999. 53-68

Bowerbank, Sylvia and Dolores Wawia. "Wild Lessons: Native Ecological Wisdom in Ruby Slipperjack's Fiction." *Homemaking: Women Writers and the Politics and Poetics of Home*. New York and London: Garland Publications, 1996. 223-37.

Brant, Beth. *Food and Spirits*. Vancouver: Press Gang Publishers, 1991.

Cornell, George L. "The Impositions of Western Definitions of Literature on Indian Oral Traditions." *The Native in Literature*. Ed. Thomas King, Cheryl Calver and Helen Hoy. ECW Press, 1987. 174-87.

Culleton Mosionier, Beatrice. *In the Shadow of Evil*. Penticton: Theytus Books, 2000.

Ermine, Willie. "Aborigial Epistemology." *First Nations Educations in Canada: The Circle Unfolds*. Ed. Marie Battiste and Jean Barman. Vancouver: UBC Press, 1995. 101-112.

Findlay, Len. "Always Indigenize! The Radical Humanities in the Postcolonial Canadian University." *Ariel* 31 (2000): 307-26.

Francis, Lee and James Bruchac, ed. *Reclaiming the Vision: Past, Present and Future: Native Voices for the Eighth Generation*. New York: The Greenfield Review Press, 1996.

Grande, John K. *Balance: Art and Nature*. Montreal: Black Rose Books, 1994.

Heble, Ajay. "Sounds of Change: Dissonance, History, and Cultural Listening." *Essays on Canadian Writing* 71 (Fall 2000): 26-36.

Highway, Tomson. *Kiss of the Fur Queen*. Toronto, Ontario: Doubleday Canada Limited, 1998.

Hooks, Bell. *Talking Back: thinking feminist, thinking black*. Toronto: Between the Lines, 1989.

Hoy, Helen. "'When You Admit You're a Thief, Then You Can Be Honourable": Native/Non-Native Collaboration in *The Book of Jessica*." *Canadian Literature* 136 (Spring 1993): 24-39.

Isernhagen, Hartwig. *Momaday, Vizenor, Armstrong: Conversations on American Indian Writing*. Norman: University of Oklahoma Press, 1999.

Jones, Manina. "Slash marks the Spot: 'Critical Embarrassment' and Activist Aesthetics in Jeannette Armstrong's *Slash*." *West Coast Line* 30 (2000): 48-62.

King, Thomas. "Godzilla vs. Post-Colonial." *World Literature Written in English*. 30.2 (1990): 10-16.

- - - . *Truth and Bright Water*. Toronto: Harper Collins, 1999.

Maracle, Lee. Interview. *Sounding Differences: Conversations with Seventeen Canadian Women Writers.* Janice Williamson. Toronto: University of Toronto Press, 1993. 160-78.

- - - . "Preface. You become the Trickster." *Sojourner's Truth and other stories.* By Lee Maracle. 11-13.

Mukherjee, Arun. "Teaching Ethnic Minority Writing: A Report from the Classroom." *Literary Pluralities.* Ed. Christl Verduyn. Peterborough: Broadview Press, 1998. 162-71.

Owens, Louis. "Other Destinies, Other Plots. An Introduction to Indian Novels." *Other Destinies: Understanding the American Indian.* Novel by Owens. Norman and London: University of Oklahoma Press. 1992. 3-31.

Ridington Robin. "Happy Trails to You: Contexted Discourse and Indian Removals in Thomas King's *Truth & Bright Water.*" *Canadian Literature* 167 (Winter 2000): 89-107.

Rooke, Constance. "Praise, the Academy, and the Common Reader." *Relocating Praise: Literary Modalities and Rhetorical Contexts.* Ed. Alice G. den Otter. Toronto: Canadian Scholars' Press, 2000. 131-44.

Ruffo, Armand G. *Grey Owl: The Mystery of Archie Belaney.* Regina: Coteau Books, 1996.

Shohat, Ella and Robert Stam. *Unthinking Eurocentrism: Multiculturalism and the Media.* London and New York: Routledge, 1994.

Taylor, Drew Hayden. *alterNatives.* Burnaby, B.C.: Talonbooks, 2000.

Weaver, Jace. *That the People Might Live: Native American Literatures and Native American Community.* New York, Oxford: Oxford University Press, 1997.

Wigston, Nancy. "Nanabush in the City." *Books in Canada.* March 1989: 7-9

Begin with the Text: Aboriginal Literatures and Postcolonial Theories

Debra Dudek

"Home was a young girl rushing through a meadow, a cedar basket swishing lightly against dew-laden leaves, her nimble fingers plucking ripe fat berries from their branches, the wind playfully teasing and tangling the loose, waist-length black hair that glistened in the autumnal dawn while her mind enjoyed the prospect of becoming . . . becoming, and the words in English would not come. She remembered the girl, the endless stories told to her, the meanings behind each story, the careful coaching in the truth that lay behind each one, the reasons for their telling, but she could not, after fifty years of speaking crippled English, define where it was all supposed to lead. Now all that remained was the happiness of her childhood memories against the stark emptiness of the years that stretched behind them."

–from "Bertha" by Lee Maracle

In this essay, I shall focus primarily on whether it is useful to apply postcolonial theories to Aboriginal[1] literatures, especially those written in a canadian[2] context. I base this work on my experience as a non-Indigenous university academic entering into my third year of full-time sessional teaching as an Assistant Professor. Throughout this paper, I shall be cognizant of Len Findlay's command to "Always Indigenize!" and I hope that it will be apparent that the strategies I outline will indeed be informed by that command and by Findlay's "doublet, vision and conspiracy," (307) as a means of Indigenizing the classroom.

Overall, this paper questions how to contextualize canadian Aboriginal literatures with literatures by other colonized peoples, while at the same time ensuring cultural and socio-political specificity. Can postcolonial theories open discussions between such literatures? I illustrate these questionings primarily through the issue of language. I begin by briefly outlining some of the problems that Indigenous writers, teachers, and critics have voiced about the position and usage of postcolonial as a term, a discourse, and a theory. I will address some of these concerns and will also put them to work by highlighting the importance of being attentive to how texts interact with each other. This attentiveness is especially important when teaching literatures by Indigenous writers; I will say more about this point later in this essay. To conclude, I shall argue that it is useful in literary analysis, and especially in the classroom, to introduce postcolonial theory when studying a text by an Indigenous author, but, more importantly, I argue that readers should always begin with the text and should listen to what the text asks of the reader.

The ways in which I understand and use theories are heavily informed by my background in feminism. I see theory as both critique and construct. It is both personal and political. Theory is both a method of analysis and a strategy for social change. It can move between dense didactic discourse and powerful purposeful poetry. Following from Gayatri Spivak's essay "Can the Subaltern Speak?" in which Spivak locates a conversation between Michel Foucault and Gilles Deleuze as a site that "undoes the opposition between authoritative theoretical production and the unguarded practice of conversation, enabling one to glimpse the track of ideology" (66), I hope that this essay works—as part of a roundtable discussion invoked in the title of this collection—to be both theoretical and conversational and to continue conversations about pedagogical practices, which are too often kept private, in the academy. At times "authoritative theoretical production" may seem to teachers and academics like a safer—perhaps a more professional—practice because one might believe that theory is guarded, is a mask and that conversation is open, is faced, but this binary does not hold. Theory can be as unguarded as conversation can be masked. It *is* a risk to put theory to work as unguarded conversation, but I believe that these sites of conversation are precisely the places where people should begin meeting. For instance, we visit each other's classrooms far too infrequently. I invite you into the classroom with me so that we can share resources, experiences, knowledges, and then produce strategies for social change.

Current debates about postcolonial cultural studies and literary theory in a canadian context are lively and diverse. Over the past fifteen years, academics and writers have begun and continued discussions about canadian postcolonialisms. However, the 1990s have been especially fruitful for postcolonial studies in canada. Writings by canadian critics and teachers about postcolonial theories

1. address concerns that postcolonial theory is a homogenizing theory that groups together diverse individuals and literatures into a single colonized subject (Mukherjee 1998);
2. question the inclusion of invader-settler societies in postcolonial studies (Brydon and Tiffin (1993); Lawson (1991); Slemon (1990); Williams and Chrisman (1994));
3. and recognize the need to distinguish between the postcolonialisms of settler and non-settler countries (see especially the Special Issue on Postcolonial Writing. *Essays on Canadian Writing* Fall 1995).[3]

Many of these discussions circulate around and through definitions and usages of the fluid and contentious term *postcolonialism*. Definitions of postcolonialism range from early chronological meanings to recent manifestations as a term that signifies various political, linguistic, and cultural experiences of societies that were former european colonies. As Stephen Slemon summarizes, in "The Scramble for Post-colonialism," postcolonialism

> has been used as a way of ordering a critique of totalizing forms of Western historicism; as a portmanteau term for a retooled notion of 'class'; as a subset of both postmodernism and post-structuralism (and conversely, as the condition from which those two structures of cultural logic and cultural critique themselves are seen to emerge); as the name for a condition of nativist longing in post-independence national groupings; as a cultural marker of non-residency for a Third World intellectual cadre; as the inevitable underside of a fractured and ambivalent discourse of colonialist power; as an oppositional form of 'reading practice'; and ... as the name for a category of 'literary' activity which sprang from a new and welcome political energy going on within what used to be called 'Commonwealth' literary studies. (45)

I find it crucial to recognize and identify specificities of race and location, which work against the homogenizing effect of the term *postcolonial*. Postcolonial *theory*, then, must also be attentive to the historical, political, cultural, and economic ramifications of european imperialism that are represented in that one specific text, at least as the first approach to the bringing together of theory and literature. I believe this crucial to acknowledge and analyze the specific experiences of individuals and groups that have been affected by european imperialism.

For me, feminist and postcolonial theories are useful as languages that give voice to oppositional politics. This connection between feminism and postcolonialism is as important as it is complex, especially when the debate expands to include discussions about whether the politics of gender or the politics of race are more important factors in women's lives. Discussions about feminism are already informed by serious and valid accusations of how (Western) feminism has failed and often continues to fail to account for women who are at least doubly oppressed. Postcolonial discourses and analyses must not make parallel failures around categories of racial and ethnic specificity and must also be attentive to how colonization often affected and affects men and women in different ways. Postcolonial critics must be strategic and must—as Len Findlay argues in his discussion about the connection between "strategic research and teaching" and "postcolonial notions like 'strategic essentialism'"—"be respectfully strategic rather than presumptuously exotic, and driven by the need to benefit Indigenous people according to *their* rights, needs, and aspirations." (313, emphasis in original) Both postcolonial and feminist critiques are politically motivated to initiate social change by producing theories of agency. Postcolonial and feminist critics must foreground theory as complicated and complex critiques in order to resist reproducing and reinscribing dominant ideologies.

Does or can postcolonial theories open texts by Indigenous writers in productive ways? Several Indigenous writers and critics—such as Thomas King, Linda Tuhiwai Smith, and Kimberly M. Blaeser—argue that the term *postcolonial* neither describes nor empowers either Indigenous peoples or their literatures. Thomas King, in "Godzilla vs. Post-Colonial," addresses some of the problems of using the term *post-colonial* to describe Native literatures:

> While post-colonialism purports to be a method by which we can begin to look at those literatures which are formed out of the struggle of the oppressed against the oppressor, the colonized and the colonizer, the term itself assumes that the starting point for that discussion is the advent of Europeans in North America. At the same time, the term organizes the literature progressively suggesting that there is both progress and improvement. No less distressing, it also assumes that the struggle between guardian and ward is the catalyst for contemporary Native literature, providing those of us who write with method and topic. And, worst of all, the idea of post-colonial writing effectively cuts us off from our traditions, traditions that were in place before colonialism ever became a question, traditions which have come down to us through our cultures in spite of colonization, and it supposes that contemporary Native writing is largely a construct of oppression. Ironically, while the term itself—post-colonial—strives to escape to find new centres, it remains, in the end, a hostage to nationalism. (242-43)

And Smith, in her book *Decolonizing Methodologies: Research and Indigenous Peoples,* claims,

> post-colonial discussions have ... stirred some indigenous resistance, not so much to the literary reimagining of culture as being centred in what were once conceived of as the colonial margins, but to the idea that colonialism is over, finished business.... There is also, amongst indigenous academics, the sneaking suspicion that the fashion of post-colonialism has become a strategy for reinscribing or reauthorizing the privileges of non-indigenous academics because the field of 'post-colonial' discourse has been defined in ways which can still leave out indigenous peoples, our ways of knowing and our current concerns. (24)

Similarly, Blaeser, in her article "Native Literature: Seeking a Critical Center" in the collection *Looking at the Words of our People: First Nations Analysis of Literature,* argues that

> [t]he insistence on reading Native literature by way of Western literary theory clearly violates its integrity and performs a new act of colonization and conquest.... [When] Native American literature ... is approached with an already established theory ... the implication is that the worth of the literature is essentially validated by its demonstrated adherence to a respected literary mode, dynamic or style. (55-56)

All three critics—King, Smith, and Blaeser—make clear some problems of categorizing either literature, method, discourse, or theory as postcolonial when speaking about Native literatures. Blaeser suggests using dialogue that arises within and between Native texts as a way of creating a critical language wherein "texts in their richness quote and comment on one another." (60) Instead of utilizing only postcolonial theories that come from outside a primary text, I suggest that non-Native critics and teachers employ Blaeser's strategy as a starting point which then can be respectfully supplemented by postcolonial theories. It would be not only detrimental to Native literatures to ignore these concerns but also detrimental for those of us who teach Indigenous writing to ignore a theorizing voice that organizes, for teachers and readers, a pedagogical context.

Bell Hooks, in *Teaching to Transgress: Education as the Practice of Freedom,* states, "Theory is not inherently healing, liberatory, or revolutionary. It fulfills this function only when we ask that it do so and direct our theorizing towards this end." (61) The classroom is neither a static site for updated history nor the place for teachers to presume "healing." However, it is the pedagogical moment—that unplanned moment of unguarded conversation that teaches—that offers both teachers and students an entrance into text, into theory, into context. Jo-Ann Episkenew, at the 2001 CACLALS Annual Conference, spoke in her paper, "The Problem of Hybridity in Mixed-blood Identity: Whose Problem Is It Anyway?" about the need for non-Native critics to be cognizant of the ideological baggage they bring to a Native text. How can non-Native critics be cognizant and make visible this ideological baggage? How can non-Native academics who are committed to teaching Native literatures ensure that any use of (Western) theory does not commit the treachery of colonizing Native literatures? How do I make sure that theory can be "healing, liberatory, or revolutionary?" I shall listen. Invite. Envision. Strategize. Conspire. Question. Revise. Begin again. I shall not answer the questions but keep asking them.

One of the processes in preparing a course outline is to be attentive to the ways in which texts speak to each other, as I mentioned at the beginning of this essay, or in Blaeser's words how texts in their richness "quote and comment on one another." (60) This is important for all literatures but perhaps is even more important for me when I teach Native literatures, when the texts being read are already informed by such course titles as *Contexts in Canadian Literature* and *Canadian Regional Literature.* In these instances, I find it especially important to engage in analyses of canon formation, the nation-state, and other imagined categories of identity such as region.

Figure 1 (see Appendix) is a condensed but complete example of a course outline I have used for a first-year introduction to english course. For the purposes of this example, I shall focus on some of the ways in which we read the last six texts individually and in connection with each other. I would like to emphasize that my course descriptions state, "Our first priority will always be to begin with the texts and then move out from the experiences represented by those texts. We will also engage with postcolonial, feminist, and other literary theories in order to, perhaps, deepen our understanding of the primary texts." This aspect of my course description is to bring attention to the importance of first discussing how texts interact with readers and then moving into how texts interact with each other and with theories.

In the second class discussing *The Tempest,* I do a brief introduction to literary theory by summarizing nine critical and textual approaches and then providing examples of how one might read the play via each of these theories. I emphasize that the theories are not always mutually exclusive; indeed they often overlap and interweave with each other, and each approach in itself is not homogeneous. One of the approaches I introduce is postcolonialism. Following a brief introduction to postcolonialism, as a class we participate in what is now a well-known reading of *The Tempest,* looking specifically at Prospero's takeover of the island and his enslavement of Caliban. We also discuss education and language, focusing on the different ways in which each teaches the other (1.2.325-31). We talk about the divisions of labour on the island and the different ways of knowing what each character embodies. Prospero names while Caliban shows, and Caliban's famous rebuttal demonstrates his understanding of naming as both a gift and a curse: "You taught me language, and my profit on't / Is, I know how to curse. The red plague rid you / For learning me your language" (1.2.362-4). This dialectic is further complicated because arguably, Caliban speaks some of the most beautiful prose in all the play (3.2.130-38). Only Caliban could say this speech because he knows the island and accepts the magic of it without knowing of Ariel. Prospero can educate Caliban by teaching him english language, but, based on his experience, Caliban makes it poetry.

These openings of *The Tempest* provide a language with which we might analyze the texts we study next. One might argue that using Shakespeare as foundation is dangerous because of the possibilities for further textual colonization. However, I stress the importance of starting anew with each text and then opening the readings up to conversations with other texts. I realize that this is an idealistic stance and that a reader is never a blank slate, but I find it crucial not to separate text from context, and I emphasize this as a reading strategy.

However, I also believe it is important to work between local and universal knowledges, in the sense that Ngugi wa Thiong'o, in his essay "The Universality of Local Knowledge," emphasizes the dialectic between these two forms of knowledge, in order to look at similarities and differences in patterns of colonization, always returning to the local to test the general. We talk about how the apartheid South Africa, as represented in *"MASTER HAROLD" ... and the boys,* is different from the Zimbabwe represented in *Nervous Conditions*, which is different from the canada represented in *Dry Lips Oughta Move to Kapuskasing*, which is different from the canada represented in "The Loons," which is different from the canada represented in *Keeper'n me*. However, it is possible—and I believe useful—to look at both the particular and the general ways in which colonization works and is resisted in each of these representations.

While each of these texts deals with the ways in which colonization has affected Indigenous communities, we can look at similarities and differences by narrowing the focus to a particular issue. By focusing on the general issue of language, for example, we can talk about dancing as a language of resistance in *"MASTER HAROLD" ... and the boys*; the loss of the Shona language in *Nervous Conditions*; the use of Cree and Ojibway languages in *Dry Lips*; stereotyped language in "The Loons"; and oral-written language in *Keeper'n me*. However, when we test the general statement that colonization often results, to some extent, in the loss of an Indigenous language against the particular texts, we see that each text complicates this statement by showing the variety of ways in which individuals have lost, kept, and/or are relearning their languages.

In the first upper-level course I taught, *Contexts in Canadian Literature*, the class—which was composed of primarily white women from a variety of class backgrounds[4]—looked at postcolonialism in a more concentrated way. The course itself was structured around considerations of canada's complex colonial, and arguably postcolonial, positionings and intersected with other issues such as multiculturalism, imperialism, and nationalism. The complete course outline can be found in the appendix to this paper, but I would like to focus my discussion here on just three of the texts that we studied: *Halfbreed* by Maria Campbell, "Bertha" by Lee Maracle, and *Blue Marrow* by Louise Bernice Halfe. These three texts began a section of Native literatures, wherein each text stood on its own, responded to each other and to non-Native writer's representations of Native peoples, precluded discussions of *The Diviners,* and ended our first term.

We began this section with a discussion of Blaeser's comments about the ways in which she urges readers to approach Native literatures, as I have outlined previously in this essay. I then provided the students with Janice Acoose's article, "*Halfbreed*: A Revisiting of Maria Campbell's Text from an Indigenous Perspective." Acoose argues that Campbell's text "intervene[s] in the Canadian literary tradition that had, until then, constructed Indigenous women in ways that were contrary to our real lived experiences.... Inevitably, she helps other Indigenous women to begin the same kind of reclamation and re-connection of their selves." (139-40) Acoose speaks of the importance of Campbell's language as a site of resistance as it "shifts from English to Mitchif to Cree." (141) By introducing these two articles to the students, I hoped to provide a reading strategy for non-Native students and a context in which Campbell was writing. From here, I divided the class into groups of four or five students and had each group do a close reading of particular passages from the first six chapters in order to listen closely to Campbell's words as she tells her story and history. By listening closely to the text and by hearing what other Indigenous writers have written about that particular text and about Native literatures in general, one can be attentive to a primary text and to the reading strategies of Native critics as the primary grounding for the rest of this section of Indigenous literatures.

From *Halfbreed,* we moved into discussions about Lee Maracle's short story "Bertha." After small group discussions about the story, it seemed to me that many of the students were frustrated and silenced by what they perceived to be hopeless and tragic circumstances being represented and reproduced in the story. Continuing from Acoose's emphasis on language as a site of resistance and from my own interest in language as an aspect of identity, I introduced Ngugi's article "The Language of African

Literature" as a way to open discussion about different ways of thinking about language. Ngugi argues that language as communication is made up of the language of the hand, the language of the mouth, and the language of the eye. The language of the hand, or the language of real life, is the way in which a community cooperates and communicates through productive labour. The language of the mouth is the spoken word, and it enhances communication between people as they work together to create community. The language of the eye is the written word, which developed after the simultaneous evolution of hand and mouth communication. (288-89) Ngugi stresses that the health of a community is based on the interrelationship between these three aspects of language as communication. I offered students a background in Maracle's text, which gives some understanding of the concerns that Native writers and critics express regarding theory that comes from outside of the text, and I then introduced Ngugi's article as a way of thinking differently about how Maracle was exploring language and silence and silence as language. The class looked at how Maracle describes the ways in which Bertha remembers the community working together, the ways in which stories were told, and finally at Maracle's own writing of this story. Ngugi's article gave students an analysis of language of the hand, ear, and eye that allowed them to speak of the structural resistances in Maracle's story, without dismissing (or even safely packaging) its content.

The next text we looked at was Louise Bernice Halfe's *Blue Marrow*. Again, the students expressed some difficulty with reading the text because they were unable to differentiate between the voices in the text. We spoke about why Halfe might choose not to name the voices, and in the third class I furthered the conversation by placing Halfe's poetry in a context of Native and Cree literatures and by arguing that Halfe uses the english language in conjunction with Cree in order to reject the political power of english.

The class also looked at another piece of writing by Lee Maracle in order to hear her speak theoretically about writing as resistance, as a way of refusing erasure. In *I Am Woman*, Maracle states,

> I wanted to be a writer when I was still a "wharf rat" from the mud flats. That was a long time ago. I did not want the "fame" that went with it. The result of being colonized is the internalization of the need to remain invisible. The colonizers erase you, not easily, but with shame and brutality. Eventually you want to stay that way. Being a writer is getting up there and writing yourself onto everyone's blackboard. (8)

Maracle overcomes her "need to remain invisible" when she realizes that the sounding of one voice often leads to many other voices being spoken and heard. She replaces the need to remain invisible by the refusal to be made invisible.

Like Maracle, Halfe makes visible both contemporary voices and the voices of ancestors. As a subversive strategy, she uses english and Cree in her poetry to represent her realities and to reject the political power of english. This rejection both creates a new language and proves that the dominant language is not unchangeable: "In Chinua Achebe's words this is a process by which the language is made to bear the weight and the texture of a different experience. In doing so it becomes a different language." (Ashcroft 284) Halfe demonstrates how both Cree and english transform as experiences, time, and place change.

Louise Halfe was born to *onihcikiskwapiwinihk*, Saddle Lake, Alberta, in 1953. She writes from the influence of two cultures—a traditional Plains Cree culture and a colonial canadian culture—and she appropriates english to make it reflect this dual inheritance. The dedication in her 1994 collection of poems, *Bear Bones & Feathers*, connects her voice to the voices of her ancestors and to the *âcimôwin* literary tradition to which her poetry belongs:

> This book is dedicated
> to the memory of my brother
> Peter Ivan Halfe,
> 1950-1975,
> and my daughter
> Soogaymoo, 1978.
>
> To my Grandmothers & my Grandfathers
> and to those who've danced before us.

Ni tipeyihtenan ôhi acimôwina
We own these stories.
The Marrow.

Her poems, like her dedication, are written primarily in english with some Cree words. The first poem in the collection, "Bone Lodge," connects to both the dedication; the afterword, "Comfortable in my Bones"; and her next collection, *Blue Marrow*:

I sleep with *sihkos.*
In the fog she untangles my braids.
. . . .
Of these I know
in the bones of the lodge. (3)

Halfe repeats the bone imagery throughout her collections, drawing attention to the embodied nature of the stories. People and animals are the bones and marrow of the poems. The speaker's body is her house of bones is the bones of the lodge is the source of interconnected knowledges. These knowledges are owned by the poem-beings but are also shared, to some extent, with the reader, for Halfe has included a brief glossary at the end of the collection arranged in the same order as the words appear in the text. The glossary opens the book to readers who do not speak or read Cree but does not necessarily aim the book at those readers. Halfe refuses invisibility. She is writing herself on everyone's blackboard.

In addition to her inclusion of Cree words and phrases, Halfe also employs what Kinkade and Mattina call "'Red English,' a distinctive dialect of english commonly heard from older Indians. This has the effect of giving a purposely exotic rendering and is intended to convey a positive view of differences of expression." (260) I do not think Halfe combines colloquial english with so-called "Red English" for exotic purposes. Instead, she takes the english language and makes it represent the "othering" and the harmful exoticizing of the body:

My brown tits
day shame me
My brown spoon
fails me.

. . . . .
A dongue in dair mouth.
A dongue in dair pants.
No nothin 'bout the heart.
No nothin 'bout my soul. (53)

She names this ironic and parodic poem "Valentine Dialogue." It speaks to the violence done to the body, the violence done to the soul. With the "dialogue" in the title and the use of repetition, Halfe is recalling an oral tradition, and the way the "Durty priest" violates that tradition because he "Jest wants da durty story / Needs to shine his rocks." Yet, beyond all the hurt, she is reclaiming a tradition that she hopes will heal. She makes english work for her by making it fit her context, her experience, and her Cree literary tradition. She takes a language forced onto Cree speakers and rewrites its corporeal colonizing effects.

In *Blue Marrow*, Halfe names her *âcimôwin* in syllabics on the first page. There is no glossary. The poems contain voices in english and Cree. They are voices of the present and voices of the past. They are voices of the ancestors and voices of the colonizers. They are names in the form of prayer:

> Cardinal Woman, Mud Hen Woman, Old Woman. Pray to them. Fire Thunder Woman, Kicking Horse Woman, Big Swan Woman, *Kytwayhat* (She Who Says So Woman). Pray to them. To all my *Nechi* Women throughout this country whose spirit and songs haven't been heard. Who will be heard. All my Relations. Amen. (5)

Halfe employs the ritual, the repetition, the naming, the prayer, the emotion, the detail of the oral narrative. It is on the pages. It is thick on the pages. Between the linguistic signs are non-linguistic signs: black and white photographs of relatives. There are no glossy insert pages; instead, the photographs stand as another text to be read and translated, offered as a testament to those who are here now, to those that came before, and to those that Halfe's words insist come after.

Among these pages the reader also finds a song heard before in the pages of *Bear Bones & Feathers*:

Waniskâ.
Pê-wâpan ôma.
Âsay Piyêsîsak
Nikamowak
Miyôhtâkwan.
Kitaskînaw. (*Blue Marrow* 78, *Bear Bones* 50)

In this song, Halfe relates the fluidity of language because she translates the song in three ways. She not only performs changes in english, she performs changes in Cree: "Arise. / Dawn has come. / Already the birds / sing. / The beautiful song. / Our land" (78). "Arise / dawn has come / already the birds sing / and the earth / delights with life" (*Bear* 51). "Get up / dawn arrives / already birds / sing / a beautiful sound / of our earth, our land" (*Bear* 128). Language is not static; it does not stay still on the page or in the mouth.

Part of an *âcimôwin* Cree literary tradition, Louise Halfe's poetry connects her contemporary voice with the voices of ancestors that exist both on pages and in memories. As a subversive strategy, she owns, takes over, translates, appropriates, reverses the english language by combining it with Cree words, Cree syllabics, songs, prayers, colloquialisms, dialect, places, names, pictures. This english represents her history, her present, her future, her choices and rejects the one-dimensional political power of english. This rejection both creates a new language and proves that a dominant language is not uninvadable. When Louise Halfe translates her poetry into a performative event, she puts the blanket of her grandmothers over her head and shoulders. I have seen her on stage with the words in her mouth, the blanket embracing her, the boots on her feet ready to walk the paths before her. In that public moment, she sheds her private self and becomes the grandmothers, speaks the voices of her history, the voices of the unheard women who are now named into visibility.

If non-Indigenous teachers and critics continually attempt to complicate postcolonial discussions, to introduce the concerns that many Indigenous writers have with the term *postcolonial*, to give postcolonial contexts while simultaneously attempting to teach, for example, Cree literatures, to trouble categories such as canadian literature and Native literatures, to be open to those unguarded pedagogical moments, to see the possibility of theory as both arising from and responding to a text, then students will more fully understand that any singular approach to reading a text, and specifically a text written by an Indigenous writer, is not the only way to hear stories being told.

Appendix

Figure 1:

English 1: Textual Interactions and Reactions (Sample Course Outline)

September 14, 16	from *The Metamorphoses*
September 21, 23	from *Paradise Lost*
September 28, 30	"The Rape of the Lock"
October 5, 7, 12, 14	*Frankenstein*
October 19, 21	"Goblin Market"
October 26, 28	*No Fixed Address*
November 2, 4	*No Fixed Address*
November 9, 16, 18	*Haroun and the Sea of Stories*
November 23, 25, 30	*Lion's Granddaughter and Other Stories*
December 2	*Lion's Granddaughter and Other Stories*
January 4, 6, 11	"The Yellow Wallpaper"
January 13	"Story of an Hour"
January 18, 20	"A Rose for Emily"
January 27	*The Tempest*
February 1, 3	*The Tempest*
February 8, 10	*"MASTER HAROLD ... and the boys*
February 22, 24, 29	*Nervous Conditions*
March 2	*Nervous Conditions*
March 7, 9	*Dry Lips Oughta Move to Kapuskasing*
March 14, 16	"The Loons"
March 21, 23, 28	*Keeper'n me*

<u>Figure 2</u>:
Contexts in Canadian Literature (Sample Course Outline)

September 10	"Introduction" in *Making a Difference*
September 13-20	*The History of Emily Montague*
September 22-Oct.1	*The Imperialist*
October 4-15	*Settlers of the Marsh*
October 18, 20, 22	*Tay John*
October 25, 27, 29, Nov.1	*Half-Breed*
November 3, 5, 8	"Bertha" by Lee Maracle
November 10, 12, 15, 17	*Blue Marrow* by Louise Bernice Halfe
November 19, 22, 24, 26	*Dry Lips Oughta Move to Kapuskasing* by Tomson Highway
November 29	"History Lesson," "Magic Woman," "Wind Woman," "Indian Woman" by Jeannette Armstrong
December 1	"The One About Coyote Going West" by Thomas King
January 3-14	*The Diviners*
January 17	"The Fairy Tale Spinners"
January 19, 21	from *The Republic of Whores,* "The Army Creativity Contest"
January 24, 26, 28, 31	*In the Skin of a Lion*
February 21, 23	"Doing Right"
February 25	"Discourse on the Logic of Language"
February 28	from *No Language Is Neutral*
March 1	"Her Head a Village"
March 3	"Big Nipple of the North"
March 6, 8	"Beena"
March 10, 13	"A Pass to India," "Another Country," "Could Have Danced All Night"
March 15, 17	"Pigs Can't Fly"
March 20, 22	from *Obasan*
March 24	"Night"
March 27, 29, 31	*Moon Honey*

Notes

[1] Throughout this paper, I alternate between the terms *Indigenous, Aboriginal, First Nations,* and *Native* in my discussions. I try to use the term that best suits the context I address. For instance, the editors of this collection use the term *Aboriginal.* Thomas King and Kimberly M. Blaeser employ the term *Native.* Janice Acoose, Linda Tuhiwai Smith, and Len Findlay prefer the term *Indigenous* (Smith uses a lower-case). Jeannette Armstrong speaks of First Nations Literature.

[2] I use the lower-case version of canadian and english following from Janice Acoose, who "deconstruct[s] the authoritative centre of the white-eurocanadian-christian patriarchy by using lower case letters to signal a politically motivated de-authorization in [her] life and thought of the concepts that had for too long held too much power" (13). While an extensive investigation is beyond the scope of this paper, I would like to signal the need for a critical nationalism.

[3] For a partial chronology that provides a sense of how diverse and extensive the contributions to postcolonial studies are in Canada, please see the "Is Canada Postcolonial?" web-site, http://home.cc.umanitoba.ca/~mossl/canadapoco/. This chronology, as well as an annotated bibliography, was compiled as part of my research with Dr. Laura Moss at the University of Manitoba in preparation for the "Is Canada Postcolonial?" conference that took place in Winnipeg, Manitoba 14-16 September 2000.

[4] In a class of thirty-seven, one quarter of the students were men and less than one seventh were people of colour. There were no students that self-identified to the class as First Nations or Métis.

Works Cited

Acoose, Janice (Misko-Kisikawihkwè). *Iskwewak – Kah Ki Yaw Ni Wahkomakanak Neither Indian Princesses Nor Easy Squaws.* Women's Press: Toronto, 1995.

Armstrong, Jeannette, ed. *Looking at the Words of our People: First Nations Analysis of Literature*. Penticton, BC: Theytus Books, 1993.

Ashcroft, Bill, Gareth Griffiths, and Helen Tiffin, eds. *The Post-Colonial Studies Reader*. 1995. New York: Routledge, 1997.

Blaeser, Kimberly M. "Native Literature: Seeking a Critical Center." *Looking at the Words of our People: First Nations Analysis of Literature*. Ed. Jeannette Armstrong. Penticton, BC: Theytus Books, 1993. 51-62.

Brydon, Diana, and Helen Tiffin. *Decolonising Fictions*. Sydney: Dangaroo, 1993.

Findlay, Len. "Always Indigenize! The Radical Humanities in the Postcolonial Canadian University." *ARIEL: A Review of International English Literature* 31.1&2 (January - April 2000): 307-26.

Halfe, Louise. *Bear Bones & Feathers*. Regina: Coteau Books, 1994.

- - -. *Blue Marrow*. Toronto: McClelland & Stewart, 1998.

Hooks, Bell. *Teaching to Transgress: Education as the Practice of Freedom*. New York: Routledge, 1994.

King, Thomas. "Godzilla vs. Post-Colonial." *New Contexts of Canadian Criticism*. Eds. Ejay Heble, Donna Palmateer Pennee, and J.R. (Tim) Struthers. Peterborough, ON: Broadview Press, 1997. 241-48.

Kinkade, M. Dale, and Anthony Mattina. "Discourse." *Handbook of North American Indians*. Ed. William C. Sturtevant. Washington: Smithsonian Institution, 1996.

Lawson, Alan. "A Cultural Paradigm for the Second World." *Australian-Canadian Studies* 9.1-2(1991): 67-78.

Maracle, Lee. "Bertha." *Making a Difference: Canadian Multicultural Literature*. Toronto: Oxford UP, 1996. 344-50.

- - -. *I Am Woman: A Native Perspective on Sociology and Feminism*. 1988. Vancouver: Press Gang, 1996.

Mukherjee, Arun. *Postcolonialism: My Living*. Toronto: Tsar, 1998.

Ngugi, wa Thiong'o. "The Language of African Literature." *The Post-Colonial Studies Reader*. Eds. Bill Ashcroft, Gareth Griffiths, and Helen Tiffin. 1995. New York: Routledge, 1997. 285-90.

- - -. "The Universality of Local Knowledge." *Moving the Centre: The Struggle for Cultural Freedoms*. Nairobi: EAEP, 1993. 25-29.

Slemon, Stephen. "The Scramble for Post-colonialism." *The Post-Colonial Studies Reader*. Eds. Bill Ashcroft, Gareth Griffiths, and Helen Tiffin. 1995. New York: Routledge, 1997. 45-52.

- - -. "Unsettling the Empire: Resistance Theory for the Second World." *World Literature Written in English*. 30.2 (1990): 30-41.

Smith, Linda Tuhiwai. *Decolonizing Methodologies: Research and Indigenous Peoples.* London: Zed Books, 1999.

Williams, Patrick, and Laura Chrisman, eds. *Colonial Discourse and Post-Colonial Theory: Reader*. New York: Columbia UP, 1994.

Storying The Borderlands: Liminal Spaces and Narrative Strategies in Lee Maracle's *Ravensong*

Karen E. Macfarlane

"Our spirit, our sweat, our tears, our laughter, our love, our anger, our bodies are distilled into words that we bead together to make power."
Beth Brant, *"The Good Red Road" (177)*

Lee Maracle has suggested that First Nations writers "believe the proof of a thing or idea is in the doing. Doing requires some form of social interaction, and thus *story* is the most persuasive and sensible way to present the accumulated thoughts and values of a people." ("Oratory" 7) The act of "storying" for Maracle is simultaneously personal, cultural and political. Telling a story asserts and affirms identity, resists artificially imposed boundaries, and transmits and sustains history. Beth Brant has similarly noted that First Nations writing by women "utilizes the power and gift of story, like oral tradition, to convey history, lessons, culture and spirit." (183) For both Maracle and Brant, the contemporary act of storying is a complex one. Working within the context of the written text, storying asserts its immediacy as narrative process, while playing out its alternate role as written artefact. Storying, then, as a verb, becomes interwoven with the static negotiations of the western text. What results is a form of narrative that asserts the mutually constitutive relation between static (written) and dynamic (oral) forms of verbal interaction. In *Ravensong*, Maracle explores this relation by deploying two ostensibly discrete narrative tropes: storytelling and the image of boundaries or border spaces. While each functions successfully as a separate, distinct element of the narrative (Stacey becomes a figure that negotiates the border space between the reserve and "white town", asserting the differences between the two as she defines herself in relation to them, for example), their interaction enacts what both Maracle and Brant have defined as an essential element of native women's writing: storying as a simultaneous *process* of individuation, collectivity, and resistance.

Storying, I argue here, structures the novel. Indeed, the novel *is* a story which answers the epilogue's question, "why did little Jimmy shoot himself?" (197) As Maracle's narrative demonstrates, this question can only be answered through a complex exploration of the relationship between the powers of language to provisionally order events (storying) and the multiple boundaries and border spaces that this act articulates. Described as a series of "gaps" or "chasms" throughout the novel, physical and cultural boundaries fracture the linearity of the narrative, foregrounding *relations* in the answer to this question, rather than structuring that answer through the reductive use of cause-and-effect. Central to this representation is the figure of Raven who acts in this novel as more than a trickster or a harbinger of change. As a narrative device, Raven articulates the necessary balance between stability and change, between narrative voices and cultural negotiations. Raven's voice is the voice of the spaces between times, cultures, individuals and identities. In this sense, Raven's presence in the novel acts out the text's focus on process: the act of storying.

Storying, then, is intimately connected with the negotiation of the physical border spaces in the text. The connection between conventionally discrete categories is positioned beyond existing liminal, or unnamed, "unstoried" areas. The central narrative, then, takes place in a number of border spaces: physically, in the boundary between "white town" and the reserve (signalled by the river and the bridge); culturally, between groups (native and invader); socially in the fractures within groups (Polly and her community, Rena and German Judy and the people of the reserve); and temporally, through the ghosts, Celia's visions and, perhaps most importantly for this discussion of the connection between structure, storying and boundary spaces, is the fact that the narrative takes place in a temporal in-between space: at the moment when Stacey is suspended between her life on the reserve and her movement outward to attend university. Articulating these in-between spaces is accomplished through an act of interconnected storytelling. The stories that circulate throughout the novel act *with* and *through* each other to reflect (on) the boundaries that ostensibly enforce separation, difference and cultural fragmentation.

Ravensong's character and plot, as Helen Hoy has suggested, encourage the readers of the novel to focus on the use of binary oppositions in the text: bridge/river; town/reserve; invader/native; past/present, and so on. Hoy usefully outlines the basis and strengths of reading the construction of binaries in the novel by suggesting that the use of the "two racial solitudes" (Hoy 137) illuminates the ways in which identities and relations have been, and continue to be, deployed and represented historically and culturally. Drawing attention to oppositional relations in the novel both positions the text within a continuum of invader/native relations and illuminates the position of such binaries as constructed, deployed cultural texts. So, while Maracle "constructs racial/cultural relations on a dualist model, reproducing Abdul JanMohamed's Manichean allegory of colonizer and colonized, but with the positive and negative valences reversed" (Hoy 140) she also complicates this model through both her characters' actions and interactions and through the form of her narrative. Reading the binaries in the text, then, leads to a coherent sense of "questions about collective identity" (Hoy 152) but does not adequately account for the role and function of this novel as a "trickster text" (Smith 11) which incorporates not only the actions and relations between characters and events, but also the relations between the form, its context, and its content. In this sense these ostensible binaries enact what Hoy has called a "radical inclusiveness." (152) This inclusiveness moves through and beyond the levels of story/text/character/reader/author to create an active relation between these categories which allows for a reading that accommodates oral/written narrative forms. As Hoy suggests, "Maracle's text, presided over by the figure of Raven, is trickier and more multifarious" (140) than binary models might suggest.

As Jeanne Rosier Smith has argued, a "trickster aesthetic" enacts a radical transformation in both the plot and the form of the texts which it shapes. (2) The trickster is thus "not only ... an actual figure in the novel but also ... a linguistic and stylistic principle." (14) The figure of the trickster in these texts acts in tandem with the resistant form of the work, "producing a politically radical subtext" which "involves not only recalling traditional stories but also revising them and even creating new ones." (2, 5) The form of trickster texts like *Ravensong*, then, is dynamic—like Raven, Stacey, and Celia's visions—negotiating relations and points of intersection between and within categories of definition. Smith notes that the figure of the trickster "emerges as an active agent within the text, [and through this figure] the dismantling of controlling ideologies becomes a key issue. Trickster authors privilege multivocality." (12) While Smith does not address *Ravensong* in her discussion, her notion of the dynamic interaction between reader/text/characters provides a useful way into a discussion of the relationship between form, content and politics in this novel.

Reading the act of storying the border spaces here—articulating the voices/spaces in the gaps between official narratives—belies any simplistic oppositional reading which could set the novel up as some sort of movement or negotiation between two opposing ideologies of cultural survival. While the appearance of physical/cultural borders does suggest this, a reading of the *relation* between borders and storying reveals that Maracle's complex use of border spaces as a structuring principle is a sophisticated reworking of linear narrative structures. Maracle uses this negotiation to articulate a space *at* the borders, *at* a moment of transition. This negotiation foregrounds the emphasis on process and on the interdependence of contemporary narrative forms and conventions. The politics of this novel, then, are more than a negotiation or articulation of the points of contact between Eurocanadian and Native cultures. Political strategies inform the politics of narrative and narrative construction within and between these cultures. Images of border spaces in *Ravensong* mirror and open up the fractured, multivocal structure of the text itself and, I would suggest, open up a space for articulating an alternate narrative and political position.

Central to construction of the politics in this text, then, is Raven—the trickster—who acts as both a cultural and a narrative figure. Smith argues that tricksters negotiate the space between and within form and content in trickster texts: "they reinvent narrative form. The trickster's medium is words. A parodist, joker, liar, con-artist, and storyteller, the trickster fabricates believable illusions with words - and thus becomes author and embodiment of a fluid, flexible, and politically radical narrative form." (11) Traditional representations of the trickster figure deploy him/her as "a sign, a communal signification that cannot be separated or understood in isolation." (Vizenor 189) Trickster, then, embodies contradictions, multiple positionings in relation to culture, story, and physical space. The Trickster inhabits the boundaries and *is* the boundaries — at least on a narrative level, resisting the notion of a single, authoritative story in favour of multiple, contingent and relational representations of events. In his/her position as "boundary figure" (O'Brien 82) the trickster challenges both oppositional definitions of relations and identities and conventional narrative forms. As Susie O'Brien has suggested, "to 'be the Trickster' is not just to celebrate the dissolution of discursive boundaries, but to engage, as Maracle does, with the complexities and contradictions of history" (94) and, I would add here, with the contradictions inherent in the notion of speaking within and beyond the interstices within the contradictory texts through which histories, cultures and identities are transmitted.

In her study of *Ravensong* and the shame of colonial mimicry, Dee Horne suggests that as a trickster, Raven "mediates between the town and Stacey's reserve, between the members of each community and between the past, present and future. As a catalyst for change, Raven articulates cultural differences and also signals the importance of cultural survival which involves cultural adaptability and transformation." (111-12) Horne suggests that the structuring principle of shame in *Ravensong* reflects Raven's role in the novel. Shame, she suggests, "can be destructive and/or constructive" (112) just as the figure of the trickster embodies and contains contradictory positions. Horne's focus on Raven as a traditional trickster draws attention to the ways in which shame —and Raven—function to signal a necessary renegotiation of relations between invader and native cultures. But, as Hoy, O'Brien, and Smith have suggested, the interstitial positioning of such a figure in a contemporary narrative enacts a more radical renegotiation of this relation than that acted out through the characters in the plot. This figure also renegotiates relations within narrative forms themselves. As Maracle has noted, Raven is "more than a trickster, she is a harbinger of social transformation, Raven sings when the world itself is amiss." (Kelly 85) To oversimplify the role of Raven (Kelly 85) is to oversimplify the position of Native narratives in the context of contemporary literary production. In *Ravensong,* Raven's positioning within and beyond oppositional structures resists the reduction of this figure to the role of trickster and foregrounds her place in the construction of the interdependent narratives that make up the novel. Raven's song is heard at transitional moments, in transitional spaces (specifically in the novel) and interpreted "otherwise" through un*author*ized linguistic and epistemic modes. Like the borders and stories which shape the narrative, Raven acts out the need for a provisional balance between and within oppositional categories. She therefore signals not only moments of transformation, but opens up the border space itself, demonstrating that moments of transition, translation, transformation have value beyond their articulation as signs of divisions and difference. In addition to the mythical figure of Raven as trickster, Raven functions here on a number of related, but discrete levels as a series of characteristics which react through and with the other characters in the novel. Characters, situations and stories are thus described as having "too much Raven" or "not enough." The liminality that Raven embodies, then, circulates throughout this novel and foregrounds the importance of process by drawing together oppositional elements of the border spaces through an emphasis on voice and the act of storying.

Raven's position as a figure which participates simultaneously in a number of discourses is perhaps most obviously constructed in a passage early in the novel. Here, Raven acts as an agent for change, but without power to impose those changes, she can merely orchestrate and encourage them:

> [Raven] considered her plan to drive the people out of their houses. She knew they stayed confined to their reserves for false reasons: segregation between the others and her own people had as much to do with how her own felt about the others, as it had to do with how the others felt about the villagers. Raven saw the future threatened by the parochial refusal of her own people to shape the future of their homeland. Somewhere in the fold between dark and light her people had given up, retreated to their houses in their raggedy reserves and withdrawn into their imagined confinement. She had to drive them out, bring them across the bridge. (43-4)

While Raven is clearly associated with boundaries in the early sections of the text (13, 23), her "plan" introduces another, more complex function for this character. While Raven is the harbinger of change, then, she neither orchestrates it nor imposes it. Change, like the construction of stories which are "joggl[ed] ... into place" (99) in relation to individuals and contexts, is negotiated here. Raven resists divisions and confinement and foregrounds the formative structures of the in-between places, the "fold between dark and light." While Raven's voice is part of the larger "web of knowing" (14) that forms the multivocal centre of *Ravensong*, her focus here on a necessary dis-membering of the community places her in a temporary opposition to the active re-membering that characterizes the women's voices which conclude the narrative. It is through this ostensible opposition that the connections between narratives and narrative forms are (re)inscribed in the novel.

From the beginning of the narrative, Raven enacts a position simultaneously within and between oppositional definitions. The past and present, encoded as separate in Eurocanadian discourse, for example, exist simultaneously in both —and neither—of these spaces:

> From the depths of the sound Raven sang a deep wind song, melancholy and green ... The sound of Raven spiralled out from its small beginning in larger and larger concentric circles, gaining volume as it passed each successive layer of green. The song echoed the rolling motions of the earth's centre, filtering itself through the last layer to reach outward to earth's shoreline about the deep. (9)

Raven's song moves within and beyond physical and temporal boundaries. Celia experiences it "between her moving cells." (10) It signals change by foregrounding the ways in which interconnected "songs" work in relation to each other. Raven's song enacts a progressive movement between and within physical, personal and temporal layers. It is described in terms which emphasize its complex positioning between and within divisive categorizations through its relation to elements and objects not generally associated with sound. It is insubstantial, connected simultaneously with water, light, colours, and with circularity. It is connected with centres and margins, with layers and echoes, explicating its connection with repetition, difference, multivocality, but paradoxically, through a single voice which relates itself to non- or extra-linguistic modes of expression. Ultimately, it connects with Celia who "felt the presence of song in the movement of cedar's branches." (9) Celia's visions are, as a part of this continuity and interconnection, inspired by Raven's song. Here, a single cause-and-effect relationship does not define relations. Instead, it is through a series of interconnected voices/movements/media that the message is conveyed. This mutually constituting relation allows Celia to see beyond the physical. Although she is sitting under the cedar in the narrative present, connected with linear time and the physical substantiality of cedar and the world around her, she is also seeing something "undefinable": she is watching the past and she is also in some ways sensing the future. The connection here between the past and the future in Celia's vision suggests that she is a kind of conduit between past and present, who perceives, but cannot interpret, the interdependence and slippage between the states. Indeed, the construction of this opening passage enacts the relations between the narrative form and content, the relations between voices, and the negotiation of oppositional categories that shapes and structures this novel. As in a series of transparencies laid one on top of another, these categories are separate, but related and that relation colours and informs the act of "reading" them both together and separately. In this sense, the introduction of Raven's voice foregrounds its multivocality and its function as a signal for this type of active negotiation in the novel. Raven's song, then, does not simply reflect Raven's voice: in fact this song is related to a number of different voices and is predicated on mutually constituted interpretations.

The community of voices is an important element in reading notions of "storying" (as an active, progressive, provisional process) in *Ravensong*. The central narrative itself is storying the answer to the epilogue's question. It does not propose a definitive answer, but one that explores the complexity of relations. The act of storying here both resists the rigidity of borders between past and present, generations and events, and simultaneously articulates them. This opening image, then, alerts us to the central concerns in this text: concerns with the simultaneity of past and present, and the related need to resist the oppositional (Eurocentric) notions that these exist independently of each other; and the necessary vitality of multivocality. The one signals the importance of borders (as places of change and growth) and the other of storying through this interaction between static and dynamic narratives.

Stories, both written and oral, are encoded as the centre of cultural meaning and identities. Momma notes, "I always wanted to know some of their [Eurocanadians] stories. I don't understand them people at all – how they live, what they do. Their stories must tell you something about them, eh?" (146) Framed in terms of a question, Momma's desire to understand the inhabitants of "white town" assumes the authority of stories. Stacey's reaction is to act as mediator between the two spaces, "I could read some to you" (147) but Momma's desire to have unmediated access to the books that Stacey carries effectively enables her to act out the complex interdependence between oral and written forms. Finding a way of describing the relation between the written characters and words/narratives, Stacey "concocted a story about a family named Alphabet, gave them names and work to do. She even threw in trickster behaviour for those moments when none of the Alphabets would do the right work." (175) Debates about the roles of the characters are interspersed with moments of unambiguously oral play, as when Momma imitates Madeline's accent. (175) The rigid rules of the written alphabet are reinscribed so that their capricious, changeable and inherently unstable characteristics are foregrounded. In this context, the contents of the books become "a new kind of vision" (176) that negotiates and disrupts the space between oral and written narrative forms. Ultimately, however, the cultural specificity of language and interpretation undermines this connection. At this stage in the novel, "the 'flu' [still] means illness to them. For us it means terror." (178) It is left to Stacey to "collect the magic words of white town and bring them home." (192) These words, too, will be altered within the context of Stacey's strategic negotiation of physical, cultural and narrative boundaries: "she would try to bring them home in a way that would revitalize her flagging community." (192)

As the ostensible protagonist of the central narrative, Stacey's negotiation of relations, cultures and stories parallels other transitional movements in the text. Although borders and border spaces are signalled by clear physical barriers they are not concrete, physical divisions here but fluid, provisional and necessarily malleable. So a border, paradoxically, is not clearly defined or necessarily divisive. Borders fluctuate. This is particularly evident in the two central boundaries between "white town" and the reserve: the river and the bridge. While both figure prominently in the descriptions of the two spaces and much has been made critically[1] of their significance as symbols of cultural divisions, they are, I would suggest, ambiguous symbols of this opposition. While clearly physically dividing the two cultures, the river is also not stable, but constantly changing. Its flow belies its apparently static position. The bridge, on the other hand, spans the river and ostensibly connects the reserve and "white town." The bridge, like the river, reinforces the paradoxical relation between the opposite shores and the cultural divisions that they represent. The physical borders signal, to a certain extent, the existence of cultural borders: differences in issues of education, medicine, and of commitment to community. These differences are essential to understanding the relationship between borders, narratives and political engagements with what Horne calls "notions of cultural survival." (112) They allow for comparisons between the cultures which are negotiated and resisted across this space. It is in relation to these images that Stacey describes the problematics of her relationship with Steve as a "gulf" and wonders "if any two people can bridge it." (185) The image of the bridge here connects the physical and cultural boundaries that divide Stacey and Steve with the relation between the narratives that shape and inform these spaces. Their connection mirrors other, similarly constructed relations between static and dynamic object, ideas, and elements in the text. In this sense, the river and the bridge are deployed, like the two narrative forms that make up *Ravensong*, as interdependent. By constructing the meanings of these objects as interdependent, Maracle problematises and reinscribes the notion of set border spaces through images, figures and ideas which cross and transcend them.

The strategic use of physical boundaries and border spaces is thus central to the structure of the novel. Their presence signals not only the artificiality of these divisions, the "imagined confinement" (43) that separates one group from another, but also the fact that the events that are being storied in the main narrative take place at a transitional moment in Stacey's life and in the life of the reserve: the time before, during and after the epidemic. Stacey's movement from childhood to adulthood is represented as a movement away from being "storied" to having, creating and telling her own story. Similarly, as Raven suggests, the people on the reserve must also move away from the external "stories" of

Eurocanadian authority and tell, as the women do in the epilogue, their own story and encourage others to similarly story themselves. Articulating these in-between spaces becomes an act of recuperation and resistance. Being storied, as Momma's brother Benny is within the government's imposition of definitions of citizenship (46-49) is to be silenced and defined. Connections to nation and national text are enacted here through the (incomprehensible) written word.

Identities which cannot be defined in the terms of the dominant narrative are enacted through counter discursive storying. As the structure of the community changes, debates about roles, specifically roles which have been strictly defined according to gender, are deployed through stories which reinforce the shifting nature of these definitions. The "struggle for understanding" (97) is storied, and the stories themselves are told in different voices at different times and contexts. The "story of a warrior woman from long ago" (97) reinforces the shifting definitions of gender and is initially told by Grampa Thomas and re-told to Stacey by Momma. The central figure in this narrative is paradoxically a definitive gap, "nameless not out of disrespect but for want of definition." (97) She is described as simultaneously mother and warrior, a woman whose "duality inspired fear and reverence in her fellow villagers." (97) This story finds a place within the larger, cultural story of the reserve, helping to "joggle [Nora and Rena] into place" (99) by finding a lineage to which they belong. The act of storying, then, shapes and renegotiates personal and historical relations throughout the novel, just as the epilogue (re)aligns the relations between Polly, little Jimmy, Jacob and the women who are telling the story.

The mutually constitutive relation between stories as they appear in the epilogue are enacted throughout the main narrative. Momma's stories of herself connect and inform Stacey's attempt to understand Polly. Stacey's struggle to understand her mother's relationship with Jim and Ned leads to "the story of Snot Woman, a story of risqué humour and passion." (105) The focus here is on the *act* of telling this story: on the context from which it arose, and the context in which it is heard. The story is "retold" but "it started to read differently to Stacey" whose interpretation changes within the context of the narrative present. (105-6) "Snot

Woman's" story folds into Momma's story which informs and shapes Polly's which, in turn, shapes and defines Stacey's growing ability to story herself.

The interdependence of stories, identities and physical border markers similarly illuminates the significance of the structure of the novel. Linear order, causal relations and narrative divisions are disrupted as the narrative present in Stacey's story is revealed, in the epilogue, to be an active re-membering (storying) of the past. In the same way that the opening scene with Celia is simultaneously narrative present and narrative past, the novel problematizes temporal relations in order to foreground the *process* of storying as a way of articulating relations between past and present, and between individuals.

The opening sequence of the novel leads us to the liminal spaces between past and present, dream and waking, vision and sight. The sense, then, of continuity, of interconnection and multivocality that has been introduced within the story of Stacey's coming of age is revisited in the epilogue and the story that has informed it. This structure leads the reader back into the text, thus resisting any closure and reinforcing the resistant non-linearity of the preceding narrative. The epilogue works, then, to reinforce and foreground the central elements in the body of the novel. While ostensibly answering the reader's implicit question "and then what happened?" it also poses, and stories, other questions about the narrative's structure, its focus and the ways in which the story has been developed and continues to develop. This section, then, reinforces the importance of change as it stories a fundamentally transitional moment, one that is full of Raven as harbinger: "Over the next decade the village fell apart. Women left to marry after that. They left in droves. No one knows why; it was as though the whole consciousness of the village changed at the same moment ... Now we are caught in an epidemic of our own making and we have no idea how to fight it." (197) This passage is constructed around the gap left by the main narrative's ostensible closure, the gap between the "conclusion" of this episode and the epilogue. Perhaps most importantly, this section reveals the multivocal construction of the preceding narrative: "The story had begun as an answer to [Stacey's] son's question, 'Why did little Jimmy shoot himself?' ... It took all winter for

Celia, Stacey, Momma and Rena to recount that summer. Young Jacob sat in silence listening to the women." (197) The intersection of a number of voices enacts a re-membering of the dis-membered community and its histories. Orality is foregrounded as an essential and dynamic part of the women's *act of* (active) storying. Telling the story through the four women allows it to be told within and beyond, as opposed to against, the definitive structure of a linear narrative. These women "come to the culture from four directions ... they were able to give a story that was rich and in which you could seek the answers, which is what Raven's stories do." (Kelly 86) The folding of these narratives into each other is further reinforced by framing the narrative with unstable, transformative songs. Songs are ways of "searching for memory" (97) as well as enacting and articulating change. Raven's transformative song at the beginning of the text is echoed and reworked in the women's grieving song at the end. Both songs ultimately negate any definitive, oppositional rendering, though both signal transformation, grief and the importance of interdependent narrative forms.

Ultimately, the physical end of the novel resists closure and leaves Jacob (as audience and as 'inheritor') to "unravel the answer" (199) to his question himself. Jacob's question, engendered by the women's narrative, asks "how 'not enough Raven' decided their fate" (199) collectively and individually. This question leads the reader back into the novel for an answer. As both character and transformative agent, then, Raven's liminal position at the "edge of the world" (13) negotiates change and enacts the positioning that opens a space for active and provisional re-membering. The border space between "too much" and "not enough" Raven that Stacey and her community inhabit allows for an exploration of the process of unravelling the complex relations between questions and answers through the act of storying. Drawing the narrative back to the opening song articulates the relation between narrative forms that shape this novel. The answer to Jacob's question can only be answered through the complex exploration of the relationship between the powers of language to order events and the acceptance that this process of ordering is provisional. The stories that circulate as answers to this question act with and through each other to reflect (on) the boundaries that ostensibly enforce division, difference and cultural fragmentation.

Note

[1] See, for example, the useful discussions of the bridge and the trope of cultural divisions in Hoy, Leggatt, and Horne. Each discussion, while recognizing that the bridge allows Stacey to mediate between cultures, foregrounds its function as a way of signalling divisions.

Works Cited

Brant, Beth. "The Good Red Road: Journeys of Homecoming in Native Women's Writing." *New Contexts of Canadian Criticism*. Ed. Ajay Heble, Donna Palmateer Pennee and J.R. Tim Struthers. Peterborough: Broadview Press, 1997. 175-187.

Horne, Dee. *Contemporary American Indian Writing: Unsettling Literature*. NY: Peter Lang, 1999.

Hoy, Helen. *How Should I Read These?: Native Women Writers in Canada*. Toronto: University of Toronto P, 2001.

Kelly, Jennifer. "Coming out of the House: A Conversation With Lee Maracle." *Ariel: A Review of International English Literature*. 25:1, January 1994. 73-87.

Leggatt, Judith. "Raven's Plague: Pollution and Disease in Lee Maracle's *Ravensong*". *Mosaic* 33.4. December 2000. 163-178.

Maracle, Lee. "Oratory: Coming to Theory." *Essays on Canadian Writing*. 54. Winter 1994. 6-11.

- - - - . *Ravensong.* Vancouver: Press Gang. 1993.

O'Brien, Susie. "'Please Eunice, Don't Be Ignorant': The White Reader as Trickster in Lee Maracle's Fiction". *Canadian Literature*. 144. Spring 1995. 82-96.

Pratt, Mary Louise. *Imperial Eyes: Travel Writing and Transculturation*. London: Routledge, 1992.

Smith, Jeanne Rosier. *Writing Tricksters: Mythic Gambols in American Ethnic Literature*. Berkeley: University of

California P, 1997.

Vizenor, Gerald. "Trickster Discourse: Comic Holotropes and Language Games". *Narrative Chance: Postmodern Discourses on Native American Indian Literatures*. Ed. Gerald Vizenor. Norman: Oklahoma UP, 1993. 187-211.

Comic Relief: Pedagogical Issues Around Thomas King's *Medicine River*

Renée Hulan and Linda Warley

The most memorable moment at the round-table organized by Renate Eigenbrod and Peter Rasevych at the 2000 meeting of CACLALS, for me, was when Armand Garnet Ruffo shared an insight on the recent critical turn to the study of humour in Native literature. When asked recently about this comment, he added, "not only does all the critical attention to humour in Native literature create the impression that all Native literature has to be funny, but it unwittingly literally hacks off the roots of Aboriginal literature by concentrating on one narrow aspect of the oral tradition" (personal communication). The remark sent me back to a paper Linda and I first presented at the 1997 MLA convention in which we try to understand the relationship of humour to our experiences teaching King's work. [1] What follows attempts to deal with that experience in light of Ruffo's insight.

Since the publication of his first novel *Medicine River* in 1989, Thomas King has become a household name in Canada. He is perhaps *the* representative Native writer in Canada for literary critics and teachers of English, as well as members of a mainstream reading audience. Unlike many Native writers in Canada, whose works quickly disappear from store shelves (if they are there at all), Thomas King enjoys both popular and academic success. His CBC radio series the *Dead Dog Café Comedy Hour*, short stories, works for children, and two subsequent novels have all been the subject of commentary. As the appearance of the special issue of the journal *Canadian Literature* devoted almost entirely to King's 1993 novel *Green Grass, Running Water* seems to indicate, however, this attention to King's work has not been evenly distributed. In fact, compared to *Green Grass, Running Water*, King's *Medicine River* has received relatively little critical attention, although it has been enthusiastically reviewed.[2]

By King's own definition, *Medicine River* can be classified as "associational," not "polemical" writing ("Godzilla" 14); that is, it is a novel written for a Native audience and, as such, it does not thematize the relationship between Natives and whites or instruct readers in their own ignorance. While there are many references to the Native identity of the characters and to details that are specific to Native people's lives - for example, references to the nearby reservation, the band council, the Friendship Center, characters who were involved in the American Indian Movement (AIM), and so on – these references are not overtly explained in the novel for the reader. As we have witnessed, students gratefully consume this novel: they are content to appreciate the text and they resist *analysing* it. Ironically, by writing for the audience depicted in the text, King enables other readers to appreciate the work all the more. While *Green Grass, Running Water* "drives its readers to the library" (Fee "Introduction" 9) to look up allusions to historical events and literary texts and to learn more about Native languages and stories, *Medicine River*, by contrast, seems to inspire only exuberant appreciation. The ease with which students can consume the novel tends to mitigate against the critical view that associational literature "allows non-Native readers a limited association with a Native world but reminds them they are not part of that world nor in possession of its truths." (Davidson 192) If *Medicine River* fits King's definition of associational literature because "non-Native readers are, in short, not the primary intended audience" (Davidson 192), then how are we to understand our students' responses, or, for that matter, the reviewers' satisfaction?

As teachers, we can complicate such responses to King's work by showing how the cultural modes used to process Native imagery in mainstream culture produce resistance to analysis. "Native stories and identity," as Kimberly M. Blaeser points out, has long been a "commodity" exchanged through and "for non-Native representation" ("Writing" 56-57), and non-Native readers learn how to approach Native arts and culture from this representation. We argue that another important reason for this resistance is the author's choice of genre and mode: the comic realist novel. Reviews indicate that readers tend to feel relieved that the text is non-polemical, a response that is accentuated by the fact that it is funny. Teaching *Medicine River* means teaching students to be competent readers conversant with the historical and cultural contexts that inform the work. It also means promoting reading vigilance, the ability to examine one's position with regard to the text. In particular, we wish to complicate the desire to consume rather than to study King's writing by raising questions concerning readers' expectations and responsibilities.

The reception of Thomas King's creative writing in Canada has been overwhelmingly laudatory. Reviewers and critics alike have showered praise on the work and the writer, and the language of that commentary is remarkably consistent. A composite paraphrase of reviews demonstrates the point. Thomas King, the critics say, tells stories that are "marvelous," "bent," "original, witty and stylishly executed," written with a "deft narrative touch." Some have commented that Indian writers "aren't known for being funny;"[3] therefore, King's voice is "fresh." His work is "playful and droll ... sophisticated satire;" he writes "benign humour" that represents "gentle resistance" and "tolerant hope." King "maintains a light, mischievous touch throughout." "His revisionist history [while] delightful and irreverent ... is also thought-provoking." Yet he is to be commended (repeatedly) for avoiding "self-righteous finger-pointing," "diatribe," or "polemics." In fact, "He succeeds where polemics would surely fail." There are "few put-downs, no snide counter-racist jibes, no speechifying." His stories are "perfect." Even by other "Native cultural activists," he is voted among "the best of the best."[4]

King's reputation as a talented and important contemporary writer is secure. He is profiled in literary periodicals such as *Books in Canada, Paragraph* and *Studies in Canadian Literature* and invited to read at writers' festivals. He is interviewed and performs his work on CBC radio, and the movie version of *Medicine River* (for which King wrote the screenplay, in collaboration with Ann MacNaughton) was shown to a national audience on CBC television. An adaptation of his short story "Borders" was part of a CBC television series featuring Native stories, "Four Directions," and King has also written for the popular drama series "North of 60." Published by mainstream North American presses—Penguin and HarperCollins, for example—King's books remain in print and can be bought at most bookstores. King has been nominated for two Governor General's Awards, and his writing is frequently taught at the post-secondary level, in general introductory English courses, practical criticism courses, and Canadian literature courses, as well as courses more specifically focused on Native literature. No other Native writer in Canada is this visible or this available.

King's visibility conditions the reception of his work both in popular and academic spheres. Students with little knowledge of First Nations literature may have encountered his name or persona before they read his fiction, especially if they follow the Canadian literature scene. The reception of his work has been shaped by trends in popular culture as well as in the public evaluation of literature: reviews, book sales and best seller lists, word of mouth and media exposure. Yet, King's popularity, and his position as perhaps *the* authority on Native matters within the Canadian academic institution, situate him outside the general ambivalence towards First Nations that makes them highly visible in some spheres and virtually invisible in others, an issue that we discuss elsewhere.[5] Canada's history of *not seeing* Aboriginal people leads to the ambivalence that fosters the continued marginalization of First Nations in the political sphere even as they are most visible in the popular one. Thus, the visibility of Native imagery in popular culture cannot, in itself, account for the reception of books by Native authors, including *Medicine River*, as public interest points to this ambivalence.

King is both a producer of literature and a critic and editor of it. His academic credentials include a Ph.D. from the University of Utah, where he wrote a dissertation titled "Inventing the Indian: White Images, Native Oral Literature, and Contemporary Native Writers," and he has gone on to hold various academic positions, including at the University of Minnesota, where he also served as chair of the American Indian Studies program, and the University of Lethbridge, where he taught Native Studies. Currently he is Associate Professor in the School of Literature and Performance Studies in English at the University of Guelph, teaching courses in Creative Writing and Native Literature.

Situated as he is within both literary and academic communities, King occupies a position that only a few First Nations writers share. For students and teachers of King's fiction, the author's critical works offer a valuable source of secondary materials, creating a scholarly context for the literature. Inevitably, students and teachers will explore the way each position shapes the writing and how it is read, just as details of the writer's biography and experience will be discussed. King's editing and critical work include a seminal collection of essays, *The Native in Literature*, co-edited by Cheryl Calver and Helen Hoy, in which critics examine the representations of Native people in works by non-Native authors. He has guest-edited a special issue of the literary journal *Canadian Fiction Studies* that features writing by Native writers, and he has published an anthology of Native literature, *All My Relations*. The introductory essays to both collections are frequently cited. King's article "Godzilla vs. Post-Colonial," in which he discusses the irrelevance of postcolonial theory to Native texts and proposes more appropriate critical categories, has been widely consulted and was republished in *New Contexts of Canadian Criticism*. In fact, King is part of a long tradition in Canadian letters that both accommodates and perhaps even promotes writer/academics. One need only think of the lingering presence in high school and undergraduate courses of Margaret Atwood's thematic study *Survival*, or the way in which some of Robert Kroetsch's pronouncements about Canadian writing turn up as epigrammatic quotations in Canadian literary criticism to recognize the effect the critical statements made by writers can have on shaping critical discourse. E.J. Pratt, Earle Birney, Frank Davey, Aritha van Herk, and George Bowering are some other examples of writers who also teach and produce influential literary criticism. Such figures have historical importance in Canadian letters, as they have been integral in defining and legitimizing the field. Similarly, the words of Native writers who also write literary criticism have weight and authority. King is also aware of contemporary trends in literature and literary theory. In an interview with Karl E. Jirgens, King credits his partner, Helen Hoy, with keeping him informed as to what is going on in critical theory, and postmodernism in particular. The postmodern qualities of *Green Grass, Running Water*, King remarks, explain "why the book sells so well on college campuses." (Interview with Jirgens 19)

As for the academic interest in *Green Grass, Running Water*, King remarks, with his characteristic sense of humour, that it is "the kind of novel, that is a little bit of fun for the academics who live such a dull and boring life." (Interview with Jirgens 19) Many would agree with King that it is "the book to work with because it has everything an academic can possibly want stuffed in there." ("Border Trickery" 177) Indeed, the critical articles collected in the special issue of *Canadian Literature* suggest just how much academic fun that novel can be. Margery Fee and Jane Flick describe "the pure pleasure of getting the point or the joke, the pleasure of moving across the border separating insider and outsider." (132) To cross that border, they argue, means "getting" the jokes that require detailed cultural/historical knowledge for full appreciation." (133) Like Atwood, they call this humour "subversive" (134) and recognize the text as "polemical" in King's sense of the term. ("Godzilla" 14) Yet, beyond the pleasure of satisfying critical curiosity, Fee and Flick assert that this humour is also what they call "coyote pedagogy," teaching Native history "in a Native way" (138):

> King's strategy for writing for an audience primarily composed of the uninformed is not to pander to its preconceptions or to produce explanations, but to entice, even trick this audience into finding out for themselves. (132)

On this view, King's novel is not *merely* funny; it is funny with a purpose.

Medicine River, and King's latest novel *Truth & Bright Water*, have not seemed to send the critics to the library, or at least, they have proved to be less popular with academics.[6] It may be that the absence of allusions to the stereotyped characters in canonical works or the exclusions and biases of history makes *Medicine River* and *Truth & Bright Water* relatively less appealing to critics eager to ferret out such references. Because King's intended audience for these novels is Native rather than specifically academic, the novels create a fictional world that takes for granted the cultural knowledge needed to understand. In Native communities, as Kimberly M. Blaeser argues, there can be tacit understanding by those who share the same worldview. ("Writing" 63) This understanding is not only evident in oral tradition, which relies on the listener's knowledge, but also informs an "oral aesthetic" that shapes written stories. Native readers will know where the text comes from; non-Native readers will not necessarily. Paradoxically, this associational method tends to invite rather than to alienate cultural outsiders, and therefore, does not explicitly challenge the ambivalence towards Native issues in Canadian culture. As the reviews suggest, works possessing non-threatening, non-judgmental humour will attract praise.

Not only is a novel like *Medicine River* funny, but the plot moves to a resolution that comforts rather than unsettles. As experience teaching his work to undergraduates suggests, readers follow these romance and comedic plots like well-worn paths, turning to the appreciation of the author's skill rather than to critique. The comedy that seems to make *Medicine River* readily accessible to non-Native readers is even more pronounced in the film version of the novel. Adapted as a made-for-TV movie that was shown on CBC television and is available for home consumption on video, the screenplay fits firmly within the generic paradigms of the romantic comedy. Again, humour prevails, as the headline titles of the reviews reiterate.[7] Will, played by the well-known actor Graham Greene, is more gullible and easily manipulated than the original fictional character, and Harlen Bigbear, played by Tom Jackson, is a much goofier and uncomplicated version of the character than we get in the novel. Furthermore, while the emphasis in the novel is on Will's coming to terms with what it might mean to stay in Medicine River and to re-acculturate himself as a Native person who belongs to a particular place and people, the movie version of the character is always ready to return to a more glamorous white world in which he feels more comfortable.

The screenplay also flattens out the narrative line, maintaining a simple chronological plot, which minimizes the complexity of the novel's treatment of the past. The novel is structured as a series of fragments, which emphasize the way the past permeates the present, and in the novel, Will confronts some difficult memories, especially about his father's abandonment of the family. This emotional pain is easily compensated for in the movie if not outright ignored. On screen, the plot focuses on the romance between Louise and Will, complete with a happy ending. The novel leaves the question of whether or not Louise and Will marry open-ended, which King says was intentional ("Border Tricks" 165-66); in the movie, however, Will is the putative husband to Louise and father to the baby South Wing, a representation that plays to western notions of the nuclear family unit and aptly concludes the romance narrative. That this new family unit is accepted by the community at large, is indicated by their front-and-centre position in the group photograph, which provides the closing image of the movie.

Certainly, what works in a novel may not work on the screen: movies are rarely as complex as written texts and often go for the love story over other possible choices. Yet by over-emphasizing the romance plot and by keeping the narrative in the present time of the story, the movie simplifies the main themes of the novel, dilutes its moments of conflict or pain, and minimizes its broader cultural and political meanings. What the audience gets in this version is a much softer, nicer story. John Haslett Cuff, television critic for the *Globe and Mail,* likens the movie to a sitcom and finds it "barely credible," "a politically correct fantasy that presents all its aboriginal characters as cute and uncomplicated as sitcom creations." (C9)[8] He charges the writers with presenting Native characters as too happy, thereby simply substituting one stereotype for another. Interestingly, this was also the assessment of one reviewer of the novel, *Medicine River,* who found fault with the ending because it was "almost too warm and comfortable." (Carolyn King, 51)

Representations of Native people in mainstream media tend to focus on trauma and conflict. The implication is that Native people are either sick or angry or both. In this context, it is hardly surprising that stories that depict a functional community of Native people might seem to be unrealistic. Yet Native writers are caught in a double-bind. Jo-Ann Thom remarks that Native writers "have quickly become cognizant of readers' low tolerance for seeing Aboriginal people portrayed as victims and white people as victimizers, even though those are the positions that each has historically occupied" and writers who enjoy current recognition are less likely than an earlier generation to focus on traumatic experiences of the past. (304) Thom suggests that "Influenced by readers' responses to their predecessors' works, this generation of writers experiments with literary strategies designed to make their texts more congenial to readers and to make their subversion more covert." (304) The question is: how do readers come to recognize and to understand that covert subversion?

Ironically, it may well be that King's skill as a writer forecloses the in-depth analysis of his work that would reveal it.

Margaret Atwood, for instance, finds two of King's short stories to be "perfect," by which she means "that as narrations they are exquisitely timed, that everything in them appears to be there by right, and that there is nothing you would want to change or edit out." (244) Consumers of print and film media may be gratified by such perfection; literary critics, however, usually like to find texts to be less than perfect. This is perhaps especially true in the contemporary moment, when deconstructive and psychoanalytic theories have trained critics to attend to what is problematic or repressed in a text. If a work seems "perfect," what more can there be to say? If a book pleases rather than challenges, it does not readily lend itself to the kind of resistant reading "against the grain" that is currently practiced in academic discourse. That *Medicine River* is a funny book may also prohibit critical analysis of it, especially for students who want to avoid "ruining" a book by "picking it apart." As Atwood and many others note, King is a skilled practitioner of comedic writing, but analyzing *how* the humour works risks ruining what made it funny in the first place. This is a comment frequently made by students.

The use of humour by Native writers seems to relieve non-Native readers rather than challenge them. For example, in a recent review Wayne Tefs writes: "*Truth & Bright Water* is a masterful, comic book, one which points beyond itself to larger issues of cultural suppression and exploitation." (87) Tefs remarks that Native people "laugh off" oppression and exploitation:

> By allowing [fears and anxieties] to emerge as self-reflexive fun, rather than as fury and anger, oppressed groups give themselves a chance to alter their conditions without resorting to violence and bloodshed. (87)

While non-Native readers may interpret humour as a writing strategy with social significance, King notes that Native and non-Native readers tend to laugh at different things and for different reasons. (Interview with Rooke, 71) In this regard, humour is integral to King's representation of Native communities:

> For instance, I don't think that I need stay away from some of the problems that Native communities face—alcoholism, drug abuse, child abuse—but I do have a responsibility not to make those such a part of my fiction that I give the impression to the

> reader that this is what drives Native communities. I'm very much concerned about that. It's my responsibility to make my readers understand what makes Native communities strong.
>
> It doesn't serve the community to constantly have it held up for ridicule because of those problems. Those problems exist within non-Native society too. (Interview with Canton, 4)

Certainly the humour is what many readers find most memorable about King's work, but in light of King's stated desire to "emphasize that the range of 'Indian' is not as narrow as many people try to make it" (Interview with Canton, 3), the interpretation of humour as a vehicle for social realism can hardly stand. While tough issues face the characters in *Medicine River*—such as the exodus of young Native people like Will from their home communities, or internal disputes over "real" Native identity—these do not seem to be King's primary concern or the concern of his readers. In fact, readers seem to be able to walk away from the text relatively unaware of many of the topics it raises. Perhaps this explains why King has recently stated that he is trying to alter his reputation as a comic writer. Comic writers, says King, "aren't taken seriously. Comic writers are enjoyed, and even if you're a satirist people have a good time with it but they don't ...." ("Border Trickery" 165) King leaves the sentence unfinished, but one can surmise that he is pointing to precisely the issue we address here: readers don't fully "get it" because they are reluctant to analyze works of comic realism. Paradoxically, the comic realist mode facilitates the easy consumption of the text within a curriculum and society that have been shaped by multiculturalism. However, it also masks the difficult cross-cultural learning that the text requires without demanding. *Medicine River* is, in this respect, an incredibly subtle book.

Consider, for example, the story of Joyce Blue Horn's family photo. The story of the photo session is woven with Will's remembrance of the family photo his mother had taken when he and James were boys. In the photo, it is just the three of them, not the fifty-four plus that swell out of Will's study and continues to grow as the crowd moves down to the river. The humour stems from the chaos that ensues as Will loses control of "the ocean of relations" and the spectacle of a harassed Will "red-faced and aglow" running from behind the camera to his place in the group twenty-four times. (215) In the end, all the pictures turn out, and Will hangs it and his mother's family photo on the kitchen wall. By weaving together the story of the two photos, the structure offers a comparison that emphasizes the bonds of pride and belonging that a family photo represents while signaling the difference between the nuclear and extended families. The scene compares not just two families, the one Will has lost and the one that is now claiming him, it also compares different ideas of community. As a child, Will's immediate family was loving and close, but disconnected from others. The significance of connection beyond the nuclear family becomes clearer after reading King's "Introduction" to *All My Relations*:

> "All my relations" is at first a reminder of who we are and of our relationship with both our family and our relatives. It also reminds us of the extended relationship we share with all human beings. But the relationships that Native people see go further, the web of kinship extending to the animals, to the birds, to the fish, to the plants, to all the animate and inanimate forms that can be seen or imagined. More than that, "all my relations" is an encouragement for us to accept the responsibilities we have within this universal family by living our lives in a harmonious and moral manner.... (ix)

Such explanation is not offered in the novel. What you see when you look at Will's pictures will depend on your perspective.

The reading of humour as subversive, as outlined by Margaret Atwood, or as pedagogical, as argued by Fee and Flick, suggests a polemical dimension to all of King's work, including his associational works. Native literature generally plays subversive and pedagogical roles when received in the mainstream, yet this role depends on the reading audience. How teachers can understand this reception without suggesting that Native societies are defined by the political struggles in which they are engaged is the challenge. One way to begin this process is by engaging students in a practice that they are well-acquainted with, that is, the reading of stereotypes. Because students are prepared by a highly visual culture to be visually literate, they tend to be skilled at recognizing and analyzing images. Thus, they are apt to understand the stereotypes against which a novel like *Medicine River* works.

In "'Tell Our Own Stories': Politics and the Fiction of Thomas King," Priscilla [Percy] Walton writes: "Because violence is the trait most commonly associated with the native Other, it is violence that receives most attention in *Medicine River.*" (79) Walton draws on the work of critics who have studied representations of Native people in literary texts written by non-Native writers. Discussing the damaging effects of such representations and assuming that Native writers consciously set out to resist them, Walton contends that "*Medicine River* is a metadiscursive text, in that, rather than trying to refer to a 'reality' outside of language, it refers to a discourse about discourse, and, as such, it foregrounds the constructedness of the semiotic field of the indigene" (78, the latter phrase is Terry Goldie's). Positioning *Medicine River* in opposition to this "semiotic field of the indigene," the article focuses on how the text deals with its main constituents, that is, stereotypes.

The particular incident in the book under examination here concerns the altercation between David Plume, a former AIM activist, and Ray Little Buffalo. As it turns out, Ray receives his injuries by landing on a beer bottle and was not shot by David for taking his AIM jacket as the newspaper reports. Walton emphasizes the newspaper report, which she reads as a symbol of how white discourse reproduces false images of Natives, and interprets the scene as an example of how the narrator's and, through him, the readers' expectations concerning the violent male Native are overturned. Arnold Davidson extends this reading by noting that, in an interview with Walton, King reveals that he "originally wrote the episode as the newspaper, in the novel, misrepresents it" and describes realizing this as a "sobering moment." (193) In the context of the book, however, the meaning of the anecdote seems to lie in the notion voiced by Harlen that "A jacket ... is a poor substitute for friends and family." (255) In the text, then, the emphasis seems to be on why David Plume is estranged from others in the community in the first place, and what might need to happen, in terms of a shift in David's perception and attitude, in order to bring him back home. In fact, violence is not represented directly in the action of the novel; even the secondhand report refers to shooting but not to anyone getting shot, and the mention of the newspaper is one of the few references to the world outside the community of characters.

Arnold Davidson stresses the impact of stereotypes on the community when he notes that "Harlen Bigbear's friends all assume that he has succumbed to alcoholism instead of recognizing that he has merely come down with a serious case of the flu." (193) The text does undermine the stereotype of the drunken Indian, but perhaps more importantly, this scene establishes Will as gullible and, once again, apt to misunderstand or misjudge his friend Harlen. Such scenes are important both in terms of their challenge to stereotypes and in terms of the comedy they produce. Much of that comedy is ironic: Harlen, the main gossip in the book, the character who is always sticking his nose into other people's business, is now himself the subject of gossip. From the community's point of view, this is funny. Reading these scenes *only* in terms of stereotypes would undervalue the structural and thematic relevance of gossip in the text. As Gerry William notes, "while gossip abounds as it does in all communities, there is rarely any malicious intent involved, just a state of confusion in which no one is sure of the truth." (125) That state of confusion is hilarious. In fact, the book shows us how to read these scenes without making them refer to the dominant culture, because they repeat the pattern of initial misunderstanding and eventual clarification that characterizes many of Will's encounters with Harlen. Such scenes also intimate the presence of the trickster (both King [Interview with Rooke, 67], and William [132] have identified Harlen as a trickster figure), for the trickster can be the object of jokes, rumors, and meddling as well as their instigator. Such scenes demonstrate Kimberly M. Blaeser's insight that "contemporary [Native] texts contain the critical contexts needed for their own interpretation...." ("Native" 59)

By drawing readers' attention to stereotypes, we risk repeating those stereotypes by casting Aboriginal people as eternally troubled. Taking this risk by encouraging students to begin with a response to the way stereotypes might be implied in the text will initiate discussion, but the teacher's role is to extend this analysis by turning the class back to the text and by questioning the impression of Native societies that is created by insisting on a polemical reading. While polemical reading might expiate white guilt, it does little to illuminate the full range of meanings of this or any other Native text. In particular, it fails to recognize that the book might be working with ways of being, as well as theoretical and aesthetic forms, that have little to do with the dominant culture. Such performances of inadvertent stereotyping in critical and pedagogical practices have much wider political implications. In such criticism, First Nations are limited to the concerns already represented in the mainstream, but, contrary to media representations, Native people do not live in a constant state of reaction to mainstream culture. *Medicine River* reminds us of this fact. As Gerry William remarks, "the worlds of white and Native in the book exist in parallel with no significant interaction between them." (118) We see a world that is coherent, that refers to itself, that refers only obliquely to the dominant "white" culture. Those oblique references can only be explained at a metadiscursive level, in terms of genre and narrative convention.

Yet, despite the book's content, which does not foreground polemic, the choice of humour and plot, we argue, is itself a political statement. While Walton claims that King does not create an "alternate reality"—which makes sense given that the totalizing power of dominant discourse would make any alternative unlikely—an alternate reality is exactly what King achieves in *Medicine River*. Thus, the book makes a political point by refusing explanation within the terms of the mainstream. Paradoxically, it also becomes more palatable to members of the dominant culture for its refusal to be polemical. If the book is all the more palatable for not forcing certain readers to confront their own ignorance and privilege, then its positive reception is the outcome of the absence of cultural context in the text, and the reading audience's lack of knowledge about the cultural context.

As teachers, we can complicate and unsettle comfortable responses to King's work by showing how resistance to analysis is produced by the cultural modes used by the mainstream to process Native imagery. In particular, the reluctance to analyze suggests that readers do not really see the difference between the world of the text and the world the reader inhabits. Blaeser notes that when she teaches Native literature, "most of all them [her students] tell me it is different." ("Writing" 64-65) This has not been our experience teaching *Medicine River* or some of the more "realistic" stories in the collection *One Good Story, That One*. And such a response is hardly surprising, as the historical and cultural information needed to be a competent reader, a culturally literate reader of this work, is not represented in Canada's national, mainstream culture. The ease with which Native cultural products are consumed and appropriated in that mainstream suggests that there is no meaningful difference, nothing that cannot be assimilated. Improved cultural literacy means gaining the knowledge required for reading competence; it means making cultural differences visible. For example, Harlen Bigbear is not just Will's "buddy"; he is a relation and he resembles the traditional trickster figure who influences the lives of others in ways both benign and disruptive. And the significance of Will's return to the community can only be fully understood if one reads his individual story in the context of the history of Indian removals – through treaties, through the Indian Act, through adoptions, residential schools, and other interventions. In the case of *Medicine River*, it also means recognizing the liminal identities of the book's characters and author, seeing that the stories come from the edges of two worlds.

Teachers and critics can also draw readers' attention to the epistemological, philosophical, and formal differences that undergird Native texts, and, in so doing, they must be self-consciousness about the analytical models they bring to bear on them. Yet too often critical analyses are shaped either by preconceived ideas of what Native texts are about or by imported critical paradigms. Readers outside of the culture generally expect Native texts to describe the oppression of Native people and to correct negative colonialist images. Thus, they tend to focus on the subversive aspects of Native texts, noting such thematic issues as cultural conflict, while ignoring or undervaluing other matters.

The issues of reception and analysis we identify in this paper point to the larger question of the cultural *illiteracy* of most Canadian readers with respect to Native subjects. *Medicine River* presents particular issues, because it seems to be so comforting, so "perfect." This is why King's work is often selected by teachers and happily and unreflectingly digested by students. Yet we should be wary of such responses, for they point to the ways in which Native images are commodified and consumed in mainstream culture. The complexity and sophistication of Native literary texts—including the subtleties of their humour—can only be fully apprehended if we learn to read them from the inside out. For the cultural outsider, this is no easy thing as there is no ready-made template that opens up the contexts, structures and meanings of Native literary texts. Reading Native literature requires, as Armand Garnett Ruffo argues, more than an anthropological approach; "rather, for those who are serious, it is more a question of cultural initiation, of involvement and commitment." ("Inside" 174) Teachers can model this commitment for their students while recognizing that cultural initiation is an ongoing process of listening to and learning from what Native writers have to say.

Acknowledgements

Thanks to Armand Garnet Ruffo for permission to quote his statement concerning humour.

Notes

[1] That paper was titled "Cultural Literacy in Canada: Teaching Thomas King's *Medicine River*," presented as part of the panel "To Celebrate Canada's First Nations: The Works of Thomas King," arranged by the Division on American Indian Literatures and organized by Dr. Virginia Carney.

[2] Reviews of *Medicine River* appeared in most of the major Canadian newspapers and in periodicals that focus on Canadian studies. Most are fulsome in their praise and draw attention to King's ability to present authentic "snapshots of life" (Gillies 212), to draw characters with a "keen eye and a humorous touch" (Carolyn King 50), and to evoke a "sense of place" (Kelly C19)—in other words, reviewers have been pleased by the success of King's

use of comic realism. Other examples of reviews include those by Westman, Rigelhof, McGoogan, Smith, Rayner, and D'Souza. Critical articles that analyze King's *Medicine River* in more depth have been written by Christie, Davidson, Peters, Walton, and William. A new book-length study of Thomas King's oeuvre, tentatively titled *Border Crossings: Thomas King's Cultural Inversions* and co-authored by Priscilla L. Walton, Arnold E. Davidson, and Jennifer Andrews, will be published in 2002.

[3] This comment could refer to an earlier generation of works that have frequently been labeled "protest literature" (see the comment by Jo-Ann Thom cited below), or it could be informed by the stereotype of the stoic Indian.

[4] Reviews by the following authors have been the sources for this irreverent paraphrase: Anderson, Atwood, Compton, Gillies, Jones, Martin, McCormack, Radu, Rainwater, Scheick, Smith, Taylor, and Tefs.

[5] See our article "Cultural Literacy, First Nations, and the Future of Canadian Literary Studies."

[6] Robin Ridington is perhaps the exception here. Ridington's article on *Truth & Bright Water* is aimed at explicating the numerous references to history and culture in the novel. His training as an anthropologist no doubt informs such an approach.

[7] Here is a selection of the headlines: "Native humor tops Medicine River" (Zimmerman) "CBC film boasts native humor" (Stevenson), "Medicine River: romantic comedy captures essence of Indian humour" (Blakely).

[8] Thanks to Renate Eigenbrod for this reference.

Works Cited

Anderson, Scott. Review of *One Good Story, That One*, by Thomas King. *Quill & Quire* Sept. 1993: 61.

Armstrong, Jeannette, ed. *Looking at the Words of Our People: First Nations Analysis of Literature*. Penticton: Theytus, 1993.

Atwood, Margaret. "A Double-Bladed Knife: Subversive Laughter in Two Stories by Thomas King." *Native Writers and*

Canadian Writing. Ed. W.H. New. Vancouver: UBC P, 1990. 243-50.

Blaeser, Kimberly M. "Native Literature: Seeking a Critical Centre." Armstrong, 51-62.

- - -. "Writing Voices Speaking: Native Authors and an Oral Aesthetic." *Talking on the Page: Editing Aboriginal Oral Texts*. Ed. Laura J. Murray and Keren Rice. Toronto: University of Toronto P, 1999. 53-68.

Blakey, Bob. "Medicine River: Romantic comedy captures essence of Indian humor." *Calgary Herald* 17 Oct., 1993: C4.

Christie, Stuart. "Time-Out: (Slam)Dunking Photographic Realism in Thomas King's *Medicine River*." *Studies in American Indian Literature* 11.2 (1999): 51-65.

Compton, Valerie. Review of *Green Grass, Running Water*, by Thomas King. *Quill & Quire* March 1993: 46.

Cuff, John Haslett. "Stereotype replaces stereotype." *Globe and Mail* 16 Oct., 1993: C9.

Davidson, Arnold E. *Coyote Country: Fictions of the Canadian West*. Durham: Duke UP, 1994.

D'Souza, Irene. "Characters make novel." Rev. of *Medicine River*, by Thomas King. *Winnipeg Free Press* 19 May, 1990: 24.

Fee, Margery. "Introduction." *Canadian Literature* 161/162 (1999): 9-11.

- - - and Jane Flick. "Coyote Pedagogy: Knowing Where the Borders Are in Thomas King's *Green Grass, Running Water*." *Canadian Literature* 161/162 (1999):131-39.

Gillies, M.A. "Temporal Interplay." Review of *Medicine River*, by Thomas King, and *Of Desire*, by David Helwig. *Canadian Literature* 131 (1991): 212-13.

Hulan, Renée and Linda Warley. "Cultural Literacy, First Nations, and the Future of Canadian Literary Studies." *Journal of Canadian Studies/Revue d'études canadiennes*. 34.3 (1999): 59-86.

Jones Jr., Malcolm. "Life Off the Reservation." Review of *Green Grass, Running Water*, by Thomas King. *Newsweek* 12 Apr., 1993: 60.

Kelly, M.T. "The subtle Trickster." Review of *Medicine River*, by Thomas King. *Globe and Mail* 3 Feb., 1990: C19.

King, Carolyn. "As the river flows." Review of *Medicine River*, by Thomas King. *Western Report* 3 Sept., 1990: 50-51.

King, Thomas, ed. *All My Relations: An Anthology of Contemporary Canadian Native Fiction*. Toronto: McClelland and Stewart, 1990.

- - -. "Border Trickery and Dog Bones: A Conversation with Thomas King." By Jennifer Andrews. *Studies in Canadian Literature/Études en littérature canadienne* 24.2 (1999): 161-85.

- - -. ed. *Canadian Fiction Magazine* 60 (1987).

- - -. "Godzilla vs. Post-Colonial." *World Literature Written in English* 30.2 (1990): 10-16. Report in *New Contexts of Canadian Criticism*. Ed. Ajay Heble, Donna Palmateer Pennee and J.R. (Tim) Struthers. Peterborough: Broadview, 1997. 241-48.

- - -. *Green Grass, Running Water*. HarperCollins, 1993.

- - -. "In the Skin of the Trickster: An Interview with Thomas King." By Karl E. Jirgens. *Rampike* 8.2 (1997):17-21.

- - -. Interview. By Constance Rooke. *World Literature Written in English* 30.2 (1990); 62-76.

- - -. Interview. By Jeffery Canton. *Paragraph* 16.1 (1994): 2-6.

- - -. "Inventing the Indian: White Images, Native Oral Literature, and Contemporary Native Writers." Dissortation University of Utah, 1986.

- - -. *Medicine River*. 1989. Markham: Penguin, 1991.

- - -. *One Good Story, That One*. Toronto: HarperPerennial, 1993.

- - -. *Truth & Bright Water*. Toronto: HarperFlamingo, 1999.

- - -. Cheryl Calver and Helen Hoy, eds. *The Native in Literature*. Toronto: ECW, 1987.

Martin, Sandra. "This Land is Whose Land?" Review of *Keeper 'n Me*, by Richard Wagamese, *Green Grass, Running Water*, by Thomas King, and *The Bingo Palace*, by Louise Erdrich. *Quill & Quire* May 1994: 24.

McGoogan, Ken. "Novelist's debut impressive." Review of *Medicine River*, by Thomas King. *Calgary Herald* 10 Feb., 1990: C8.

McCormack, Eric. "Coyote Goes Slapstick." Review of *Green Grass, Running Water*, by Thomas King. *Books in Canada* Apr. 1993: 40-41.

Medicine River. Dir. Stuart Margolin. Teleplay by Thomas King and Ann MacNaughton. Medicine River Productions, 1992.

Peters, Darrell Jesse. "Beyond the Frame: Tom King's Narratives of Resistment." *Studies in American Indian Literature* 11.2 (1999): 66-78.

Radu, Kenneth. "Comical and Economical." Review of *One Good Story, That One,* by Thomas King. *Books in Canada* Oct. 1993: 36-37.

Rainwater, Catherine. "Negotiating Cultural Boundaries." Review of *One Good Story, That One,* by Thomas King, and *The Native Creative Process,* by Douglas Cardinal and Jeannette Armstrong. *Canadian Literature* 149 (1996): 170-73.

Rayner, William. "Engaging tale of survival tinged with sadness." Review of *Medicine River,* by Thomas King. *Vancouver Sun* 24 Feb., 1990: H5.

Ridington, Robin. "Happy Trails to You: Contexted Discourse and Indian Removals in Thomas King's *Truth & Bright Water.*" *Canadian Literature* 167 (2000): 89-107.

Rigelhof, T.F. "Medicine for the spirit." Review of *The Ancient Child,* by N. Scott Momaday and *Medicine River,* by Thomas King. *The Gazette* 23 Feb, 1991: K3.

Ruffo, Armand Garnet. "Inside Looking Out: Reading *Tracks* From a Native Perspective." Armstrong, 161-76.

Scheick, William J. "Grace & Gall." Review of *Green Grass, Running Water,* by Thomas King, and *The True Life Adventures of Sparrow Drinkwater,* by Trevor Ferguson. *Canadian Literature* 138/39 (1993): 155-56.

Smith, Stephen. "Modern native images that counter cliches." Review of *Medicine River,* by Thomas King. *Toronto Star* 24 Mar., 1990: M10.

Stevenson, Jane. "CBC film boasts native humor." *Calgary Herald* 15 Dec., 1992: D8.

Taylor, Drew Hayden. "The Best of the Best in Native Arts." *Windspeaker* Feb. 1997: 9-10.

Tefs, Wayne. "Reaching and Grasping." Review of *Truth & Bright Water,* by Thomas King. *Border Crossings* 18.4 (1999): 85-87.

Thom, Jo-Ann. "The Effect of Readers' Responses on the Development of Aboriginal Literature in Canada: A Study of Maria Campbell's *Halfbreed*, Beatrice Culleton's *In Search of April Raintree*, and Richard Wagamese's *Keeper 'n Me." In Search of April Raintree: Critical Edition*. By Beatrice Culleton Mosionier. Ed. Cheryl Suzack. Winnipeg: Portage and Main, 1999. 295-305.

Turbide, Diane. "A Literary Trickster." Review of *Green Grass, Running Water*, by Thomas King. *Maclean's* 3 May, 1993: 43-45.

Walton, Priscilla L., Arnold E. Davidson, and Jennifer Andrews. *Border Crossings: Thomas King's Cultural Inversions*. Toronto: University of Toronto P, forthcoming 2002.

Walton, Percy. "'Tell Our Own Stories': Politics and the Fiction of Thomas King." *World Literature Written in English* 30.2 (1990): 77-84.

Westman, Marybeth. Review of *Medicine River*, by Thomas King. *Canadian Woman Studies/Les cahiers de la femme* 14.4 (1994): 115-16.

William, Gerry. "Thomas King's *Medicine River*: A Review." Jeannette Armstrong, 1993: 115-36.

Zimmerman, Kate. "Native humor tops Medicine River." *Calgary Herald* 18 Jul., 1992: B6.

"You Can't Get Angry with a Person's Life": Negotiating Aboriginal Women's Writing, Whiteness, and Multicultural Nationalism in a University Classroom

Jennifer G. Kelly

The focus of this article is a complex, undertheorized, heavily charged, typically frightening, and often-exhilarating space commonly known as the "University Aboriginal Literature Classroom."[1] I draw on my experiences as a white Canadian feminist, graduate student and novice anti-racist teaching Aboriginal Literatures to a predominantly white class at the University of Calgary, and on the responses of course participants to the materials and pedagogy.[2] I am concerned with understanding how the unmarked operations of whiteness, assumptions about Aboriginality, literature, particularly autobiography, nationalist ideologies of multiculturalism, and Christian morality converge and are reproduced in the Canadian university Aboriginal Literature classroom, and how critical pedagogy might work to resist and transform these discourses. I am interested in exploring the complexities of the location of the white instructor of Aboriginal materials, and how Aboriginal women's lifestorytelling, in entering visibility in the university classroom, is itself pedagogical in how it "exists, insinuates itself, and thereby 'teaches' in the worlds it inhabits." (Mathur 8)

My goals in teaching this course were multiple (and in retrospect, optimistic): to counter one of the major obstacles in the analysis of Aboriginal literatures—the vast lack of knowledge regarding the histories of global and local colonization; to resist the commonsense sexism and racism that attend the production, reception, and criticism of Aboriginal literatures; to engage participants as active critics and producers of knowledges, as subjects and agents of history; to begin to lay some of the groundwork necessary for a rigorous critical analysis of "Aboriginal" cultural production to even begin.[3] Many dynamics and responses emerged that I had not anticipated (for a number of reasons),[4] including the vexed desire of white students to "relate to" and "identify with" Aboriginal characters, autobiographers, and fiction writers, a desire enmeshed with literary inheritances, ideologies of multicultural nationalism, whiteness, and Christianity. As I have learned through this course, Christian morality shapes not only how many students in an anti-racist Canadian university classroom construct themselves when faced with the histories and current realities of colonization and racism—often in essentialized terms of personal "goodness"/

"badness" and innocence/guilt, especially—but how (to my surprise at the time) they read and construct the instructor as "moral guardian" on these issues. These concerns have raised for me broader questions about the limits of critical race theory regarding Aboriginality in the classroom, about the extent to which Christian paradigms are profoundly constitutive of national and individual identity as it circulates in (supposedly secular) university structures, and about how multicultural ideologies function as promises of individual and collective redemption regarding past and present injustices conducted in the name of nation. I begin to explore these issues by locating this "Aboriginal Literature" course in terms of its systemic and institutional marginality, and my position in it. I then consider responses by white women to Mohawk/white Beth Brant's *Writing as Witness: essay and talk* (1994), which evoked the most powerful, vehement, and gendered, negative responses—responses that combined white defensiveness, individualism, Christianity, and the ideology of multiculturalism. I then discuss the responses to Métis Beatrice Culleton's *In Search of April Raintree* and Métis Maria Campbell's *Half-breed,* which indicate dominant assumptions about autobiography and authority, history and truth, and Aboriginal women's agency in relationship to poverty and addiction. I conclude with some further reflections on the potential role of "identification" in anti-racism work, and on the vexed construction, by white students, of me, as white anti-racist instructor, as the moral guardian on racism.

With its history in imperialism, nationalism, and the production of loyal citizenship, the Canadian educational system remains involved in the production of social categories and the claiming of space/territory according to those categories (Schick 5). The classroom, an extension of the public sphere, is a site "for the re-affirmation of bourgeois, racialized identity and the constitution of the 'not-Other'" (6), that is, for the production of whiteness as norm. This process manifests in a number of ways, including the marginal status assigned most Aboriginal Literature courses, appended as electives to the core curriculum. Canonical, disciplinary, and popular assumptions about literature, particularly autobiography, and their relationships to history and "truth" also shape the conditions of the Aboriginal literature classroom. Ideologies of autobiography as a denigrated form (as biased and/or personal) often transform when they converge with ideologies of race; in the case of liberalism and multiculturalism, the text from a racialized location is often viewed as cultural and historical artefact, representative of a collectivity (race, culture, nation), and its writer as spokesperson. In conjunction with the operations of white guilt, it may be viewed as having an altered or increased purchase on truth and referentiality. (In climates of entrenched conservativism, however, the denigration of the form as "biased" is often reinforced.)

Moreover, the Aboriginal or "international literature" classroom, like most Canadian university populations, generally comprises white middle-class individuals whose ideological inheritance includes what South Asian Canadian critic Aruna Srivastava calls the "cult of multiculturalism, that is, the wholesale and largely uncritical acceptance of Canadian multicultural ideology as a fact, rather than a questionable construct with a distinct history." (2-3) Part of the pervasiveness—the *persuasiveness*—of multiculturalism as a national ideology rests, especially for those privileged by whiteness and middle-class status, on how it poses racism and systemic inequality (often coded as "cultural diversity") as mere echoes of the past in a mythic current climate of equal economic opportunity and "tolerance" of difference. It is manifested in polite denials (by white people) of the existence of systemic racism and the concomitant reduction of racism to the level of individual attitude, and arguments about how minority groups "should" conduct themselves in relationship to the dominant culture. Codes of tolerance, "niceness," and the abhorrence of anger (these are codes of gender and class as well as of whiteness), assertions of white feminism in terms of universal sisterhood, and the refusal to accept responsibility for racial privilege through charges of the minority voice unfairly making the innocent white person "feel guilty" are all part of this script.[5]

When the issue of racism is raised in the university classroom, where participants are well-versed in ideologies of the superiority of rationalism, white students often register their discomfort (and channel their emotional responses) through arguments about civility, rationality, reason, and self-control.

Their insistence that "differences on issues of race and gender can be discussed as intellectual topics" (Schick, 12) constructs the university as a site of whiteness and Western rationalism, "quite unlike 'out there' where others belong and which participants describe as political, embodied, and not necessarily rational." (2) When literatures by Aboriginal writers and writers of colour comprise the subject matter of the university classroom, writes South Asian Canadian critic Louise Saldanha, multiculturalism "permeates reading practices wherein textual representations of race and ethnicity are managed through Eurocentric normative ideals." (3) Texts are labelled

> with the rather dubious honour of universalism or, forgiven [their] rather unfortunate subject matter by representing racism tastefully. If, on the other hand, readers of these texts do not, or cannot, read the representations of "difference" ethnocentrically, within established multicultural interpretations, the books in question are reprimanded for being polemical ... not believable ... or downright rude. (3)

Much of my pedagogy was directed at making "whiteness" visible as a social category with profound effects on the history of colonization, current inequalities, reading practices, and classroom dynamics. I felt that for a predominantly white class, in a white university, it was urgent to foreground how most authorized knowledge "about" Aboriginal peoples is filtered through European/ white perspectives. I saw this process as supplemented not by my "authority" or "knowledge" as lecturer *per se* but by the introduction of crucial issues regarding racism, the foregrounding of perspectives of Aboriginal theorists, and the facilitation of discussions on a range of issues.[6] Central to my teaching was the use of journal writing as a critical process that connects the particularities of individual responses to systemic processes and cultural/historical inheritances. In the words of Aruna Srivastava, from whom I have energetically borrowed this practice, the journal writing process supports a "politicized reader-response approach to cultural texts" that engages participants in "self-reflection and critique of the repertoire of beliefs they bring to reading literature and their world." ("Cult" 3) It opens students "to the possibility that their literary reading strategies are remarkably similar to, and often informed by the same presuppositions as their 'reading' of people, other cultural texts, different cultures, races, genders." (3)

One of the dangers of journal writing when viewed as a "personal" form is that it may be interpreted as a site of freedom to be a racist (Asante), and in order to forestall this I was very clear from the outset that the journal was not "personal" but critical, and would be assessed as such. Central to the process is the concept of "unpacking," which requires participants to persistently critique (rather than simply "explain" and therefore justify) their responses and their historical/cultural sources, such that, particularly in the case of whiteness but also in terms of other forms of privilege, retreat (usually unconscious) into defense strategies and the reassertion of dominance are explored and resisted. In enacting a process that is in many ways autobiographical, critical journalling enables a reconsideration and a reconceptualization of the discourses that shape the individual's responses as cultural, historical, and therefore open to change. In linking "knowledge, social responsibility, and collective struggle" (Mohanty 192), it can generate a transformation of "subjectivity" that is individually empowering, as many of the participants indicated, but also politically vital for systemic change. "I don't know what to do," and "What can I do?" were common questions posed by white participants grappling with the new awareness of the immensity of historical, institutionalized, and personal processes of oppression.

Clearly, the location of the white anti-racist feminist teacher in a predominantly white Aboriginal literature university classroom is a complex mix of negotiations with power, authority, and history. While women university teachers do have institutional authority in the classroom, this authority "is undermined constantly by existing gender relations that operate in society at large" (Ng 135), in the university structure, and in the hierarchy of faculty seniority. At the same time that women instructors' knowledges are devalued, we are expected to "play the role of the all-forgiving nurturing mother whose approval is unconditional." (S. S. Friedman, qtd. in Ng 138) The dance with patriarchal institutional authority in the anti-racist feminist classroom is a difficult one, particularly when the interrogation of emotional responses is a constitutive feature of the pedagogy, and is located in a larger institutional context that is likely to read the pedagogy derogatorily as "therapy" and "anti-intellectual." Anti-racist pedagogy can unleash a torrent of emotional response: anger (sometimes directed at the instructor), confusion, grief, frustration, denial, defensiveness, often-paralysing guilt, and sorrow. Though experience and allies are invaluable in this regard, one perhaps cannot be entirely prepared (I certainly wasn't) for the mix of dynamics that might emerge among any particular group in an anti-racist classroom - dynamics of open hostility, racism, sexism, homophobia, silences of defeat and of privilege, and quite understandable terror of Aboriginal students and students of colour at the prospect of being the objects of investigation and of racism yet again. Anti-racist pedagogy requires, in other words, a teacher with attributes traditionally ascribed to women within patriarchy. A constant risk, then, is that this work and its politics will simply be reincorporated into and defused by a masculinist paradigm once again. (In this case, I was a graduate student and first-time mother to a nine-week old breastfeeding daughter who accompanied me to campus and often appeared, sometimes to nurse, in the classroom. These factors, in terms of practicalities and more nebulous issues of gender and authority, complicated matters for me, to say the least.)[7]

In this course, participants recorded, perhaps for the first time in their academic lives, their shock, horror, sadness, anger, and fear upon reading Aboriginal writing. They grappled with feelings of guilt, sorrow, grief, and a sense of powerlessness in the face of overwhelming systemic processes, and understandable uncertainty about how to view the world once their previous perceptions had been dismantled. And, until they were assured that an "emotional" response is part of a critical process, many often "apologized" in their journals (to the instructor/reader? themselves?) for what they saw as their emotionalism, their loss of rational objectivity: "Am I talking in circles? I sort of feel as though I am, but I hope this all makes sense ..."; "I am embarrassed by the emotional response to the book."

In disclosing the information that they do, under circumstances in which they are not in power (though they are not powerless either), participants are engaging in a process of self-exposure that is personally risky, institutionally new (in foregrounding what they do not know rather than what they do), and requires a particular amount of trust in the instructor as audience of the journal if the process is to be effective. Nor can an anti-racist teacher entirely prepare individual students for their own unlearning processes; describing grief, anger, defensiveness, and pain *in advance* is necessary but the description of emotional responses is not the same as experiencing them. As Sharilyn Calliou of the Michel Band in Alberta suggests,

> racism must be named, and teachers must know that in doing so emotion will emerge from the underground of denial within individuals, lunch rooms, classrooms, textbooks, media, or schoolgrounds. These events can provide the occasion for lessons to unlock the cycle of denial and begin the dialogue to generate awareness. The emotional content enables both parties to link experience to the theoretical knowledge of racism's poor science, overt consequences, and continuing denial of full citizenship to some members of society. Racism cannot be unlearned like mistaken geographical knowledge can be unlearned. Instead, emotional life history needs to be relived and re-examined and emotional impacts felt in the presence of compassionate teachers and learners who wish to understand and confront what happens when denial stops. ("Peacekeeping" 58)

Anti-racist pedagogy requires persistent clarification, to administrators and to classroom participants, regarding how our pedagogy is a *critical* process that interrogates the mind/body, rational/irrational binarism underlying academic and popular thought, to ensure that our praxis is not reduced to the emotional, even as we insist on the necessity of the inclusion of the emotional in the classroom. It involves, too, as Chandra Talpade Mohanty suggests, "taking responsibility for the material effects of these very pedagogical practices on students." (49) This may include, for example, providing information that participants may find helpful regarding resources (books, articles, counselling services), being available for further discussion outside of the class time, and being a role model for working through such processes.

One of the most vexing and challenging inheritances of imperialism involves the negotiation with powerful social categories, such as Aboriginal and non-Aboriginal, which, while shown to be arbitrary (i.e., historical) in their construction, continue to have damaging material effects and are intimately involved in and constitute unequal power relations. The complex location of the non-Aboriginal teacher of Aboriginal materials is a case in point. (Many participants of English 385 indicated that they had expected the course to be taught by an Aboriginal instructor.) In terms of this specific classroom context, and in teaching about the histories of misrepresentations of Aboriginal peoples, for example, I am wary of reproducing those misrepresentations; yet, in order to critique constructions of Aboriginality and to introduce Aboriginal perspectives and theories into the classroom, I am in some ways still "representing" Aboriginal peoples (as "them"). Even the deconstruction of the histories and assumptions behind dominant concepts of "Aboriginality" in the anti-racist Aboriginal Literature classroom continues to invoke the category Aboriginal, and in doing so, re-names and re-locates particular individuals in the classroom as "Aboriginal" and "not white," in a location in which, in terms of race, they are already less privileged than the white participants. This can be and often is profoundly empowering for minority students; for many, for the first time in their educational lives, systemic oppression is overtly named and identified in the classroom. But it can also have the negative effect of re-naming and reinforcing oppressions and categories in ways that are less than liberating. Moreover, it has the effect not only of eliding the very multiplicity of subjectivities, and therefore of both multiple oppressions and privileges, and potential sites of alliance among individuals, but of erasing the reality of mixed-race identity in the classroom by collapsing race back into a binarism.

In the broader university context, the promotion of hiring Aboriginal faculty to make the institution more reflective of the population, and to introduce alternative forms of knowledge and practices into educational systems (which I support), can also be used to reinforce systemic racism, if: the faculty members are seen as Native Informants and/or as qualified to teach Aboriginal subject matter *only*; if they are assumed to be responsible for anti-racist work in the university, and/or, are used as evidence that the predominantly white faculty and the system they inhabit are not involved in systemic racism and that the "work" is done. Conversely, arguments that non-Aboriginal teachers should not teach this material can function to marginalize it as separate from the Canadian social, historical, and political fabric, and can absolve us from our responsibility to do the cultural and historical homework necessary to teach the materials effectively. Our systemic privilege does not disappear, after all, if we teach something else.

This issue, too, extends to the question of adopting or adapting Aboriginal pedagogical practices as part of an anti-racist praxis. Calliou intriguingly proposes a pedagogy based on medicine wheel philosophy, for example. Yet I find myself uneasy about adopting such a strategy in my own classroom for fear of misinterpreting and appropriating an Aboriginal philosophy. And yet I am also uneasy with the (apparent) alternative of teaching only through the (often problematic) methods and philosophies of my own inheritance, however radical from within they might be. To remain in such pedagogical either/or, however, is an indication once again of the power of the binarism Aboriginal/non-Aboriginal to reassert itself. And, "[l]ike all dilemmas, it is too neat and false when it implies I must do one or the other." (Dibernard 150) In this case, reliance on the givenness of the binarism Aboriginal/non-Aboriginal not only elides the specific identifications of Aboriginal peoples, including the Métis, but can lead to troubling arguments: that white feminists have no place in anti-racism; that we cannot simultaneously explore the social construction of identity and foreground their material and institutional effects—in all of our classrooms, regardless of subject-matter—advocate for equitable representation of Aboriginal faculty and faculty of colour in universities, *and* be prepared to move over as necessary to realize that goal.[8]

At the personal level, among the many related complications that arise in "teaching what you're not" is "teaching what you're not in the presence of those who are" (Dibernard 132), and for me this became the challenge (and fear) of encountering the emergence of my own racism yet again (as in constructing these individuals within the category of Other/I'm not). In this course, I was very anxious about the responses of the Aboriginal students, noticing and worrying about their occasional absences from class in ways that I did not consider for the white students. My concerns were in many ways valid (was there something racist going on that I wasn't noticing, in a course that labeled them so directly?) but also indicative, I think, of more problematic dynamics – was my own racism emerging here, in assumptions about these students as Native Informants who (naturally?) could challenge my authority, insight, or expertise because of their cultural and racial difference? How did my *desire* that they see me/construct me as an ally (my desire to be seen as a "good" white woman) emerge, in my hope that they willingly play the role of caretaker of the white anti-racist? As a white woman in authority in the classroom, it was not likely that an Aboriginal student or student of colour would challenge me on the ethics or effects of my practice.

One of the biggest advantages for the white anti-racist teacher in the predominantly white university classroom, nonetheless, is her/his whiteness. Unlike Aboriginal instructors and teachers of colour, white instructors do not have to face the charges that our anti-racist work is a personal vendetta, as it is more easily viewed within the framework of the university as an intellectual and rational exploration of dominant ideologies and power relations. It is a valuable location in terms of being able to provide examples of how the personal is political, and of how whiteness operates, from a location within whiteness, especially when that pedagogy involves "naming, witnessing, and accounting for [our] whiteness in the same way that [we] account for other politicized identities." (Mayberry 16) Speaking from a position of authority and from within whiteness, articulating some of the systemic difficulties and personal struggles of the work, can go a long way in defusing defensiveness and guilt, particularly when systemic analysis is accompanied by strategies for action. White professors who "are willing to examine and question" their own locations within whiteness can "help engage white students in similar kinds of critical analyses" and demonstrate to Aboriginal students and students of colour that "allies can be found to fight the war against racism." (Peterson 35)

In this course, the predominance of white-middle class participants in conjunction with my location as a white instructor (and inexperienced anti-racist teacher at that), did determine the class dynamic to a large extent. Even as I attempted to critique whiteness, its processes of defensiveness, individualism, anger, guilt, grief, and genuine frustration at a process and pedagogy that were new and unsettling ultimately took over most class discussion. As one small discussion group including Aboriginal students astutely asked of the course, the course materials, and the issues these raised (and did so only partially "anonymously" in an exercise in which participants wrote on the chalkboard questions coming up for them), "Why is everything focused on white ...? Why is it always 'white against ...?" Further, an Aboriginal man often addressed the entire class and spoke of his personal experiences and those of Aboriginal peoples generally. His contributions to class discussions were invaluable and powerful; and yet there was a Native Informant dynamic operating that I was unprepared to negotiate effectively, to name and critique without re-naming this student in troubling ways. (As such, I did not connect the/his personal voice to systemic processes, as I had been urging participants to do in their journal responses to the texts we were reading.)

I was also not prepared for the intensity, complexity, and vocal nature of the negative responses of white women in the course to Beth Brant's *Writing as Witness: essay and talk,* which intervenes powerfully into dominant discourses, expectations, and reading practices. The responses so intricately embedded defensiveness, guilt, anger, genuine confusion, and the reassertion of whiteness as norm through ideologies of liberalism/multiculturalism that they were extremely difficult for me to recognize, separate out, and deconstruct, at least initially, and if ever, during the too-short semester. The inclusion of the text early in the course, however, in conjunction with Daniel Francis's *The Imaginary Indian: The Image of the Indian in Canadian Culture,* was perhaps one of the most productive aspects of the course.[9] It evoked and provoked a critical process for many of us that continued through the semester, although at that point it was difficult for participants to see this very unsettling and rigorous process as positive, as in the comment of one white woman feeling "more confused than ever about what 'Native literature' is supposed to mean" (Prpich).[10]

What I found particularly surprising (at the time) is how deeply personally many of the white women responded to Brant's usage of the pronoun "you" (a response not registered by the three white men in the course). Overwhelmingly, the white women in the course interpreted—individualized—Brant's use of the second-person plural pronoun "you" as singular, as addressing them directly, and many indicated a feeling of being "personally attacked" by Brant. In response to this experience of being named as part of an oppressive group, they vehemently (and quite emotionally, in fact) dismissed Brant's argument through charges of *her* emotionalism, unnecessary anger, reverse racism, blatant charges of stereotyping whites and manipulating guilt. Many made appeals to their essential "goodness" as individuals, and arguments about objectivity as the appropriate modality for dealing with racism and systemic oppression. Some projected the problems of imperialism and racism as facts of (completed) history of which they have no part—the familiar "I-am-not-responsible-for-my-ancestors'-actions" argument—or by analysing Brant as having personal problems that she needs to deal with before she can effectively participate in the "proper" way to deal with racism. This process of dismissal of "anger" as intellectually and politically unacceptable intertwines white defensiveness (in fact, it is a reassertion of whiteness) with the liberal ideology of multiculturalism that "accepts" difference but only on the terms of the dominant, in terms of politeness, "tolerance," and "respect." Embedded in these assumptions about the "Other" is the production of the white middle-class national subject as ideal. Brant was read as "needing to move forward" ("past" anger, militancy) towards the ideal "Multicultural Other", i.e, as polite, rational, and non-threatening, "like" the ideal, objective white rational self (but *never quite the Same*).[11]

And while participants' responses are of course nuanced and shaped by a multiplicity of discourses, these multicultural codes none the less emerged in their first responses (and I would like to stress that these were *initial* responses that participants were required to critique.): 1) in terms of the appropriate teleology of the multicultural Other: "The expression of anger is a good way to invoke guilty feelings.... Beth Brant would do well by getting past her anger and telling her readers more about the Good Red Road" (Prpich); 2) in terms of the appropriate manner in which the Other should teach white society (and on whom the responsibility for social change rests): "I cannot help but feel, though, that I would have been able to understand better where Brant was coming from if I had not felt so personally throttled after reading this book;"[12] 3) in terms of a feeling of a betrayal of (white) feminism and arguments of being "excluded" because of Brant's refusal to homogenize all women's experiences under a white rubric:

> Right away I was feeling very insecure and unworthy, not unworthy that I'm not good enough, but rather that I didn't *know* enough. She outright laughs at white women trying to connect and understand. (26) If she doesn't want to let us in, who will read the book? She says the writing is for her sisters, but she only claims sisterhood in being Aboriginal or being lesbian. I am neither, but isn't sisterhood about being a woman? ....she discludes anything universal. It is frustrating to see this from a woman trying to increase tolerance and awareness;[13]

4) in charges of "reverse racism":

> It seems to me that she is acting in a racist manner towards Whites. I didn't directly impose these things on Native people. It seems she constantly doesn't give people a chance. We are not mind readers. Her attitude frustrates me. I wonder, do Natives know everything about White culture? ... She is stereotyping us. I don't use Native people ... I didn't personally take from the Native peoples;[14]

5) here coupled with the appropriate teleology and required "niceness" of the Other:

> The book's focus wandered from her hatred of the white race to her lesbianism. It is a personal and ethnocentric view of whites, religion, and sexuality.... Her search for healing and wholeness is apparent, but holding onto her anger, victimization, and hatred will not help her to break free.... I believe it is important to look at one's past as to understand

> one's self, but to remain in the past does not benefit anyone ... I can't say that I liked this book because of its anger and attack that was aimed at whites. Brant is hypocritical in her stereotyping of whites.... She was making it out to be every white person's fault for her problems as a Native lesbian.... I think that Brant's book is an example of perhaps the first or second stage of recovery that a people or person goes through when victimized. (Leggett)

In this course, the prevailing response of most, if not all, participants was to try to "identify" with the characters, narrators (often the "autobiographers") of the texts by saying "I can relate to that experience"; when they (typically white participants) could not find easy connections, a common complaint was "I found this book hard to relate to." Many white women responded to the texts initially by seeking gender identification. Many noted that they had experienced sexism in their lives, and, as they had a systemic analysis to critique sexism, this not surprisingly was the lens through which they tried to make their readings intelligible. Prior to teaching this course I (thought I) had understood this desire for identification as an imperialist gesture, what Gayatri Spivak refers to as the attempt "to 'identify' (with) the other as subject in order to know her," even as "knowledge is made possible and is sustained by irreducible difference, not identity." (254) But the responses of participants in terms of this process of "identification" were deeply knotted and challenging for me. I did not clearly see at the time how this process worked in the materiality of classroom praxis, how the desire to identify "with" was not only an inheritance of canonical literary traditions (and perhaps an effect of the autobiographical aspect of the journal writing) as well as a function of gender but was simultaneously overlain and intertwined with recognitions, assertions, and constructions of difference. (And I had rather conveniently forgotten how this is part of my own history of reading Aboriginal literatures.)

Writing as Witness forces white readers to experience being marginal, excluded, while uncomfortably categorized. As one student observed, "[t]rying to put my personal thoughts aside, I now have had a taste of what it is like to read lies about yourself"

(Lahey). White participants found it extremely difficult to find a comfortable subject position from which to "safely" read the text. "We are all individuals and we should just treat each other as individuals" was a common refrain in class discussions on Brant's text (which for many was a discussion on Brant *as individual*), an indication of both discomfort and defensiveness in response to being named directly as part of a dominant, oppressive group. One woman wrote: "My reaction to this book was anger, defensiveness, and that I was being stereotyped. It was like someone was sitting me down and blaming me for all that was wrong with the native people and I was not allowed to defend myself.... I took it fairly personally.... Is this a form of racism?" (Lahey).[15] Michelle Kruhlak recorded that she felt "continually under attack.... When the word "you" is written I assume it is directed towards me. I am offended because she assumes all people act in this manner. I feel as if I have been wrongly accused."[16]

Several white women who identified themselves as Christian had particular difficulty reconciling Brant's arguments about the exploitation and oppression in which Christianity has participated historically with their own affiliation with what they saw as a primarily positive and liberatory faith and practice, and their self-constructions as "good" people. This is understandable, given the overtly secular nature of academic institutions, which do not discuss religion except as an "object" of study (often an object of unstated subtle derision) as if separate from its actual operation in a predominantly Christian culture. This indicates in particular the need for more critical investigation into Christianity as constitutive of a majority of students' subjectivities (and as an inheritance many instructors, myself included, carry as well), and the recognition that it too is transforming in some contexts even as it is being further entrenched in others. Such a critical language would also provide a starting point for an investigation into the role of the ideology of "guilt," not only in terms of multiculturalism as a process of purging national remorse through a promise of collective redemption but in terms of the location of Christianity as both an enabling and limiting (often paralyzing) factor in anti-racist activism and pedagogy.[17] Clearly, white women's articulations of overwhelming feelings of responsibility for all of the "wrongs," past and present (the white men didn't register feelings of personal responsibility or guilt), are an indication, too, of how gender and Christianity overlap and complicate the construction of the white national citizen.[18] The responses of the women, I suspect, are powerful echoes of white women's historical roles as moral guardians (and reproducers) of the white/colony nation. As I discuss in more detail in my conclusion, I have come to view this complex desire to "identify with" the text/character/writer as neither surprising, given inherited histories of autobiography, nor a necessarily homogeneously imperialist process – it may in fact function as an effective *starting* point for white feminists to explore our *relationships*, as readers, to the systemic contexts of the production of texts. Certainly, the process of identification carries a different political valency for Aboriginal participants in the course, and by extension, for broader Aboriginal constituencies reading Aboriginal literatures.

In recording their anger and uncertainty about Brant's *Writing as Witness*, several white women opened up transformative avenues of investigation and ways to critique their responses and appreciate the text, as Haley Wilson suggests:

> My first reaction to reading Brant was "Hey, what are you talking about, you don't know me." I felt defensive, accused, unable to speak up for myself. Like it wasn't fair to categorize me like I am not responsible for all this stuff – it's not *my* fault. Then it occurred to me that this is just a small sample of how it must feel to deal with this every day. To be stereotyped, misjudged, not given a voice. I think this is a brilliant literary technique Brant uses. But it is also more than that. I don't think her accusatory tone is simply meant to give me a brief sense of the racism she has lived with. It is also meant to accuse. And rightfully so. After all, I *am* part of the dominant group, and this has given me advantages. And I also either participate in maintaining a power imbalance (through denial, or outright racism) or I am part of the solution.
>
> Many of my classmates who I spoke to about the book hated it. I believe that this is because it brings about a sense of personal responsibility and most of us don't know what to do with it. It's overwhelming. Pretty shitty to feel helplessly

> guilty. It is therefore much easier to consider Beth Brant as a bitter, whining woman, who, as one classmate stated, needs to "Get over it."... Everything she states I believe to be true. And being able to accept all of that was a very humbling, saddening, yet also liberating experience ... In being able to own this history, I feel empowered to move beyond it.

The unsettling of paradigms and unconscious strategies of resistance to this pedagogy and to the alternative forms of knowledge and histories it entails, however, not surprisingly continued to resurface throughout the course as especially thorny questions arose, as particular issues hit particular nerves, as participants grappled to analyze their individual and our collective histories in a new light, and as I grappled with the class dynamics and my location in them.

In the journal responses to Maria Campbell's *Half-breed* (1973) and Beatrice Culleton's *In Search of April Raintree* (1984), for example, there is an unspoken sense of relief, indicating that participants, at first at least, felt they had the analytical tools with which to engage, to "know," the texts (and the authors). This more easily recognizable reader's position was one from which dominant assumptions about autobiography, truth, Aboriginality, whiteness, and middle-class ideologies surrounding addiction, recovery, and individualism emerged as unconscious reassertions of dominance. Unlike Brant's *Writing as Witness*, these texts, which participants comfortably recognized—and in the case of *In Search of April Raintree,* mis-recognized, as "autobiography"[19]—initially provided a more familiar position for readers, a position in which ideologies of multiculturalism as the nice and proper way to discuss racism, were re-asserted:

> What I appreciated in the way Campbell told her story was that while she clearly and articulately spoke of both the horrendous treatment she has faced, and her anger towards her oppressors, she did not target me with her anger. As I read, I felt only compassion and understanding for Campbell and her people, and outrage towards a society that would treat and oppress fellow human beings in such a way. This is a contrast from how I felt when I read Beth Brant's "Writing as

> Witness." Brant's uncontrolled rage, not unjustified however, seemed like it was targeted right at me.[20]

The predominant initial responses of participants to *In Search of April Raintree* were emotional, visceral: participants consistently registered surprise, horror, shock, and sadness. Many reported that they hadn't been aware of the historical events and circumstances recounted, and that they had cried while reading Culleton's text. One white man recorded he was "was sick to [his] stomach while reading the rape scene" (Paul). This outpouring of emotional response is instructive. It is a powerful reminder to those of us whose careers involve the reading of painful narratives of oppression and survival, readings to which we may become rather de-sensitized, that literary texts can have profound intellectual and emotional effects. The strategies and subject-matter of the texts proved pedagogically important, in terms of increasing awareness of the location and struggles of the Métis people in Canada, of their absence or demonization in official national narratives and educational curriculum, of systemically produced historical amnesia, and of issues facing mixed-race people, including the desire to "pass" as white in supposedly tolerant Canada. As a white straight English/management major noted: "Through 20 years of life, 12 years of public school and two years of post-secondary, all in Canada I might add – I have never really heard much about Métis people."

What I find interesting in these emotional responses of non-Aboriginal participants is how canonical assumptions and ideologies about the "personal," "individual," and therefore acceptable and even *expected* emotional nature of autobiographical writing might be at work. Here, these are further complicated by ideologies of "Aboriginality," of the racialized Other as "naturally" irrational (and emotional) and their lifestories as cultural artefact rather than creative discourse. White Canadian critic Helen Hoy has countered students' and critics' dismissals of *In Search of April Raintree* that are based on literary and poststructuralist arguments regarding the text's "artlessness" and "simplicity." Initial critical responses, she suggests, "at best evince a difficulty in devising an aesthetic language to account for the text's emotional power; at worst, condescension and nostalgia for the unmediated authenticity of the speaking 'Other'." (155) In the multidisciplinary undergraduate classroom that I am exploring, there were no dismissals (in the journals or in class discussions, at least) of *In Search of April Raintree* or *Half-breed* based on poststructuralist critiques of realism. Rather, assessments of the texts, and of Culleton's in particular, were overwhelmingly positive, if complexly and problematically so, in their reinforcement of ideologies of the transparent and knowable "Native Other," of Aboriginal autobiography as unmediated (albeit 'personal') truth, and of the representativeness of the Aboriginal author/narrator. What Hoy refers to as the tendency to assign the label of "uncrafted testimony to the 'Native informant'" (154) surfaced in a number of ways, but most concisely perhaps in one white woman's initial response to Campbell's *Half-breed*: "It is simply her story, written in her own words, almost like having a conversation with her. Her honesty in conveying the most traumatic and least dignified times of her life immediately makes me trust her." [21] Or as one white woman, a fourth-year English major, wrote of *Half-breed*:

> I find her text extremely moving. I get a sense of universality of emotions—we are all human regardless of race. I agree completely that 'we have to set aside our difference and come together as one.' Oppressing someone is not an option. I love the book. There are so many circumstances that I relate to – feelings of emptiness, self-disgust. No one should have to feel that way because of the system."[22]

Not all participants recorded that they felt emotionally involved in these two texts, particularly *Half-breed.* In registering their *lack* of emotional response, these participants in fact indicated the desire for identification and ideas about autobiography as primarily personal and emotional disclosure. One participant writes that she was "rather annoyed" by Campbell's text as it "seemed to be written with a lack of emotion," and the response of another white woman is revealing in this context: "I'm only just starting *Half-breed.* It is *cold.* Written as an autobiography, yes, but shrouded and *distant.*" Another, who identifies herself as white/Blackfoot, dealt with her uncertainty about the literariness (which she does not define) of

Half-breed by asserting the text's historical rather than literary value:

> I was not too pleased with the literary quality of this book. I think that the story could have been written in a way as to incite empathy, not just sympathy. It just seems a bit tiring to keep reading, "And then I did this, and then this happened, I felt this way, and then"...However, the value of the book does not lie in its literary quality, the value lies in providing insight into Canadian History of the Métis people, and to their plight.

Some participants were revealingly disappointed to discover the "fictional" nature of *In Search of April Raintree.* As Tiffany Leggett wrote, "[s]omehow thinking that a book was a real account of someone's life seems to make me embrace it more. I like finding out about peoples' lives, about their history. I want to know about people, about cultures and about history." Haley Wilson commented that she had assumed the text was "all true" and had felt a sense of disappointment, as if she had been "tricked."

I attempted to problematize assumptions regarding "Aboriginal autobiography" by pointing out that Culleton's text defines itself as a novel and by asking participants to discuss and describe the relationship between truth and autobiography. Many participants struggled to reconcile their inherited assumptions about the "truth" in autobiography (as in Wendy Fehr's words, "an autobiography is supposed to be real not just someone's imagination") with their awareness of the possible self-interestedness and therefore "less-than-truthful" or inaccurate nature of an autobiography by a person in a dominant location (as Fehr also puts it: "The question of what is truth and according to whom often get in the way of the writing of an autobiography"). This issue was further complicated by participants' genuine desire to grant the minority voices (in a manner that homogenized narrator and writer) representational authority and their uncertainty about where to draw the lines among the narrator and author as "real," and text, history, and truth. This desire emerges from a critical recognition of the deconstructive energies of the texts (if not of their creativity or literariness). But it is overlain with white liberal guilt and a genuine confusion (productively so) about how to "critique" works from minority locations, particularly when the author and text, in the ideology of autobiography, are often merged, and in the absence of non-oppressive critical approaches that do not rely on dominant ideas of literary aesthetics. A white man in the course, for example, intriguingly introduced his commentary on Rita Joe's *Song of Rita Joe: Autobiography of a Mi'kmaq Poet* and her poetry collection *L'nu and Indians We're Called* in the following way: "****WARNING—I AM NOT A RITA JOE FAN. The views expressed in this entry are mine and mine alone and are not meant to offend or in any way diminish my views of Rita Joe as a person****."[23] While these questions were not resolved, the raising of these issues is pedagogically and politically important in terms of unsettling dominant expectations and market pressures regarding what constitutes "Aboriginal literature" and "Aboriginal autobiography."

Moreover, the strategic negotiation of Aboriginal lifestorytellers with the dominant ideology of autobiographical form may in fact be part of the very pedagogy of their writing practices. The following is part of an intriguingly knotted response to *Half-breed*:

> This book was much more easy to look at systemically [than *Writing as Witness*]. I think this may have been easier for me to do because I kept looking at it as if I was reading a story of a person's life, from a long time ago, a long way away. This is probably more comfortable because society continually says we are progressive and learn from our mistakes. I internalized this into meaning the problems in this book are no longer as big an issue.
>
> One interesting part of this book is how non aggressive it is. *You can't get angry with a person's life.* She states very clearly in the beginning how she is going to tell *her* story. She is simply stating what happened to her.... I had a hard time imagining the harshness of some of her living conditions. Even when she was explaining all of her responsibilities and worries I did not feel sorry for her. She worded it in such a factual way that feelings were not involved ... she is not asking for anything or trying to get our interest through emotional appeal.

> As I reread that last statement I asked myself why would I assume in the first place that an autobiographic native writer is trying to get something from me (whether emotional or monetary)? I think that this is due to my limited exposure to Native literature. Most are political or angry and are blaming white society, which as I have explained in previous journals, makes me defensive (something I need to work on). (Lahey, my emphasis)

There is much that is troubling here, but the statement "you can't get angry with a person's life" is particularly intriguing, as it collapses autobiography, writer, reality, truth, and ideas about multicultural tolerance so efficiently. On the one hand, Lahey seems to suggest that "anger" is not the appropriate mode for addressing racism in polite Canada. On the other, she might also be suggesting that part of the effectiveness of this text, its "pedagogy" (Mathur), lies in how it gets inside and manipulates the form's popular connections to truth and history. In other words, it actively deflects the defensive anger underlying the veneer of multicultural "tolerance"—anger usually directed at the individual who dares to talk about racism—towards a larger, less easily dismissable target—the history of the colonization of what is now Canada shared by Aboriginal and non-Aboriginal Canadians. *Half-breed* works to productively transform white defensive anger into rage at historical and systemic injustice, because, logically, rationally, "you can't get angry" at the person recounting this undeniable history nor at the life she has lived because of it. As Campbell writes in her introduction: "I write this for all of you, to tell you what it is like to be a Halfbreed woman in *our* country." (2, my emphasis)

Both *Half-breed* and *In Search of April Raintree* address issues of alcoholism, primarily by detailing how internalized and systemic oppression function in poverty, depression, and substance abuse. It was in responses to these issues that middle-class and individualist assumptions about Canada as an equal economic and health-care playing field emerged in participants' journals. The awareness of addictions recovery theory that suggests recovery must begin with the addicted person's commitment to change combined with liberal individualism in troubling condemnations of April's and Cheryl's parents (apparently as "real" people) as failures who did not deserve to keep their children. Here, binaristic thinking regarding addiction prevailed in assumptions that one cannot be addicted *and* desperately love their children, and in the failure to recognize that addiction, by definition, is the loss of choice or control over the substance. Several participants in the course made comments such as the following, but only the following participant granted her permission for quotation in my work:

> This is the first book (*In Search of April Raintree*) that I've read in the course that has held a person accountable for his/her decision to drink. I'm glad to see this.... She [Cheryl] tries to reason that it was because what they "once had has been taken from them." (216) So does that justify one for drinking oneself into oblivion? Because one has faced some kind of adversity one is *made* to drink? That's what she is suggesting, and again is trying to run away from taking responsibility, as if to justify alcoholism. It seems that this excuse has worn itself out; "the white man took away everything, therefore I'm going to drink to take away the pain, to avoid dealing with reality and facing the future." It's not only Natives who feel as though everything has been taken away. What makes their problems harder than someone else's? Everybody faces adversity and everybody deals with it differently. I don't respect anyone, any human being, ie: black, white, beige, etc. that blames their failures on the past or on someone else. I feel very strongly about this because I have lived with an alcoholic and know people who have overcome alcoholism.... Everyone has a will and therefore has choices to make, and are held accountable for those choices. April and Cheryl's father poured the "medicine" down their throats by choice and will. No one forced them.... Why weren't they sent to a detox centre? Or at least offered that option?

Significantly, the issue of alcoholism among Aboriginal peoples did not emerge in larger group discussions. My failure to tackle one of the biggest stereotypes and socio-economic issues facing Aboriginal peoples is certainly a mark of my own uneasiness with the topic. It also indicates a larger concern, a general liberal multicultural uncertainty (which I shared) about how to discuss such an immense problem without reducing it to stereotypes. As Aboriginal Australian critic and activist Marcia Langton suggests, however, the avoidance of discussion among liberal academics of this "major icon of Aboriginality, 'the drunken Abo,'" is part of a refusal to recognize and theorize the location of alcohol in race and economic relations. This resistance can function to reinforce the "popular explanation for the extraordinary arrest rates of Aboriginal people, for the continuing removal of Aboriginal children and the continuing exclusion of Aboriginal people from employment, education, health services, rental accommodation, and a range of other services." (83) The critical analysis of the "drunken Aborigine," she continues, "is an excellent starting point for examining the identity attributed to Aborigines and the inter-subjectivity of the European and Aboriginal identity constructions." (86)

Culleton's text nonetheless was a powerful catalyst to discussions regarding the role of government and social services in terms of foster care and adoption.[24] Participants grappled with their inherited assumptions about the essential "goodness" of government and social services, their "good intentions" in attempting to protect children from abuse, and the actual effects of the foster care system on and in Aboriginal communities, where every child fostered outside of that community is a loss to that community. What emerged in this cluster of responses is the operation of a middle-class assessment of poverty as the personal failure of individuals to work hard enough, and of middle-class privilege as the product of personal effort rather than an effect of imperialist capitalist relations. Again, there was the unconscious though powerful consolidation of the white self through a production of a racialized, classed, and demonized other. The individualism here operates to erase the history of colonization in Canada and to reinforce the liberal multicultural ideology of Canada as an "equal opportunity" nation, where addictions treatment and social services are assumed to be readily and equally accessible to all, and what is available is assumed to be culturally suitable for all. Some participants, however, worked to dismantle these assumptions through the increased historical awareness the framework of the course provided, including class presentations and guest speakers on the history and effects of the Residential School System.

What discussions around the deaths and the incidents recounted in Culleton's text also revealed in terms of university structures, the reproduction of whiteness, and multicultural nationalism was a desire to re-constitute the ethical white bourgeois subject in relation to the "needy" Aboriginal Other, a desire enacted through the history of the paternalism of government policy and the residential school and foster care systems. Culleton's text, however, in detailing the systemic process producing a class of dispossessed peoples actively refuses the reconstitution of this white subject as separate from these histories. Several participants, in critiquing their initial responses, came to recognize that both *In Search of April Raintree* and *Half-breed* detail the internalization of systemic oppression, in which we all participate. This is not to suggest, however, that the desire to "identify with" the narrative subjects did not resurface in responses to these texts. Paul's astute analysis of the class and gender implications of his reading, for example, quickly slips back into the normativity of the scripts of multiculturalism, individualism, gender, and imperialist identification:

> I wanted to help April. My class upbringing probably influences this by tending to want to help others. Our culture loves fairytales. To take April out of the book and give her a better life would be a fairy tale. Our culture believes in helping those who can't help themselves. It's a white middle class ideology. Its also a way for middle-class people to know that there are people below them. I believe it creates a sense of superiority and identity for the middle class.
>
> I like Cheryl because I see a lot of myself in her.... Through her knowledge of history Cheryl is developing character. I like people with character.

The vast majority of participants (I can think of only two exceptions in a class of 45) in this course energetically took up the challenges of anti-racist pedagogy, posing and thoughtfully exploring for themselves the vital question "what can I/we *do* to fight racism?" This is a mark less of my personal success as instructor (though I would like to claim that) than a telling indication of how traditional pedagogy stifles the exhilarating agency of university students. While participants' journals by the end of the semester often reverted to paradigms they had earlier critiqued (a function of the time constraints and end-of-semester pressures of the university), the final projects that participants produced for this course were stunning in their creativity and commitment to the exploration, from their own locations, of histories of the oppression of Aboriginal peoples in Canada and ways to understand and intervene in those processes.[25]

Our shared grappling with the immensity of systemic racism against Aboriginal peoples has foregrounded for me the need to name racism in the classroom, and to make multiculturalism a subject of critique, in a location where these operate as "commonsense" practices. And I have come to reconsider the *potential* of the desire for and processes of "identification" of white women students with Aboriginal narrators/characters/authors/individuals in anti-racist pedagogy. Certainly, such identification, as I've suggested, is problematic when non-Aboriginal readers attempt to deflect our implication in white privilege and racism by finding points of connection with the text, by "relating to" specific representations through the lens of individual experience at the exclusion of all else. And certainly, this process of identification also often works to elide the specific narrative and generic functions and strategies of given texts. Having said that, however, I think it is also crucial to consider how an anti-racist feminist pedagogy *might* work in conjunction with this desire for identification. This desire in many ways indicates a genuine wish to "understand" and "learn" cross-culturally (even when the language for systemic analysis is absent), in support of the politics of decolonization of the texts themselves. It is not surprising that for white middle-class readers a comfortable initial position in discussions of race and class privilege is "me-too-ism"—the defensive desire to identify with the oppressed rather than with the oppressor. But if an anti-racist pedagogy is able to engage participants in the recognition of our locations as multiply constituted, as locating us in both positions of privilege and of oppression, and accepting that our own experience is perhaps an appropriate location from which to *begin* the unlearning of privilege, then the process of identification need not be a political or theoretical taboo. There is a crucial distinction to be made, then, between desires to "relate to" the characters of literary texts as defense strategy, and the complex articulation of one's *relationship,* as reader, to the systemic contexts of the production of the text, particularly when (as in most university classrooms) there is a lack of a concrete language surrounding whiteness and the processes of racialization.[26] Moreover, as the one Aboriginal (white/Blackfoot) student in the course who gave permission to quote from her journal suggests in her response to *In Search of April Raintree,* "identification" from particular and previously occluded locations is pedagogically and politically crucial:

> This book triggered within me a sorrowful, empathetic memory. I can find many parallels between April's experiences and my own on several planes. Reading literature such as this is truly an experience where I can relate my trials and tribulations as a "half-breed" to the greater forces that created them. Am I making sense? I'm not certain. However, I shall continue. This book made me cry, not little tears of sympathy—"Oh dear, how sad!" But a release of sorrow. On a personal level, I related to April's experience of castigation and ostracization directly. I recalled, as I read, the humiliation and stupefying shock of being called "squaw" and other unflattering names, only because I was part Indian. Yes, I remember sitting at my desk, as April sat on the bus, the burning of self-esteem within and the stoic expression without whilst the whole classroom resounded with Indian war cries. The teacher only smiled.
>
> I seem bitter, I know. It is difficult to believe in the ideology that one of mixed descent can be a bridge between two worlds when one is viewed disparingly as taking on the image of the detested cultural group. Squaw-white bitch. Same dif. It hurts equally on both sides.... What is very sad about this book is the reality that the afflictions of First Nations can be traced back through history to a causal, primordial event. It is true for all First Nations people, including myself. For I have as well experienced the angst of the street claiming and re-claiming a close family member.... But what is the message to non-Natives? I'm not certain, but I can testify that her writing

in this book creates a window of insight into the reality of being of aboriginal ancestry in this society.

My experience of teaching this course, and my subsequent grapplings with it, have clarified for me how teaching the "Aboriginal Literatures Course" drawing on anti-racist feminist pedagogy and aimed at dismantling some of the operations of imperialism, nationalism, and racism is at once fraught, daunting, and urgent. While my own academic training is within postcolonial studies, this process has foregrounded for me some significant gaps in the field. By remaining focused on textual politics, for example, it has yet to clarify how literary production and analysis are related to anti-racist activism, pedagogy, and to the material social transformation it claims to espouse. In critical race theory, the absence of attention to the specifics of Aboriginal histories and the locations of Aboriginal students in the anti-racist classroom, and the absence of Aboriginal pedagogy theory are among the biggest concerns. The very question of how feminist anti-racist pedagogy affects men (white, Aboriginal, and of colour) also indicates that critical race theory needs to engage not only with Aboriginality as produced and reproduced in the classroom, but with gender studies and critiques and transformations of masculinity as well.

It was also not until my experience of this course that I became acutely aware that, as anti-racist instructor and audience and grader of individual journals, I had a personal and ethical authority I had not entirely recognized or theorized. Part way through the course, and after the formal class had ended for the day, one white woman said to me, in reference to the self-censoring she enacted in the process of journalling (and to which several white women around her nodded their agreement), "I don't want you to think I'm a racist." My initial (unspoken) response was that she was correct, and that this was positive in the larger scheme of anti-racist politics. My actual response to the participant was that the important thing in the journal is to critique one's initial reactions as a process of moving through them—not that it was "okay" to say racist things, but to record your response, however problematic, in order to interrogate it. I have struggled with her comment ever since. It highlights for me the processes of surveillance that undergird the university structure as a whole but which are foregrounded in a course such as this, in which personal information and histories constitute the pedagogy. I had not, however, considered the journal or the pedagogy to be sites through which participants saw or constructed *me* as a moral guardian on racism, particularly as I felt that I was just beginning my own processes of unlearning racism. (Though I wonder to what extent I "liked" the comment in how it somehow elevated me in terms of ethical and professorial authority, i.e., "the good, white anti-racist...").

This brief but telling moment in the classroom has made visible to me how predominantly Christian perspectives of (individual) judgment, guilt, punishment, and redemption (which in my history have been normalized to invisibility) are structured into the education system's evaluative criteria and circulate as norm, despite the overtly secularly nature of the university. It suggests, too, how much of Christian ideology, and its threat of moral judgment and punishment, is built into multiculturalism's assertions of "tolerance" and "acceptance," how much official multiculturalism is undergirded by Christian concepts of guilt, and how its popularity with white Canadians may rest on its unspoken promises of personal and collective redemption. There is a need, then, for a critical language that clarifies on what ethical ground we (postcolonial theorists, feminists, anti-racist workers) theorize and enact transformative agency, the role that Christianity plays in that process (and an awareness of what that focus excludes), and the risks and limits of pedagogical authority in anti-racist pedagogical practices. As Métis writer and critic Emma LaRocque puts it, "[t]o study any kind of human violation is, *ipso facto,* to be engaged in ethical matters. And we must respond—as scholars, as men and women, Native and white alike." (12) Literary, cultural, and even critical pedagogical theories will struggle to meet their goals of social justice if they are not accompanied by the development of a clear language of ethics and a praxis of activism, of what to do with this transformative knowledge recognized and created in the classroom.

Notes

[1] This paper is a revised version of a lengthy chapter of my Ph.D. thesis, "'Analyze if you wish, but listen': Aboriginal Women's Lifestorytelling in Canada and Australia and the Politics of Gender, Nation, Aboriginality, and Anti-Racism" (University of Calgary 2000). I would like to acknowledge the Social Sciences and Humanities Research Council of Canada, and the Department of English and the Faculty of Graduate Studies of the University of Calgary, which provided funding for my doctoral studies. I would especially like to thank Aruna Srivastava, my Ph.D. supervisor, mentor, friend, and teacher in so many ways, for her support, guidance, and example of embodied anti-racist work in the university and beyond. I would also like to thank Jeanne Perreault for her helpful critique of the original thesis chapter, and Louise Saldanha and Ashok Mathur for their insights, support, and friendship.

[2] I am grateful to each participant in the course for her/his involvement in the process and pedagogy of the course. I have learned from each of them, their perspectives and processes, and in particular from those 17 participants (12 white women, three white men, one Aboriginal woman, and one South Asian woman) who granted me their permission to quote from their journals. Their interests, responses, and insights have profoundly influenced my thinking on these issues. In a class of 45, four participants identified themselves as Aboriginal or Métis, two identified as women of African-Caribbean ancestry, and one as South Asian. The remainder of the class comprised white women and three white men.

[3] English 385 is a non-core half-credit undergraduate English course offered by the Department of English at the University of Calgary, and until very recently its position in the curriculum was consistently tenuous; it was offered only when an instructor (usually tenured faculty) expressed an interest in teaching it. Moreover, the course is multidisciplinary, serving as an English elective for a diversity of programs across campus, such that it is institutionally and unofficially considered less serious or rigorous

than core courses. (For many participants, 385 serves as the only English course of their university careers.)

[4] I taught this course in the Winter 1998 semester, as a Ph.D. candidate in the Department of English granted a Graduate Teaching Fellowship. That I was a graduate student with a good deal of personal and professional investment in this course certainly had an impact on how I set up the course. In retrospect this investment indicates to me how many of the norms of the academic institution I had internalized. I felt that this was my "one shot" to show my knowledge and skills, and that I needed to make the course "marketable" in my prospective job hunt. I wanted to show that I could teach a "postcolonial," a "feminist," *and* a Canadian-Australian Aboriginal literature comparative course, and be an anti-racist instructor as well—all in thirteen weeks.

I put Aboriginal Australian material on the course to provide participants with a sense of the global context of imperialism (following our study of the Canadian context). I scheduled this material for late in the semester hoping that by then participants would have developed some systemic analysis of imperialism that might forestall some of the problems outlined. I deal with the mixed results of this strategy, and some of the attendant problems of the Australian-Canadian comparative mode, in my thesis.

[5] Aboriginal peoples are not located clearly in the official policy of multiculturalism but awkwardly positioned as both "beyond" the purview of the multicultural context and, yet subsumed by it. While the fact that official multiculturalism does not clearly "include" Aboriginal peoples in some sense appears to be a recognition of the specificities of Aboriginal peoples (i.e., the extensive legislation circumscribing Aboriginality, such as The Indian Act) and their prior occupation of the land, it also indicates the vexed relationships among nationalism, multiculturalism and Aboriginal history and ongoing land claims. It is perhaps not surprising, then, that official multiculturalism emerged alongside increased Aboriginal activism.

Attempts (desires) to create national identity by absorbing Aboriginal cultures and histories—and lands—into the dominant myths, as in claims that "we are all immigrants"—have proven both factually incorrect and unacceptable to Aboriginal peoples. And while proponents of official multiculturalism like to suggest that it posits a new national identity separate from Canada's imperial history, "the present multicultural reality," as Daniel Francis writes, "cannot deny the fundamental significance of British traditions to our history and institutions … it is the context of these institutions and traditions that multiculturalism now operates" (drawing on Donald Akenson *National Dreams* 86).

[6] The course structure included a series of group assignments and class presentations on historical events and current issues, such as the Oka Crisis, the Métis in Canada, residential schools, Aboriginal languages, and the report of the Australian Royal Commission into Aboriginal Deaths in Custody (1991). As well, an Aboriginal speakers series on campus that semester facilitated the inclusion of a number of Aboriginal speakers (writers, educators, and cultural workers/researchers) in the class schedule. Aside from framing some introductory classes with lecture-style overviews on cultural assumptions and the necessity of historicizing our locations as readers, I did not conduct formal lectures. Rather, most class discussion took place in small groups, so that the familiar dynamics of professorial authority, individualism (a few vocal students claiming most of the discussion time), and the tangible reinforcement of the categories Aboriginal/non-Aboriginal would be mitigated (somewhat). I facilitated most classes by setting up general questions for the groups to discuss (and I required that each group record their responses); I visited each group a number of times throughout the semester and reviewed their group journals.

Course participants selected their own groups. While the Aboriginal students were given the option of forming their own group, they did not choose to do so. I never asked why. This could be an indication of their resistance to the reinforcement of the categories of Aboriginal/non-Aboriginal and/or an effect of the materiality of classroom we were in at the time. It had fixed seating, and when I suggested an arbitrary counting off for the creation of groups, participants instead selected their groups according to proximity of other students and the linearity of seating—the first four in the first row made one group, the next four, the next, and so on.

[7] Aruna Srivastava and I have written about the various negotiations and complexities of our institutional locations, as an academic, Ph.D. supervisor, and woman of colour and as a white graduate student, new mother, and novice anti-racist, respectively, in our article "Dancing on the Lines: Mothering, Daughtering, Masking and Mentoring in the Academy."

[8] See Lee Maracle's "Moving Over" on the role of white women as allies in Aboriginal politics.

[9] Francis's *The Imaginary Indian* is an excellent and highly readable analysis of white Canadian cultural history from the nineteenth century and of the production and prevalence of dominant images and ideologies of Aboriginality through legislation, art and literature, official history, the Hollywood film, and so on.

[10] Prpich identified herself as a white straight 37-year-old woman of Croatian and German descent in her fourth year of General studies.

[11] A cogent example of this dynamic appeared in one white woman's response to Lee Maracle's *Bobbi Lee: Indian Rebel* (not on the primary reading list): "My intuition tells me that Lee Maracle bases her political views on emotion. This is not necessarily a bad thing since it equips her with the essential passion and strength to move forward" (Kruhlak). Another white woman (a fourth year English major) responded to Rita Joe's *Song of Rita Joe: Autobiography of a Mi'kmaq Poet*: "I like Rita Joe's positive outlook. The pain is evidently there, but I think people are more likely to listen if this is the kind of attitude a person conveys." And as another white woman suggested regarding Brant, "I feel [books like this] are a step back and an excuse made by people" (Lahey).

[12] This participant identifies herself as a 21-year-old white straight Canadian graduating in nursing, who was raised in National Park communities across Canada by Alberta-born and raised parents.

[13] This white woman gave her permission to quote from her journal but did not provide in her permission form information as to how she chose to be named/identified in this study.

[14] This participant identifies herself as a 22-year-old fourth-year English major, born in England and raised there to the age of 18

by her Canadian parents, and holding dual Canadian-British citizenship.

[15] Lahey identifies herself as follows: a 21-year-old white female Canadian of Greek and French ancestry, and a geography major in the faculty of Social Sciences.

[16] Kruhlak identifies herself as a 22-year-old third-year visual arts major, married, and of Scottish and Irish ancestry.

[17] Following these rather charged discussions about Brant, the class engaged in a target group exercise in which participants move across the room in relation to specific categories of privilege and oppression (sometimes leaving a few people on the side of the oppressed and feeling particularly vulnerable). Several students later commented in their journals that the exercise was highly instructive in that it helped them to recognize, and physically embody, the multiplicity of oppressions and privileges they inhabit, but had not recognized. My attempts afterwards to engage the class in a productive discussion about racism, however, was clogged by my lack of experience and critical language for the dynamics the discussion took—a litany of stories by white individuals as to how they (or close family members) had been the victims of "racism," a discussion in which the students of colour and Aboriginal students were noticeably silent.

[18] For a further discussion of the dynamics of white liberal guilt that considers it outside of the Christian framework, see Jeanne Perreault's "White Feminist Guilt, Abject Scripts, and (Other) Transformative Possibilities."

[19] Significantly, the final page of the text includes a note by Culleton stating that the work is fictional.

[20] This participant is the nursing major quoted above.

[21] This participant is the nursing major quoted above.

[22] This woman, previously quoted, was born in England and raised there to the age of 18 by her Canadian parents.

[23] This participant identified himself as a major in molecular biology.

[24] Discussions about the historical role of non-Aboriginal social services in particular took on a heightened and painful significance as, during the semester, an Aboriginal mother and her nine-year old son, Connie and Ty Jacobs, were shot and killed by a

white RCMP officer on the T'suu Tina reserve near Calgary, as social services attempted to remove her children from an alcoholic and potentially violent situation. One of the course participants lived on that reserve. Again, however, I did not at the time have an effective language in which to discuss the tragedy, nor the relationships among alcoholism, "Aboriginality," and systemic oppression, even as the media and RCMP justification for the removal of Jacob's children was based in alcohol abuse and a history of physical violence in the home. Rather, while trying to engage in such a discussion (and we were all, I think, troubled by the events), I merely addressed my lack of language in discussing such a loss and the complex of power relations in which the event was embedded.

[25] Several white women, for example, took up Paul Kivel's *Uprooting Racism: How White People Can Fight for Social Justice* and Anne Bishop's *Becoming an Ally: Breaking the Cycle of Oppression* in writing personal/critical essays of their own histories and privileges as white middle-class women (work which also functions to articulate the specificities within the general category of whiteness). Two education majors did a collaborative project that developed anti-racist activities for a primary classroom, and two others developed anti-racist activity centres on Aboriginal and Canadian culture and history. Another white woman conducted a photography tour of Calgary, documenting the pervasiveness of the stereotypes of the "Imaginary Indian"; a white woman interviewed a local Aboriginal artist, invited him to class as a guest speaker, and prepared a thoughtful response on the politics of marketing Aboriginal art. An Aboriginal woman raised in white foster care conducted interviews in her family and community to compare the benefits and costs of white foster care versus remaining in impoverished reserve conditions (a project emerging from the readings of *In Search of April Raintree*).

In a class in which white and Aboriginal men comprise a striking minority, it is difficult to assess my feminist, anti-racist pedagogy without dangerously generalizing from the course work of five men. Yet, that each of the three white men in the course granted me permission to quote from their journals, and that the two Aboriginal men in the course felt safe enough to pursue projects that had a personal component (the writing and critique of autobiographical pieces, in one case, and the exploration, from a gay Aboriginal perspective, of gay Aboriginal writing) suggests to me a certain degree of success in creating an environment of safety for Aboriginal men in a predominantly white classroom, and in engaging white men in the processes of feminist, anti-racism. One of the white men (invited by an Aboriginal participant) attended a sweat lodge as part of a final project (and powerfully critiqued how his own assumptions and history shaped his perceptions of the experience); another, while not doing "well" in the sense of a high final grade, did a class presentation critiquing how he had unknowingly perpetuated racism in his high school years, and went on the next semester to do a similar course in international literatures with an anti-racist focus.

[26] For one white woman (an English/Management major), imagining what it would be like to be constructed as a "Native informant" proved a useful starting point for addressing her white privilege:

> My lack of knowledge about Métis life allows me to accept any information as all encompassing. But I think it is more than just lack of knowledge. I keep thinking back to the article we read [Peggy McIntosh's "Unpacking the Invisible Knapsack"] with the questions about being a minority/majority. One of the statements that I clearly recall is "I never am asked to speak on behalf of my race." It seems to be true that dominant culture (white) wants to hear a single voice representing a specific group. It is an extreme attempt to oversimplify. Imagine how white society would react if we were told we were allowed one or two speakers to speak on "white life." People would be appalled. And yet we expect this from others, as though they are not complex societies comprised of many individuals.

Works Cited

Asante, Yaw. "Student Journals as a Teaching Tool." Panel Discussion with Janis Svilpis, Roberta Jackson, and

Vivienne Rundle. The Department of English, The University of Calgary. 2 December 1996.

Bishop, Anne. *Becoming an Ally: Breaking the Cycle of Oppression.* 1994. Halifax: Fernwood, 1995.

Brant, Beth. *Writing as Witness: essay and talk.* Toronto: Women's Press, 1994.

Calliou, Sharilyn. "Peacekeeping Actions at Home: A Medicine Wheel Model for a Peacekeeping Pedagogy." *First Nations Education in Canada: The Circle Unfolds.* Ed. Marie Battiste and Jean Barman. 1995. Vancouver: UBC Press, 1998. 47-72.

Campbell, Maria. *Half-breed.* 1973. Halifax: Goodread Biographies, 1983.

Culleton, Beatrice. *In Search of April Raintree.* Winnipeg: Pemmican Publications, 1983.

Dibernard, Barbara. "Teaching What I'm Not: An Able-Bodied Woman Teaches Literature by Women with Disabilities." Mayberry 131-54.

Francis, Daniel. *The Imaginary Indian: The Image of the Indian in Canadian Culture.* 1992. Vancouver: Arsenal Pulp Press, 1995.

- - -. *National Dreams: Myth, Memory, and Canadian History.* Vancouver: Arsenal Pulp Press, 1997.

Hoy, Helen. "'Nothing but the Truth': Discursive Transparency in Beatrice Culleton." *ARIEL* 25.1 (January 1994): 155-84.

Kelly, Jennifer, and Aruna Srivastava. "Dancing on the Lines: Mothering, Daughtering, Masking and Mentoring in the Academy." Forthcoming in *The Madwoman in the Academy: Songs from the Ivory Tower,* an anthology on mothering and the academy, edited by Debbie Keahey and Deborah Schnitzer, Department of English, The University of Winnipeg.

Kivel, Paul. *Uprooting Racism: How White People Can Work for Racial Justice.* Gabriola Island, B.C.: New Society Publishers, 1996.

Langton, Marcia. "Rum, seduction and death: 'Aboriginality' and alcohol." *Race Matters: Indigenous Australians and 'Our' Society.* Ed. Gillian Cowlishaw and Barry Morris. Canberra: Aboriginal Studies Press, 1997. 77-94.

LaRocque, Emma. "The Colonization of a Native Woman Scholar." *Women of the First Nations: Power, Wisdom, and Strength.* Ed. Christine Miller and Patricia Chuchryk, et al., Winnipeg: U of Manitoba P, 1996. 11-18.

Maracle, Lee. *Bobbi Lee: Indian Rebel.* Rev. ed. Toronto: Women's Press, 1990.

- - -. "Moving Over." *Trivia Magazine.*

Mathur, Ashok. Brown Gazing: The Pedagogy and Practice of South Asian Writing in Canada. Ph.D. diss. University of Calgary, 2000.

Mayberry, Katherine J., ed. *Teaching What You're Not: Identity Politics in Higher Education.* New York and London: New York UP, 1996.

McIntosh, Peggy. "White Privilege: Unpacking the Invisible Knapsack." *Independent School.* (Winter 1990): 31-36.

Mohanty, Chandra Talpade. "On Race and Voice: Challenges for Liberal Education in the 1990s." *Cultural Critique* 14 (Winter 1989-90): 179-208.

Ng, Roxana. "Teaching against the Grain: Contradictions and Possibilities." *Anti-Racism, Feminism, and Critical Approaches to Education.* Ed. Roxana Ng, Pat Staton, and Joyce Scane. Toronto: OISE Press, 1995. 129-52.

Perreault, Jeanne. "White Feminist Guilt, Abject Scripts, and (Other) Transformative Necessities." *Colour. An Issue.* Special Double Issue of *West Coast Line.* Ed. Fred Wah and Roy Miki. 13-14 (Spring-Fall 1994): 226-38.

Peterson, Nancy J. "Redefining America: Literature, Multiculturalism, and Pedagogy." Mayberry 23-46.

Saldanha, Louise. "Bedtime Stories: Canadian Multiculturalism and Children's Literature." Conference paper presented at Midwest Modern Languages Association Conference. Chicago, Ill. Nov. 7, 1997.

Schick, Carol. "'By virtue of being white': Racialized identity formation and the effects on anti-racist pedagogy." Ph.D. diss. Ontario Institute for Studies in Education, 1998.

Spivak, Gayatri Chakravorty. 1987. *In Other Worlds: Essays in Cultural Politics.* London and New York: Routledge, 1988.

Srivastava, Aruna, Ashok Mathur, and Louise Saldanha. "The Cult of Multiculturalism: Obstacles to AntiRacist Teaching." UBC Centre for Research in Women's Studies and Gender Relations ConferenceProceedings: Race, Gender, and the Construction of Canada. 5.1 (1996). Vol. 2.28: 1-15.

A Moose in the Corridor: Teaching English, Aboriginal Pedagogies, and Institutional Resistance

Sharron Proulx and Aruna Srivastava

This piece is at one level a dialogue in which our voices alternate, punctuated by Sharron's poetry and the quotations, almost all from indigenous writers, which also signal a shift from Aruna's voice to Sharron's. At another level, we hope that it emulates a circle, or at least a polyphony of voices, in which even our own comments may not always be linear or consistent, where even our two voices are many: such is the nature of our experiences over the past year, and of the complexities of some of the issues we are imperfectly trying to work through.

rest when you can and you'll live a long life

heartwords
whose heart to whose heart
there's something in the air
prolonging winter and very warm
talking winds
the talk of the town

today a raven hangs around
sounds like a duck with a cold
back and forth back and forth
yapping telling
tells a secret
secret of the day and the wind so strong

follow with your shadow
follow with your spirit

Aruna begins...: I recall the roundtable on teaching aboriginal literatures last year. It seemed huge to me. A huge audience too, perhaps a testament to the popularity of this topic or idea. But I wondered, a trifle cynically, about commitment as well: what were people all there for, there to see? Would this roundtable revolutionize the teaching of Aboriginal literatures? Certainly not at my university – of which I and a few colleagues, of course, were representatives. But I wasn't there, officially, to talk, just to listen. The usual tensions and differing points of view, epistemological and pedagogical, especially about the role of humour, perhaps a misunderstanding fed by whiteness about humour being the best way to get students (read "white students"?) to appreciate Aboriginal stories and perspectives. This is an old story, and a story I hear constantly from my own white students especially. Certainly never from aboriginal ones, the charge that this is all too depressing. Too guilt-inducing. So, the tension in the circle seemed to be about that, and my own inner tension was also about how it does not matter at all about what we teach in those classrooms anyway: like a broken record, I think, I said my piece when the invited speakers had said theirs, because I feel passionate about this. We can see any number of interlopers and appropriators and do-gooders and strong-minded radical change-the-systemers want to teach Aboriginal studies in mainstream (and other) postsecondary institutions, but we get obsessed by the what and not the how. It is perfectly possible (and is often done) to teach Aboriginal literatures in deeply racist, colonialist, ahistorical and disrespectful ways—often unintentionally—and, I said then, and maintain still, it is possible for students and teachers both for us to read the literature and to take in the knowledge of Aboriginal and Indigenous people in such disrespectful and close-minded ways that it is infinitely more harmful in many ways to read these texts at all than not to. We must pay attention to the how, the process and the pedagogy and not the what, the curriculum, the texts, the course outline, in what I maintain is that peculiarly western, categorical, strategy of naming and containment. I was feeling good then, last year, about my institution, my job, my place in it. What was to happen had not happened yet.

> I would say that if one begins to take a whack at shaking the structure up, one sees how much more consolidated the opposition is. (Spivak 71)

Sharron dreams: A couple of years ago I have a mid-summer dream. I'm a student and I'm taking a gift and a card to see a teacher. I want to thank her and to see her once more at the end of classes. Turns out there is another woman ahead of me and several more women and men of many cultural backgrounds come and we all kind of line up. The teacher opens a door to what seems like a classroom. She's surprised to see everyone and asks us can we all come in at once because she'll be needing to cry at some point and doesn't want to spend the entire afternoon with one intense moment after another but would rather if we could all share together. So in we go. I'm aware we'll each have our moment to speak uninterrupted and I feel happy I'm second in the circle because I'm thinking in terms of myself and how I think I'll remember stronger and more fully with the first few people. I am happy to have a fresh and open start rather than listen to many others first. I'm aware of the advantages of both and I'm happy about the timing.

That's as far as the dream gets. I wake up, and only then do I realize in the dream itself I am each—her feelings bodies minds—without the dream-conscious knowledge I am both the student and the teacher. That knowing comes only to my awake-consciousness, and yet that knowing is a part of the dream. I don't understand this, though at the time it seems quite ordinary.

> The acquisition of skills necessary for unearthing and then articulating meaning draws on knowledge from many areas, including oral tradition. Curriculum delivery must take into account the requirements of the primary traditional learning modes of "experiential learning" and "learning by doing." (Couture 164)

I have taught several undergraduate Aboriginal literature classes at the University of Calgary, and have been struck by how paradoxical my position is particularly as a woman of colour with a commitment to anti-racism pedagogies and various modes of student-centred learning (which already make the project of teaching in what Sharron calls the mainstream classroom an ambivalent one). In these classes, however, the always troubling issue of constituency really comes to the foreground: who are these classes for? I think as professors we often default to the notion of the classroom as a homogenous space, and when we have "trouble" in our class, we tend to assume that the minority student or students are the source of the trouble. I did this in my early days of teaching Aboriginal lit classes (or indeed any classes where there was racialized content and a minority of racialized students in a predominantly white institution); I was slow to learn that if I figured out that there were indeed different, often conflicting constituencies, and those themselves often constituted by a history of colonialism and racism that ran through the what and the how of my course and the institution we were in, *of course* there were going to be necessary failures and conflicts. Not to mention particular choices all of us had to make. My constituency, then, when I had to make those choices, had to be the Aboriginal students who had attended my class and who had rarely, if ever, had the experience of being validated by a professor. I also had to come to terms, painful terms, with the fact that this was not benevolence on my part and that neither Aboriginal or white students would necessarily *like* me for the pedagogical gestures and choices I made (learning not to be liked has been the hardest lesson for me to learn). I have not taught these courses for some time now, in part for institutional reasons I outline later. Having made that decision, I was awarded a teaching award by the Native Centre in 1999, an honour that still runs deeply for me. Note how institutional racism functions here: even on appeal I failed to convince powers-that-be that this award was significant enough to be mentioned on evaluations of my teaching, as other teaching awards would have been: a comment not so much on my teaching (although it may well be) as on the institutional significance of awards presented by the Native Centre.

> Structural barriers are illuminated to me as I slam into them head on. Equity, and the expertise I have developed, have come at personal consequence and have been very painful for me.... I have never been asked what equity concerns I have about my own position within the university. (Monture-Angus 115)

Patricia Monture-Angus writes of trickster and her place as teacher/student; "the trickster role is not just so much to teach but equally to make us think and reflect." She goes on to say tricksters/clowns "live and love dichotomy. They are contrary and I have long known I possess some contrary qualities." (101) Like Patricia Monture-Angus, I have long lived and loved dichotomy. In astronomy, dichotomy is the aspect of the moon, Mercury, or Venus, when half the disk is visible. Neither Mercury nor Venus can be seen in the round because of the sun. Because Eurocanadian, when the construction of a course is not white middle class, the round is made flat. To explain, after teaching composition into my fourth year at Mount Royal College, a university transfer institution in Calgary, an approved proposal I'd submitted (to teach an Aboriginal literature class) was finally scheduled for teaching after a two-term delay. I titled this special topics course, "First People's Words: Contemporary Aboriginal Literature in Canada," only after the literature committee insisted I keep Canada and the States as separate forty-niners.

> I say that tribal literatures are not some branch waiting to be grafted onto the main trunk. Tribal literatures are the tree, the

> oldest literatures in the Americas, the most American of American literatures. We are the canon. Native people have been on this continent at least thirty thousand years, and the stories tell us we have been here even longer than that, that we were set down by the Creator on this continent, that we originated here. For much of this time period, we have had literatures. Without Native American literature, there is no American canon. (Womack 7)

To start this paper in collaboration with Sharron has been enormously difficult, as every moment of writing and thinking through the complexities of teaching Aboriginal literature, of teaching Aboriginal students, being the friend of an Aboriginal teacher reminds me of how incredibly resistant our institutions are to some of the most apparently simple propositions we might (and are) suggesting, not just in this paper but in this collection, in our educational culture and in Canadian society at large. The centre of this paper will be to describe a course on Aboriginal literature that Sharron will likely not get to teach because of her effective dismissal in December of 2000 from the college she designed it for and was going to teach it for in the January 2001 term. Our delay in getting this paper to endlessly-patient editors is a direct result of a month's-long process (as yet unresolved) which is not new to many of us who are racialized academics in postsecondary (and other) educational institutions; that is, her specific experience is not at all unique, even as it has its own peculiar institutional ramifications, twists and turns, and very real, personal effects. How do we write about the almost-inconsequential act of teaching an Aboriginal literature course when one of us, Sharron, a Métis woman was fired for using anti-racism pedagogies in the classroom, and when her direct challenge to that act has engendered hatred? How to talk about pedagogy when her Aboriginal literature course, the first in her college's history, will not be taught. How to talk about a course when Aboriginal people applying for work at the University of Calgary are routinely being passed over? When our own faculty association will not support Aboriginal people (or racialized people) in our concerns about systemic racism, when racial equity has become a laughable issue? It is indeed odd that an institution that will find the activism that it rhetorically espouses as a valuable form of community service suddenly so heinous when it occurs within its walls.

> Even after the Second World War, when the post-colonial period was beginning according to some cultural studies theorists, many indigenous peoples around the world were still not recognized as humans, let alone citizens. The effect of such discipline was to silence (for ever in some cases) or to suppress the ways of knowing, and the languages of knowing, of many different indigenous peoples. Reclaiming a voice in this context has also been about reclaiming, reconnecting and recording those ways of knowing which were submerged, hidden or driven underground. (Smith 69)

The question of the day is rhetorical: Is my effective dismissal somehow connected to my special topics course in Aboriginal literature? The department where I work is conservative at best. The essay is revered as *the* form of critical writing, a form whose necessary exclusionary thrust just doesn't allow for the kind of learning and self-reflection among non-Natives that recognizes what Joseph Couture describes as "the gross and still-resonating destructiveness of the European contact (a)s a front-and-centre fact." (164) I did not hide my intentions in my course outline.

Students in my class would not only be required *not* to write in essay format, but would also be required to make offerings to and interview urban and reserve Elders, visit urban and reserve archives, do extensive small group work, research the Indian Act and residential schools, become informed about issues of appropriation. They would be provided with the means and advised to attend a sacred teaching sweat lodge at some point during the term and their writing assignments would involve structured critical Response Statements to the required texts, films and assignments.

Ordinarily I teach mainstream with a focus on anti-racism and awareness of oppressions such as racism, sexism, heterosexism, ageism, ableism. In these classes, students learn to write in essay format only after careful self-and cultural-reflexivity through critical Response Statement writing, a powerful and rewarding learning experience for the vast majority of mainstream students. As a Métis person I was and am encouraged by the Elders to teach this way in order to raise the awareness of non-Natives and immigrants in general, to bring the students to acknowledge the extent of the racism and oppression that exist systemically in Canadian institutions and in the materials taught in the education systems. We are encouraged to have students really examine their values and the values of the people they study. The approach is ideological, and the stress is on critical thinking and writing. I stress the importance of "voice" and "audience" to any writer through the readings near the beginning of term(s). Some of the material the students read is difficult, both academically and personally, due to the lack of familiarity with writings by Aboriginal peoples and peoples of colour, and the lack of experience with being challenged emotionally and intellectually at the same time. After about a month in my classes, students begin to value my methodologies and my pedagogy. This is clearly reflected in my student evaluations. I ask for evaluations late each term (even when I am not required to do this) in order to better serve students. I try to incorporate student suggestions in my future classes.

> Academic knowledges are organized around the idea of disciplines and fields of knowledge. These are deeply implicated in each other and share genealogical foundations in various classical and Enlightenment philosophies. Most of the "traditional" disciplines are grounded in cultural world views which are either antagonistic to other belief systems or have no methodology for dealing with other knowledge systems.... While disciplines are implicated in each other, particularly in their shared philosophical foundations, they are also insulated from each other through the maintenance of what are known as disciplinary boundaries. (Smith 65-67)

Often, of course, it is our own imperialist policing of disciplinary boundaries that takes up our energies, and the concomitant valorization of certain knowledges over others. The discipline of English literature is not going to attract Aboriginal people or people of colour—clearly does not want to—until it asks some long hard questions not just about curriculum and pedagogy but about its values around literacy as well. Take our (and of course our students') rehearsals of values around canon, for instance—what now seem to be quite tired old arguments about what is good literature and what is not, or what, in our first year survey courses we spend time on, as opposed to what we do not, or what we subtly pass on about the value of "oral" versus "written" literatures. In none of our courses, nor in our curriculum do we question the foundational assumptions of the discipline that lead to the marginalization of Aboriginal literature in the first place.

In courses on British literature, even on postcolonial literature, do we emphasize to the extent we need to how deeply our discipline is founded on sexist, colonialist, classist and racist foundations, or do we, as we do in our department tend to steer away from courses (as not literary enough) that lay bare the foundations of the history of our discipline. The cry of "where's the literature" is a sad, policing cry indeed, and would come up again and again in a course such as Sharron's in which, of course, the importance of context in a student body (both non-Aboriginal and aboriginal*) that has been trained by us culturally not to know its history* and gets enormously resentful, often, when it does.

Our student (and administrative!) evaluations often read, an echo of that imperial archive, that "this is not an English course, but a ... [fill in the blank]?", not only demonstrating that students are interpellated by an imperialist educational paradigm, and a kind of systemic arrogance that suggests that they fully know what a range of disciplines are in fact about, but more important how they interpellate us, and those with power who read our evaluations: do they believe what they read there? Or do they believe in us? This distrust in our pedagogical practice is what happened in Sharron's case. And in countless others. We don't stay within the correct boundaries.

> I will seek a literary criticism that emphasizes Native resistance movements against colonialism, confronts racism, discusses sovereignty and Native nationalism, seeks connections between literature and liberation struggles, and, finally, roots literature in land and culture. This criticism emphasizes unique Native worldviews and political realities, searches for differences as often as similarities, and attempts to

> find Native literature's place in Indian country, rather than Native literature's place in the canon. (Womack 11)

In my experience and the experience of the many educators who teach from a position of race awareness, students complain about a course that is taught this way. The complaints, though often described as outcome-based very early on in the term(s), are race-related and come almost exclusively from students who are white. There are at least 1/3 students of colour and Aboriginal students in my mainstream classes at Mount Royal College. This past fall, like all other terms, students complained about outcomes after three weeks of class. The new Chair and new acting Dean of my department supported the student complaints against me and told the students they already had problems with my teaching. Rather than do the job of supporting my pedagogy, my academic freedom, me, rather than read any of the student evaluations in my file, they both demanded I change my approach in the classroom to one that is not "thematic," that I should lecture, stop doing group work, stop doing lab work, stop sitting students in a circle, establish a mentoring/teaching relationship with a tenured person in the department, and drop the "race stuff." They then reminded me that our meetings together were informal and didn't need to be put into writing. When I asked in interview with them, both the Dean and the Chair said they didn't see where there was any connection to race here and they didn't find it odd that the students who complain are white. They understood how fifty years ago students may have deflected issues around women writers if a (then pretty much white male) professor introduced predominantly women authors in a writing class, but they could not see the connection to race now.

> I would likely go back to graduate school in a minute on two conditions. The first is if I could find a program where I could be all I dream to be. This would be a place where I could learn from a position of cultural respect. It would be a place where I could look at knowledge including how I understand knowledge from my Mohawk woman's place; a place where people would not look at me as if I was crazy when I based my scholarly work on what grandmother told me (that is one example of Aboriginal epistemology). Very clearly, that place

> does not yet exist within educational institutions that grant graduate degrees. (Monture-Angus 103)

Even with the astounding amount of scholarly work done in the United States primarily on the deep connections between composition teaching and race, gender, socioeconomic class, and so on, we labour under the assumption that to teach writing is a neutral activity. Even as we teach "postcolonial" or Aboriginal literatures in the same departments, we ask the instructors of those courses to pull back on the politics when the students get anxious, to change their teaching when students and when colleagues complain, rather than investigate the deeper causes of anxiety that are informing such complaints, and rather than remembering that we are supposed to have in place some venerable institutions, such as academic freedom, which several commentators on race and gender have noted, simply do not apply, or apply differentially, to racialized people doing political teaching and research. I quote, as an example, from Mount Royal College's clearly articulated Academic Freedom policy, which seems to have been forgotten not only in the specificities of Sharron's case, but in the predictable backlash: "academic members ... are entitled, regardless of prescribed doctrine, to freedom in carrying out research and in publishing the results thereof, freedom of teaching and of discussion, freedom to criticize the College and the Faculty Association and freedom from institutional censorship. Academic freedom does not require neutrality on the part of the individual." (*MRC 2001-02 Calendar*, 8)

Overheard in the corridor and, later, more respectfully asked me by the Mount Royal College lawyer in Sharron's case: "I don't see what race has to do with the teaching of composition." "Or gender?" I returned the volley. Well, no, he said, although I expect my colleagues (feminists) might have answered differently. And that, of course, gets to the heart of the question: we will get student and collegial complaints about our teaching of everything of composition to Aboriginal studies to (in my case) critical race theory and South Asian literature if the teaching of "English" is, as it has been passed down to us through decades of "objective" study, the cornerstone of colonial discourse, liberal individualist discourse. This strategy of denial and containment is an old colonial strategy: to suggest that we do not teach composition (or other subjects) correctly, objectively, or within our disciplinary boundaries and parallels the methodologies by which Indigenous and other people are "gatekept" out of the academy and out of dominant culture, through discourses of merit and authenticity: not only is Sharron's expertise called into question but, both implicitly and explicitly her gendered and sexualized status as a two-spirited woman and her "hybrid" status as a Métis woman (one of the stories that continues to circulate of course is that she is not "really" Aboriginal).

> As we have seen, the notion of "authentic" is highly contested when applied to, or by, indigenous peoples. "Authorities" and outside experts are often called in to verify, comment upon, and give judgments about the validity of indigenous claims to cultural beliefs, values, ways of knowing and historical accounts.... Questions of who is a "real indigenous" person, what counts as a "real indigenous leader", which person displays "real cultural values" and the criteria used to assess the characteristics of authenticity are frequently the topic of conversation and political debate. These debates are designed to fragment and marginalize those who speak for, or in support of, indigenous issues. They frequently have the effect also of silencing and making invisible the presence of other groups within the indigenous society like women, the urban non-status tribal person and those whose ancestry or "blood quantu"' is "too white." (Smith 72)

In my own department, for example, we have determined—a progressive gesture?—that we must teach a junior level Aboriginal literature course every fall or winter term, and have gone in some terms to great lengths to ensure that Aboriginal students be permitted to take senior courses if they don't have the necessary prerequisites. These are individual initiatives, however, and have not extended to a departmental (or even a faculty-level) initiative to hire Aboriginal faculty, an argument that, were it to be made would rouse arguments of tokenism, merit, credentials, and the usual feel-good liberal strategies that in effect perpetuate the status quo. The "where are they"? argument would also come into play, without any recognition of the systemic barriers that we put into place in our advertising and recruitment procedures, or long before in our graduate and undergraduate policies that in effect condition who gets in to school, and who stays in school.

> As the only female, tenured (almost) faculty member, what message does this send to graduate students? What institutional space and environment does it create for them? As students learn of my tenure experience including the fact that the two "regular" members of the department (that is, two Euroamerican men) did not support my tenure application, who does this operate to silence, foster fears instead of confidence, and exclude? If I experience the university as alienating and I have a position on the hierarchy well above students (even graduate students), then I fear the quality of their experience is negated as a possibility. (Monture-Angus 116)

As far as I know, I am one of very few Aboriginal (First Peoples/Inuit/Métis) persons to teach in the English department, all of us as sessionals. In my time, there has been one other Aboriginal person teaching an English class and my friend's term lasted only a term. And as far as I know, this is the first time an Aboriginal literature course has been offered in the English department in the ninety-year history of Mount Royal College. I was put in the same position as most Aboriginal educators today, "answering questions posed by people who did not even know what to ask" about my course proposal. There were no Native people on the committee, yet "another example of colonialism related to teaching and hiring." (Womack 8)

like a pie in the face but different

now I wait
for the end of the honey
empty jar and new moon's
full blossomed sheets
blown winter in a full spring sun

follow with your shadow
follow with your spirit

Of course, what angers me in 2001 is that we all know this, that our gatekeeping function as academics is clear to all of us, especially those of us in the so-called "humanities" disciplines who police literacy. Even as I, as an undergraduate advisor to our English programme, police and enforce rules that suggest, for example, that postcolonial literatures are optional to the programme, but some literature before 1800 is not, or that "Canadian literature" is required in our programme because it satisfies our internationalization component of our new curriculum but neither international (postcolonial) literatures nor Aboriginal literatures are. That we do not have a regular offering in our senior courses in Aboriginal literature (rather, it is offered as an open "topics" course at the second-year level, along with other non-canonical courses such as sci-fi, fantasy, children's lit, lit and the environment, detective fiction, and, oddly, a lower level Canadian lit and Shakespeare). With the huge range of Aboriginal literatures that exist, students are often not permitted to take Aboriginal literature courses twice. And so on. The real importance of Aboriginal literature to our programme as a whole is clear.

> Overall, it seems to me, Native-written fictional stories about reconnection to Native culture enjoy a much wider popular appeal than non-fiction written by Indians concerning their tribe's land claims or politics. In terms of fiction itself, take as an example the glaring difference between the attention given to Leslie Silko's Ceremony, a novel about a warrior's reintegration into Laguna society ... and the same author's Almanac of the Dead, a novel that posits that indigenous peoples through the Americas will take back their land. America loves Indian culture; America is much less enthusiastic about Indian land title. (Womack 11)

The class was scheduled for winter term, 2001, and advertised by the department only after the student registration deadline for winter courses was well over. I was told by my department Chair that the course may not "fly," to hope for the best and cross my fingers. The cap was 35 students and there would have to be 17 registered within two weeks, the end of the fall exam period. My last exam was late afternoon on December 19. Just before going to the gym I received an email from admin saying the course would "fly." Less than twenty-four hours later, the day of my "effective dismissal" from Mount Royal College, both the course and I were cancelled by the acting Dean, who refused to sign my (already signed by my department Chair) winter-term contract.

> There is no consideration given to the few of us who have been attracted to and hired by the university. The consequences are often evidenced in the retention rates of Aboriginal faculty and Aboriginal students. (Monture-Angus 115)

As English departments go, ours is reasonably savvy and politically aware, in a liberal sense, of the issues I raise here, but not willing to tackle the more difficult ones that would, in effect, challenge us to rethink our disciplinary assumptions: certainly, we incorporate (canonical and easy-to-get) Aboriginal texts in many of our courses; we tout the importance of reading Aboriginal literatures, and we teach the junior Aboriginal literature course; at one point we even suggested that an Aboriginal literature appointment might be a departmental priority (departmental discussion about whether this might be an Aboriginal person, however, revolved around the usual tired arguments of tokenism and the usual weary assumptions that we had enough people on staff to teach the course we currently offer. We did not raise queries about whether we had, for example, someone with graduate or undergraduate level expertise or the cultural knowledges required to teach aboriginal literatures (with all the Eurocentric and colonialist assumptions that attend even that designation, a failure at the start, however politically expedient it is)). We do not.

Currently, university-wide, we have two tenure-stream Aboriginal instructors. Current job searches in various faculties have routinely overlooked Aboriginal applicants specifically, just as they have historically overlooked racialized applicants generally. This effect is not news, of course, but puts the lie to the "where are they"? argument. Our own job searches, especially in creative writing, for example, did not attract Aboriginal writers; it strikes me as predictably odd that we have not asked why that is, both as a department and a faculty.

> Universities ... were established as an essential part of the colonizing process, a bastion of civilization and a sign that a colony and its settlers had "grown up." Attempts to "indigenize" colonial academic institutions and/or individual disciplines within them have been fraught with major struggles over what counts as knowledge, as language, as literature, as curriculum and as the role of intellectuals, and over the critical function of the concept of academic freedom. (Smith 65)

When I was in school I read the books of countless white middle- to upper-class European (including Canadian and American) mostly men a few women. Until I was in my twenties I'd read very few authors who weren't white. I read Maria Campbell's *Halfbreed* several times and held on so tight, but that was about the extent of my "other" reading until Beatrice Culleton's *In Search of April Raintree* and Howard Adams' *Prison of Grass*. I returned to school in my mid-thirties and the curriculum was pretty much the same – still is more than ten years later. I'm not so sure my experience was/is out of the ordinary as far as being inundated with white middle to upper class information. I grew up in Ontario and went to school from grade one to grade thirteen on an army base. Two major rivers join there, spectacular and wonder. The land buffered the violence and racism I and many others endured in that village. During high school, the principal at my school was a Jamaican Canadian man, and if I remember correctly, the vice-principal and student advisor was an African Canadian man. From these men I learned that those of us who are oppressed by the mainstream have a perfect right to be and to move in this world, that the condition of our oppression doesn't ask us to "reason;" rather, we are asked to *resist*. When we're unable to resist, we must then come to know what is stopping us.

> Problematizing the indigenous is a Western obsession. The discourse has shifted away from the cultural deficit views to

> cultural diversity views. Even within these views the indigenous can only be perceived as a problem because many are considered "inauthentic" and too ungrateful. The belief in the "indigenous problem" is still present in the Western psyche. It has been portrayed by some writers as a deeply held fear and hatred of the Other. (Smith 92)

Equally unsurprising, although just as spirit-destroying, is the swirl of stories that has surrounded Sharron's and others' determination to fight the institutional racism that led to the termination of her contract, the labelling of her as a troublemaker, and the inevitable backlash that follows such situations, the failure of both individuals and institutions to recognize, quite simply, that there is an opportunity here for something to be done. In the end, her department (faculty and college) lost not only an Aboriginal instructor, but their first opportunity to teach a course in Aboriginal literature. To date, they have not rectified this failure. This is not simply the failure of vision of one institution, however, but a deeply entrenched systemic racism, for which all postsecondary institutions are responsible if we turn a blind eye to the many manifestations of our own complicity—an often peculiarly proud complicity—in structures that would permit the continued marginalization of Aboriginal peoples, knowledges, in this case literatures.

I realize I am moving to a polemical conclusion, and my rhetoric certainly suggests a cynicism or despair that precludes possibility. This is, in part, true. The workings of systemic and institutional racism, particularly in a year when I and others have experienced them first hand, and over and over again, make foregone conclusions the most likely scenario: systemic discrimination is designed to foreclose on our options at the same time as, in a liberal individualist culture of the university, make us feel like our work, effort, and time are being valued (look at the discourses of academic freedom and diversity). But my agenda is not merely cynical; it is a call-to-arms to those of us—and there are many of us—who experience this discrimination almost daily in our academic lives and who do not speak out for fear, or because we really are persuaded to believe that nobody else experiences the chilly climate of racial discrimination. We know from the work of (largely white) feminists that this happens everywhere, and continues to do so. Why is it that some of the same feminists, and those who listened to them cannot feel the same chill of racism? And recognize that it is as deeply systemic in nature, has lasted as long as sexism, intertwines with sexism.

> If universities are ever going to practice equity beyond the level of literacy (that is, writing down good things about equity), then ... the university must come to terms with the conditions of my life as an "Indian" woman. It (still) means I more than likely got a late start at university (and this is the result of the history of educational exclusions of "Indian" people). It means I more than likely have greater family obligations including the fact that I am more likely responsible for more children and belong to an extended family in an active way. There is also a greater likelihood that I am a single parent. Further, the disposable income within my immediate family and my extended family is more than likely insufficient to support the family let alone provide additional resources to support me while I go to school. Attending university also has the unfortunate consequence of isolating me from my family if they live on a reserve. (Monture-Angus 104)

Years later I heard almost the same words from Lee Maracle, who differentiates between "oppressor logic" and the logic of the oppressed. To paraphrase her, in order to be paralyzed by oppression, you have to be a believer of oppressor logic at some level. Oppressor logic says things like, accept your oppression as human beings; men are naturally aggressive; there will always be poor; there will always be racism; my parents and/or grandparents worked hard for what we have. Oppressor logic is "truth" in mainstream consciousness. The mainstream classrooms I teach are filled with predominantly lower-middle/middle/upper-middle class young women and men whose housing, meals, transportation, entertainment, tuition, and so on, are paid by their parents. The truth of oppressor logic is passed to their folks from their parents and grandparents, from their teachers and televisions, from their literatures and histories. University is where, all their lives, these folks are told they *belong*.

Unlike oppressor logic, the logic of the oppressed is

human spiritual logic, the struggle for change. The logic of the oppressed most often comes from folks who are/told all their lives by middle-class and "upwards" language and teachers and televisions and literatures and histories/that they don't belong – not in university, not in management, not in government, not in academia, not in a million years. The all-Native classes I teach flow from the logic of the oppressed. Oppression hurts, and when folks dare to feel that pain, the healing hurts just as much. Yet, time after time, students in my Native classes go to the source of the pain. The person being hurt has the authority over the hurt; this is understood. And unlike mainstream classes, I don't have to "teach" Native students critical thinking. There is an understanding that all inhumanity is intolerable. Overall, the gap between Native students' level of *response-ability* (a living word from Toni Morrison) and that of mainstream students' is tremendous. The difference starts with the most basic of questions: ask a Native student what she or he will do with a degree and the answer will almost always be something like, I plan to work in my community, I plan to help the people, I'm going to school for my children, for my grandchildren, for the generations who follow. Ask a mainstream person the same question and s/he'll invariably start to talk about a good-paying job, a house, a car, money.

> Much of what I have read has said that we do not exist, that if we do exist it is in terms which I cannot recognize, that we are not good and that what we think is not valid. (Smith 35)

Let's return to Sharron for a moment. Is she seen as a problem? Perhaps, as a Métis woman and an activist, not quite authentic? Not a real academic because she was a sessional, not fully credentialled? Of course, if we've paid attention to ourselves, we know that this is how Indigenous people have been marginalized for centuries. She is the "problem," just as is the absence of those other Aboriginal people we lament but do so little to change. It certainly won't be long in that particularly institutional memory before she does not exist at all.

My rhetoric is also a call to persuasion, a (strong) gesture towards those who would not fully deny that our academic institutions have a gaping absence, despite our best intentions, and that that absence is the absence of Aboriginal people, of respectful and respectable Aboriginal academic programs and courses with adequate (even adequate!) resources behind them.

Most of us know the hoary old questions to ask about the continuing absence of Aboriginal faculty, students and perspectives in Canadian university and college campuses today: In a sense they are almost embarrassing to have to enumerate again and again. We also know the answers to most of these questions, the derision with which some of these questions are greeted, the blankness, the accusations of interference with academic freedom, of tokenism, of meritocracy and of gatekeeping that meet any attempt to level the playing field or to suggest that academia take a long hard look at its own whiteness, particularly in regard to the exclusion of Aboriginal people and Aboriginal knowledges. And this, in our teaching as well as our various academic processes, is where we all have to ponder what position at the gates we have taken up.

> On a given day, if you ask me where you might go to find a moose, I will say "If you go that way you won't find a moose. But, if you go that way, you will." So now, you younger ones, think about all that. Come back once in a while and show us what you've got. And, we'll tell you if what you think you have found is a moose. (Elders of Seven First Nations of Alberta, qtd. in Couture 159)

A woman in one of my all-Native classes says, as a teacher, I'm like Nanabush in Tomson Highway's *The Rez Sisters*. This is the highest compliment I've had about my teaching. In the publication notes of *The Rez Sisters*, Tomson Highway says, "the role of Nanabush is to be played by a male dancer - modern, ballet, or traditional. Stage directions for this mostly silent Nanabush are indicated very sparingly in this script. Only his most 'essential' appearances are explicitly set out." (xi) The text goes on to say, essentially a comic, clownish sort of character, Nanabush (trickster) teaches us about the nature and the meaning of existence on the planet earth; s/he straddles the consciousness of the people and that of the Great Spirit.

the grammatical construction is not white middle class English

am I living a lie
or is that lay
as in neighbour or weigh
this
or even that
is not a rhetorical question
do I sleep
which rhymes with sheep
white sheep of the family
tree
or dare I ask
what kind of tree is this
or even that
the answer being implied in the question
great white pine
do I please
do I persuade
do birds do
the art or act of declamation

more mere rhetoric
at the end of the day
the art of prose
or distant verse
or vase
at the end of the day

rhetorical oratorical
another dare I ask
in greek
a question put only
for oratorical or literary
effect
am I living a lie
or do I just plain play dead

follow with your shadow
follow with your spirit

Works Cited

Couture, Joseph. "Native Studies and the Academy." *Indigenous Knowledges in Global Contexts*. Ed. George Sefa Dei. Toronto: U of Toronto P, 2000. 157-167.

Highway, Tomson. *The Rez Sisters*. Winnipeg: Fifth House, 1992.

Monture-Angus, Patricia. "Selected University Experiences: A Preliminary Discussion of Equity Initiatives for Aboriginal Peoples." *Equity and How to Get It: Rescuing Graduate Studies*. Ed. Kay Armatage. Toronto: Inanna, 1999. 99-128.

Morrison, Toni. *Playing in the Dark: Whiteness and the Literary Imagination*. Boston: Harvard University Press, 1992.

Smith, Linda Tuhiwai. *Decolonizing Methodologies: Research and Indigenous Peoples*. London: Zed, 1999.

Spivak, Gayatri. *The Post-Colonial Critic: Interviews, Strategies, Dialogues*. Ed. Sarah Harasym. New York: Routledge, 1990.

Womack, Craig. *Red on Red: Native American Literary Separatism*. Minneapolis: University of Minnesota P, 1999.

Teaching Aboriginal Literature: The Discourse of Margins and Mainstreams

Emma LaRocque

Ashcroft, Griffiths and Tiffin (1989) have argued that the study of history and English and the growth of Empire

> *...proceeded from a single ideological climate and that the development of the one is intrinsically bound up with the development of the other, both at the level of simple utility (as propaganda for instance) and at the unconscious level, where it leads to the naturalizing of constructed values (e.g. 'savagery,' 'native,' 'primitive,' as their antitheses and as the object of a reforming zeal). (7)*

Thus, a "privileging norm was enthroned at the heart of the formation of English Studies as a template for the denial of the value of the 'peripheral,' the 'marginal,' the 'uncanonized'." (3) The standarization of "privileging norms" in Canadian historiography and literature has entailed, among other things, extreme devaluation and marginalization of Aboriginal cultures and peoples. Needless to say, Native literatures, both oral and written, have remained, until very recently, completely outside of Canadian literary and academic canons.

I well remember a debate I had with the Dean of Arts about the value of keeping two courses on Aboriginal literatures in our roster of courses in Native Studies. It was sometime in the early 1980s; the Department of Native Studies was not a decade into its existence, and I was even newer and definitely inexperienced in the politics of university teaching and canons. Because student enrolment in both the literature courses was low, the Dean took an economical approach and bluntly informed me that both courses were to be cancelled and taken off our calendar of course offerings. Besides student enrolment, it was clear that the Dean did not believe there was sufficient Native literary material to justify teaching Native literatures. Although I had just begun teaching the courses, I was instinctively horrified by the suggestion, and in the full splendour of my inexperience, argued passionately for those courses. To this day, I am sure it was my naivete and vision (and perhaps the Dean's respect for an honest exchange) that won me a compromise. The Dean cancelled the American Native Lit course but I could keep the Canadian equivalent as long as the enrolment increased. I argued then that it was just a matter of time before Native literature would grow and demand pedagogical and critical attention. As it has turned out, and not surprising to those who knew the Native experience and studies, I could not have been more right in my prediction.

Today it is with pride and pleasure to be able to state that Native literature has virtually exploded onto the Canadian intellectual, if not literary, arena, and is one of the most exciting new fields of study for those specializing in Canadian Native literature. The dramatic growth both in Native writing and critical study of it has resulted in many changes for those of us producing and/or teaching Aboriginal literature(s). This essay is not a detailed history of Native writing[1] but rather a reflective overview of pedagogical, epistemological and canonical issues arising from two decades of teaching Canadian Native Literature from the margins of Native Studies in a large mid-Canadian, middle-class mainstream university.

Location in the Empire

"To be an Aboriginal person, to identify with an indigenous heritage in these late colonial times, requires a life of reflection, critique, persistence and struggle." (McMaster and Martin 11) I begin by briefly locating myself and thus situating the Indigenous and de/colonial basis of my pedagogy. In a number of significant respects, I have unorthodox beginnings in university teaching. At home I grew up Cree with Wehsehkehcha; in schools my senses and intellect were overrun with Settlers and Savages and neither knew anything about Wehsehkehcha, rendering me an "alien" in my own home/land. Alienation and poverty do have social consequences; in Alberta in 1971 the average grade level for Status Indian and Métis children was grade four. Statistically speaking, Native children were not expected to make it to high school, let alone to university. Quite an interesting combination of factors enabled me to pursue education in an era of devastating marginalization and bleak social conditions for my community and family. It was the resourcefulness and support of my parents, along with their engaging Cree-Métis cultural literacy that instilled in me a love of knowledge and a spirit of determination and independence. By the mid-1970s I had worked my way to a graduate degree in Peace Studies. I then had come to the University of Manitoba on a Graduate Fellowship to work on an MA in (Canadian) History, which I completed in 1980.

One day while walking on campus at the University of Manitoba (and still a graduate student in History), I was approached by a Métis man who introduced himself as the Head of the recently established Department of Native Studies, a department I had not known existed. He asked me to teach the summer Intro (to Native Studies) course.

In addition to my academic qualifications, I was a writer with a Cree language background, and perhaps because of that I was assigned to teach (among other courses) the two Native literature courses that the Native Studies department offered.[2] I took to teaching, particularly Canadian Native Literature, with enthusiasm and not a little creativity. Teaching Native literature in the late 1970s and even into the mid-1980s presented certain challenges. For one thing, I was finding it difficult to fill a half term course with contemporary Canadian Native fiction. To compensate for this lack in those years, I focused on three areas: oral literatures, literature *about* Native people and non-fiction Native writing. Although the non-fiction writing (including poetry) consisted of a wide variety of styles re/mapping place, facts of biography, ethnographic explanations, legends, curriculum guides, historical and sociological expositions, responses to governmental policies or proposals and so forth, it was often lumped as social protest writing. Native writing, whether social commentary or poetry, was not appreciated as post-colonial (Ashcroft *et al*) or resistance literature (Harlow), and much of it was dismissed as parochial or undermined as angry and bitter. (Petrone 1983) As a result, there was minimal, if any, critical literary treatment of any form of Native writing; instead, reviewers concentrated on "anger," personal tragedy or ethnography. Native Literature courses in most mainstream English departments were not generally available, and only one other Native Studies department (University of Lethbridge) was offering courses on Native American writing. Even my colleagues in our department assumed Native literature consisted mostly of "folktales" and "children's literature." These are, of course, honourable subjects but the assumptions revealed ignorance about the scope of study available in Native literatures.

In various respects, we all need/ed to learn how to read Native material. For example, while I understood the colonial experience addressed by most Native writers, I did not presume to understand without study the specific cultures from which each writer expressed him/herself. Being Cree does not make me some 'natural' expert on all things Cree, let alone on non-Cree Aboriginal cultures. Certainly, students required a basis of knowledge from which to better comprehend and appreciate Native writers and writing. Consistent with the systemic devaluation of Aboriginal cultures in society, schools and textbooks,[3] such basis of knowledge had not been made available to students in most Canadian controlled educational institutions, whether in elementary or post-secondary levels, whether in residential, reserve or public schools. In fact, because of the educational system's abysmal failure in providing basic and balanced treatment of Aboriginal peoples in all areas significant to any peoples' history and cultural achievements, students have suffered from deeply entrenched conditioning to 'see' "Indians" through "stereotypic eyes" (Pakes). Cultural differences notwithstanding, both Native and non-Native students continue to arrive in universities with a disturbing combination of absence of basic knowledge *and* misinformation about Aboriginal peoples and issues. This is a significant shared experience by students which informs their approaches to the study of Native peoples.

The cultural literacy of the audience plays a crucial role in the appreciation of any particular literature. In universities students are the 'audience,' however interactive the classes may be. Educating this audience is no routine task for it entails deconstruction before even basic learning can begin. Undergraduate students were particularly ill prepared, both emotionally and intellectually, to deal with multi-racial and cross-cultural classrooms, perhaps especially with Native issues.

It soon became clear to me that I was teaching in no ordinary "cross-cultural" circumstances. Not only were there many cultures[4] represented in my classes, there were educational, socio-economic and racial chasms, as well as deeply divergent political experiences. Both the differences and the similarities derived from the common schoolground of western bias posed (and continue to pose) unique pedagogical challenges.[5] And there were no role models to pave the way for me. In the 1970s and much of the 80s, Native Studies was largely treated as a cultural sensitivity, remedial program, not as a serious scholarly field. Critical intellectual work was often misunderstood or dismissed as "biased,"[6] and the barely emerging handful of Native scholars had not yet developed methodological tools or languages by which to articulate what we, in praxis, were modeling, namely, Indigenity and post-coloniality.

De-colonizing Scholarship in the Empire

In retrospect, it occurs to me that I, per force, developed in content and approach a contrapuntal anti-colonial Indigenously-engaged epistemology and pedagogy. But it was not until the 1990s that I began to articulate this as *resistance scholarship*, a critical scholarship not only based on Aboriginality but one borne out of colonial experience.[7] Such scholarship confronts knowledge which has been privileged in a dominating society and includes the critical use of "voice," and "engaged research" as well as the exploration of the social purpose of knowledge.[8] Knowledge cannot be devoid of human values. Brazilian educator Paulo Friere (1986), for example, argued for the humanization vocation of pedagogy, a vocation that requires a conscientious criticism. Such purposeful pedagogy challenges us to use languages and styles in classrooms and publications which seeks both to demystify and to revisit western assumptions of objectivity in research and modes of distancing in teaching. Decolonizing scholarship takes to task western appearances of impartiality hidden in designatory vocabulary and methodologies which, among other things, objectifies and others the peoples being portrayed or studied, usually Indigenous peoples.[9]

My interdisciplinary work on Native resistance response to "textual strategies of domination" (Duchemin 63) in historical and literary writing has shaped how I have taught, and in many respects continue to teach, my Canadian Native Lit course. As has my Indigenous-informed knowledge. I find that this unique multidisciplinary approach and ethos offers students the possibility of a much greater appreciation of both original and contemporary Native expressions.

I should reiterate here that even though students today are generally more open and better informed, not all students are willing or able to engage with issues beyond sanctioned histories, texts or forums. Although this is to be expected, given the school system's failure to provide critical skills, it is nonetheless demanding. Teaching about the 'dominant western narrative' to those who assume its hegemonic properties as well as to those who have been 'othered' by it—all in one classroom—invites reflection on what was/is really the subtext of colonial discourse that exists in any given Native Studies class. It adds a 'racial' and political dimension to our classrooms which administration may not understand and which mainstream scholars, as a rule, do not have to deal with.[10] While many students appreciate the new perspectives, others resist re-viewing the "the National Dream" version of the Canadian self-image. Students obviously feel more comfortable with cultural portraiture which they associate with and often expect from Native Studies than with the critical work required in the revisiting of Canadian historical and cultural records. But studies on Native peoples in universities are not cultural workshops, and however "positive"[11] we want to be, Canada is centrally a colonial project and good scholarship dictates that we not teach with one eye closed. Ethnography and cultural sensitivity are of course important but not without critical awareness.

For example, Indigenous cultures have been infantilized through the linguistically literal translations of legends and myths as well as through the civ/sav interpretations. In order to demonstrate some of the problems with literal translations, I often find myself paraphrasing into modern English Wehsehkehcha stories my Nokom and Ama related to me in Cree. And of course, I make every effort to properly contextualize Native oral literatures by providing historical and cultural readings, discussions and data. But "cultural studies" alone does not address the master narrative of "the Indian" as savage and/or primitive. To help students appreciate the political environment in which scholarship develops, I encourage them to discover some of the early anthropological forays into Native communities and to explore how anthropologists gathered and interpreted cultural information.[12]

Appreciating oral literatures is also an effective means to appreciating contemporary written Native poetry. For the generation of Native poets who grew up with their mother languages, poetry reflects the transition from oral to written literatures. This, in part, may explain why so many Native writers have taken to poetry, often in conjunction with other genres. Of course, there are as many complex reasons for choosing the medium of poetry as there are poets, but poetry does seem to best facilitate the linguistic and thematic expression of many Aboriginal writers. There is in Aboriginal poetry both a Romantic and Resistance tradition.[13] Rita Joe, Chief Dan George and Duke Redbird are among the earlier poets who drew on the more romantic (both invented and reality-based) presentations of Native cultures and at the same time, protested colonial interference in their cultural and personal lives. It is also through poetry that Native individuals can express both personal and social outrage. Outrage in poetry (or poetic prose such as Arthur Shilling's *The Ojibway Dream* or Maria Campbell's *Road Allowance People*) is often exquisite. What more heart and metaphor can we find in any poetry than in the late Sarain Stump's *There Is My People Sleeping*?

> I was mixing stars and sand
> In front of him
> But he couldn't understand
> ... And I had been killed a thousand times
> Right at his feet
> But he hadn't understood.

The quality of much Native poetry should dispel any doubts critics may have about the aesthetic value of Resistance Literature.

To help students discover the raison d'etre of Native "protest writing," I still include a section on literature *about* Native peoples. I assign students to review archival sources as well as white Canadian fiction and poetry selected from various eras. For example, *Wacousta* is explored not only as a Canadian gothic novel but also as an illustration of hate literature.[14] This historio-literary interrogation helps students to better understand the imperial connection between English history and literature and why Native writers have been resisting their subordination in Canadian scholarship and society.

It also helps them better understand Native authors or characters who struggle with confusion or deep shame about their Indianness, for example, Agnes (Kane), Slash (Armstrong), Garnet (Wagamese) or the Raintree sisters (Culleton). It has been my observation that white students are often surprised by the extent of this shame. But once they learn about the dehumanizing role and power of stereotypes in the media and texts, they gain an appreciation of the Natives' struggles with internalization alongside their resistance reactions to misrepresentation, especially to the Savage portrayal. And many Native students feel an affinity with various Native characters which then leads them to new levels of awareness about their experiences.

I hasten to add, though, that while Native fiction (or non-fiction) serves a socio-political function in pedagogy and society, we must tend equally to its aesthetic value. Native literature is as much about art and nuance as it is about colonial discourse. That Native writing can best be understood as Resistance Literature does not mean that it is singularly political or that it lacks either complexity or grace. Nor does it mean that we have to subscribe to the Noble Savage construct or nativist moral righteousness in order to create a sense of beauty. The Aboriginal landscape is full of aesthetic possibilities - be it in our cultures, faces or resistance. Those of us who teach and/or write do so because our intellects are inspired by the creative re/construction of words and our spirits are nurtured by imagination. It is unfortunate that so many literary critics have focused on ethnography or politics and have overlooked the art of reinvention. Literary criticism needs to come back to the artistic essences of imagined words and worlds. "We are born into a world of light," writes Richard Wagamese, but "it's not the memories themselves we seek to reclaim, but rather the opportunity to surround ourselves with the quality of light that lives there." (1997: 3)

One of the reasons I like and teach literature is because it may be one of the most effective ways to shed light on Native humanity. Perhaps it is through literature we can best illuminate Native individuality, psychology as well as fluidity, and we can do this without compromising Native cultural diversity or the colonial experience. Were critics (and audiences) adequately educated they would have long ago recognized the multidimensionalty of Native works and personalities. Appreciating, highlighting and demanding excellence as well as what is unique in contemporary Native writing should certainly become central to Native literary criticism.

Of course, this begs the question of what constitutes Native literary criticism and the role of culture in Aboriginal Literatures. Many issues intersect here and I cannot, to my satisfaction, treat them in this essay.[15] But I will approach the issue of criticism and culture through the back door, if you will, by now turning away from art and irresistibly to the matter of mainstream English departments opening up positions in Aboriginal

Literatures. It appears that all the post-colonial theorizing about western canonical hegemony and with it the relatively recent addition of "cultural studies" in English departments has lead to certain allowances for "cultural differences" both in the study and hiring of non-Western peoples. While we can perhaps celebrate such efforts, certain problems are emerging in the treatment of Aboriginal scholars and studies.

I have greeted these new openings with some ambivalence, and raise a number of questions. On a more personal level, I am happy to see greater professional and job possibilities for scholars specializing in this field. The importance of the Aboriginal contribution to literature cannot be overemphasized, and I have long cautioned against the ghettoization of Native Studies, Literatures, or scholars. But the question arises as to what extent and in what manner these openings should be serving Aboriginal interests, be they students, scholars, or culture(s).

In my view the new openings in English departments are not necessarily meant to facilitate Aboriginal scholars (in Aboriginal literatures), knowledge or experience, but rather, to facilitate their new graduates specializing in these fields. For the most part, it has been scholars (the majority remain non-Native) in English departments who have had the luxury of advancing their studies in Aboriginal literatures. Such scholars are, of course, looking for positions in universities, most likely in English departments, and this fact puts into perspective the reason(s) why mainstream departments are assimilating Indigenous literatures. But is "specializing"[16] in Native literature within standard graduate programs in English a sufficient enough criteria for teaching this literature? I am of course suggesting that it is not.

Legitimating Aboriginal Epistemology in the Empire

Aboriginal Literatures represent languages, mythologies, worldviews and experiences which requires pedagogical and critical knowledge *beyond* standard western academic literary treatments. That is, those of us teaching Aboriginal Literatures have an extraordinary mandate to *know* both Aboriginal and western epistemologies and should, accordingly, have more than just western-based graduate training in English. This being so, English departments are challenged to consider extraordinary qualifications in the hiring of scholars in Aboriginal literatures.

Whether English departments assume this extraordinary mandate depends, in part, on what exactly English departments mean by "Aboriginal Literatures" and/or to what extent they wish to facilitate genuine cross-cultural exchange and learning. Part of the question being posed here is this: should Aboriginal literatures be fitted into the English discipline, or should English departments change to accommodate the *real* cultural differences combined with Native colonial experience suggested in Indigenous literatures? English departments will have to clarify these points in their advertisements. If English departments simply wish to offer courses on Aboriginal writing, usually fiction, with standard English literary treatments (ie plot, characterization, theme and so forth), then they should specify that all is required is Western-specific pedagogy. If however, they mean to enhance the cross-cultural, post-colonial and Indigenous-based understanding of Aboriginal literatures, then they should consider those who do not fit the standard pattern of a candidate in English, but who are informed by several disciplines, cross-cultural experience and epistemological and political understanding of Native/White relations which informs contemporary Native writing.

By opening up positions in Aboriginal Literatures, English departments are opening up the pandora's box of "cultural differences." By inviting "cultural differences," at least ostensibly, then the other part to the qualification question must centrally be about Aboriginality. But how would English departments assess Aboriginality (whether in defining a body of literature, or in assessing a candidate)? What criteria will they draw on here? While much has been written about what may constitute 'Native literature,' little has been determined as to how Aboriginality is assessed in criticism or in hiring. For example, is having a biological (however remote) and/or ceremonial (however recent) but not epistemological (land and language-based) connection to Aboriginality a sufficient criteria for hiring "Aboriginal" staff?[17] What and whose culture might be priorized?

The commodification of Aboriginal culture (Kulchyski) is a topic which requires much greater exploration and critique than I can give it here. Needless to say, the subject acts as political currency and is both unwieldy and highly charged. The fact is both the colonizer and the colonized have been profoundly informed by centuries of oppositional politics and colonial misrepresentation. Politically and intellectually, confusion reigns in a continuing attempt to uncover (or hire) the "authentic Indian." The result has been a colourful invention of oversimplified cultural typologies and social contradictions.

But it does remain for us to try to assess the role of identity and culture in the study of Native literature. As our repeated attempts indicate, this is no easy task for it is difficult to unravel what is real or what is important. We are confronted with the task of treating Aboriginal cultures which respects their integrity and at the same time taking into account colonial forces. You will note that I use the phrase "real cultural differences" throughout this paper. It is my attempt to address misrepresentation and at the same time say that there is a basis to Aboriginality, both in cultural content as well as experience. It is true that colonization has complicated and compromised Aboriginal identity, but it is equally true that there is extant a remarkable cultural ground from which and through which many of us approach our scholarship. Not all of us grew up confused or alienated from our homes, languages or lands. Dislocated characters such as Agnes, Slash and Garnet do find their way back to their cultural and epistemic home/lands. In other words, there is an Aboriginal ground to Aboriginal literature. The foundational bases to Aboriginal worldview refers to the modes of acquiring and arranging knowledge within the context of original languages, relationships and cultural strategies. This ground, though, is layered and 'unsedimented,' for there is here a complex imbrication of cultural continuity and discontinuity. The "broadening" of Aboriginal epistemology must be treated with all the interspacial nuances and contemporaneity that this implies and demands. (LaRocque 2001)

Recently, in the context of my arguing for such a ground to Aboriginality in the teaching of Aboriginal Literatures, I was taken aback by a white colleague's challenge: "But is there a Native experience?" I believe I retorted something like: "What Aboriginal literature is there if Aboriginal identity and experience is erased?" Concerns about how we define or delimit Native experience (thus literatures), which may be the basis to my colleague's challenge, are well taken but what I was trying to articulate was and is more than just about 'experience,' as such. It is about theory and praxis. Aboriginality as an identity is more than about an amorphous grouping of persons with varied experiences who happen to have some 'Indian,' it is about epistemology. To what extent modern deconstructionists can comprehend this is another debate, for many may conjecture *a priori* that this place of difference is essentialist or nativist.

As is often the case under colonial existence, there are time warps and contradictions. Even as a growing number of scholars are finally taking an inclusive or "cross-cultural" approach, Native peoples are in various phases of decolonizing. For many academics cross-cultural means their 'academic right' to use Native material in the advancement of (their) research and theory without that translating into bringing Aboriginal praxis in their pedagogy. Here cross-cultural is a one-way street. Some academics even take the direction of imposing a notion of racial sameness (not to be confused as equality), some to the extent of appropriating Native identities themselves. Let's shake hands (in a culturally-appropriate clasp, of course) and say we're all the same (with varied experiences, of course).

To Native peoples, cross-cultural means having the 'inherent right' to practice and protect their Aboriginality. Decolonization demands having to define and protect more closely their identities (languages, literatures, among other things) and what is left of their lands and resources. Aboriginal identity and Aboriginal Rights are inextricably related. But even as Native peoples are attempting to shore up their colonially beleaguered identities, they are pressured to be "inclusive" or even "transcultural." Irony seems to be a singular feature of colonialism. Using only western standards for intellectual western purposes, albeit post-colonial, is hardly a balanced equation to a truly cross-cultural exchange! In the universalized name of "literature" the Native experience is again levelled. But those of us not so alienated from our *ground* especially represent what the literati is fond of talking and writing about, namely, the *real* cultural differences.

Although there is way too much ethnographication (allow

me to coin this) in literary criticism on Native works, and although there is too much emphasis on our (oft stereotyped) differences generally, I am becoming increasingly concerned that mainstream literary treatments of Aboriginal writers and writing is losing sight of the *real* cultural differences that yet exist between Native and White Canadians.[18] For me this is an odd place to be. I am of course aware of the increasing complexities concerning Aboriginal identities. Change and adaptability inherent in Aboriginal worldviews and practices have long been central tenets to my research and writing. And certainly, I do not believe that Aboriginal cultures should in any way be pre-historicized (coin) or typologized. However, the recent post-colonial emphasis on "hybridity" (which is not to be confused with Métis Nation cultures), "crossing boundaries" or "liminalty" can serve to eclipse Aboriginal cultural knowledges, experiences (both national and individual) and what may be called the colonial experience.

I appreciate that we all want to be "fluid," and I appreciate that none of us want to be labelled as exclusionary, and I certainly appreciate the wide-ranging experiences of Native (and non-Native) peoples, but fluidity should not mean the erasing of Native identities or the Native colonial experience. Whether we like it or not, at this time in Canadian life we are all deeply colonized, white and Native alike,[19] and no amount of disassembling "the Native experience" to accommodate globalized post-colonial theories can undo this homegrown colonial burden.

Literary treatments carry political implications: whitewashing our Aboriginality means dispossessing our Aboriginal Rights. For example, the reading of "métis" in English literary treatments tends to obscure both our Aboriginality and our unique Red River Cree-Métis roots.[20] Such obscuration carries serious implications concerning Métis land rights and Métis identity. Broadening "métis" to include anyone who claims to be so (without the specific cultural and historical identity markers) merely on the basis of some biological connection (however remote or recent) confuses readings and discussions on Aboriginally-based Métis cultures and identities.[21] Take the Raintree sisters in Culleton's *In Search of April Raintree*. Most critics have assumed the sisters are "Métis." But are they? They may be "métis" or "halfbreed," that is, they may have part Indian and part White ancestry, but they quite clearly do not have Red River Cree-Métis cultural identity. Anyone looking for such cultural markers will not find them in this novel, not even towards the end where April begins to accept her Indianness (which is not the same as Métisness). One will not be able to discern Aboriginally-based knowledge systems here, yet my Cree-Métis community of Red River roots practiced (and in many respects continues to practice) Cree-Métis epistemology. I have found it troublesome that non-Métis critics use Culleton's novel as a standard of defining the Métis. Culleton's portrayal (and experience) is valid for herself and her identity search, but the novel should not be used as a history book or cultural lesson on the Red River Cree-Métis. There is no question that the Raintree sisters experience racism and mysogyny to the extreme, but I cannot say they represent my culture.

I do not think I am being a Métis "nationalist"[22] here; I am pointing out a cultural and historical point of difference significant to Métis identity (and good scholarship). Further, that I relate much more closely to Ruby Slipperjack's Owl (*Honour The Sun*) or to Jeannette Armstrong's Penny (*Whispering in Shadows*) than I do to the Raintree sisters is not just about literary preferences. As a Cree-Métis of Red River roots, I grew up with an Indigenous worldview and experience that comes only from the land and the language.[23] Both Owl and Penny exude the ethos born out of the motherlands and languages. Yet, I have faced an odd sort of discrimination (denial of my Aboriginal rights and denial of the view that "métis" does not mean "Métis") because of the confusion around the portrayal and universalization of the term "métis."

Native identities, knowledge systems and the colonial experience(s) are complex, mutable, uncongealed yet well-defined. It is true that some 100 different Indigenous cultures representing 10 unrelated linguistic families, or about 50 different languages greeted Europeans (not all at once of course) at the site of first encounter(s), and given all the historical and demographic changes experienced and yet the cultural continuity exhibited by Native peoples since this time, it may seem foolhardy to speak of a Native experience in the singular. Anthropology and History point to "a kaleidoscope" of diversities among Native peoples, but also some fundamental similarities, especially in the use of resources and spirituality. (Frideres 22) There appears to be among Indigenous peoples, a fairly remarkable shared understanding of life as a cosmo/ecological whole, enabling the human being to experience life past the sensory confines. We cannot build a canon of Aboriginal literature or criticism without appreciating what this means in terms of mythology, literature and cultural strategies. As anthropologist Ridington has discovered, land-based orally-literate peoples "code their information about their world differently from those of us whose discourse is conditioned by written documents." (275) For those of us who grew up in oral cultures, it is this 'code of information' we seek to impress upon and within modern scholarship.[24]

Besides cultural commonalities, Native people's sustained and multifaceted resistance to colonization has also bonded them and provided them with 'similarities.' Colonial time has collapsed some fundamental differences in areas such as resources, economies, technologies, education, kinship, governance, language, religions, among others. The *Indian Act* has determined legal identity and locality, defining margins and centres even within the Native community. This is not to mention, societal prejudices, industrial encroachment and urbanization. In other words, we can speak of the 'Native experience' from a number of cultural, historical and colonial bases. This though, does not imply or hold that Native peoples' experience is unidimensional. But it is there. Any panoramic study and Indigenity-based reading[25] of Aboriginal writing and writers makes this abundantly apparent.

There is an Aboriginal experience unique to the Canadian context.[26] This point comes back to (and tentatively answers) the issue and significance of qualifications and Aboriginality in the hiring of faculty for positions in Native literatures. Those who have an interdisciplinary academic training and/or who code their information Aboriginally, are particularly well positioned to teach both oral and written Native Canadian literatures. This kind of interdisciplinarity is more than about latching onto post-colonialism (Slemon), it is about putting into practice Aboriginal knowledge and knowledge systems, the origins of which predate and in some ways now co-exist with as well as sub-versely-exist to colonialism. I am not at all promoting nativism or essentialism. At issue is the legitimation of Aboriginal discourse. Having an Aboriginal, land-based, linguistic and cultural upbringing which provides a particular worldview does make a difference in teaching, research, writing and criticism. As does the on-going de/colonization.

I am not suggesting that non-Aboriginal scholars cannot treat Aboriginal literatures. Insight and understanding cannot be confined to ethnic origins. Many non-Aboriginal scholars especially those who are attuned to the Aboriginal worldviews[27] and post-colonial experience, have served to advance Aboriginal histories, cultures and contemporary peoples. However, scholars in Aboriginal literatures need to bring to their teaching and research an Aboriginal epistemological ethos *in addition to* their western academic training and credentials. I hasten to add, I am not suggesting that a candidate for a university position should have fewer academic qualifications (even as western hegemonic standards are under review); rather I am referring to those who have *more* than the academic qualifications. Indigenous literatures bears on an area of discourse and study which cannot be dealt with effectively only by standard western models or by a undisciplinary approach.

Standardization must come under review for "knowledge" cannot mean only or same as "western" under cross-cultural mandates. Nor can English departments assume to meet their cross-cultural mandates simply by re-routing Aboriginal scholars, writers and writing within the Empire's old dominant narrative or the newly sanctioned theoretical models, for these canons by themselves are insufficient in the appreciation of Aboriginal cultural productions and experience. This implies that English departments, consistent with their ads, should be particularly interested in those who do model, not just theorize, *real* cultural differences. Candidates with extraordinary qualifications would best serve, I would think, both the cultural and post-colonial mandates in the study of Aboriginal writers and writing. And of course, in the final analysis universities must hire on the basis of research and creative achievements, publication record, community service and years of teaching experience. For English departments such a dossier should, of course, be in the area of Native literatures but not confined to it. I must emphasize that a cross-cultural and interdisciplinary scholarship gained in fields such as Native Studies can only enhance the study of Aboriginal Literatures. For these and other reasons I believe that university resources for the development of Aboriginal Literatures should go primarily to the community of Native Studies. This is not to suggest that other departments cannot study Aboriginal literatures but it is to declare that Native Studies should remain the intellectual and cultural foundation to the study of Native Literature.[28] At the very least, Native Studies should be consulted and cross-referenced prior to developing literature courses extraneous to Native Studies.

Ironically, in the area of Native literatures, Native Studies departments have not kept up with the dramatic changes. Today there are young (as well as experienced) Aboriginal scholars looking for positions in Aboriginal literatures. For those looking to Native Studies, it is the sad fact that the handful of Native Studies programs or departments across Canada have not developed in this area and so will not be able to absorb such graduates. Most Native Studies programs have gone in the direction of the social sciences rather than the humanities. Most courses revolve around anthropology, history, law, linguistics (not to be confused with contemporary Native literature), governance, socio-economic issues and more recently "Traditional Ecological Knowledge" which is an amalgam of environmental and cultural (associated as 'traditional') studies. Even my own department teaches only one half-term course on Canadian Native Literature! Yet, it is my position that the study of Aboriginal literatures (and languages) ought to be among the core courses for any Native Studies program.

Pushing Paradigms

In the final analysis, our studies of Aboriginal literatures can only be advanced by the production of more Aboriginal works. Even though today a half-term of Native Lit cannot begin to touch on the literary material now available, we can never have enough Native plays, prose and poetry. And of course, our studies are enhanced by Aboriginal literary criticism. Non-Native teachers and critics should no longer dip into Native material just for ethnographic or personal information in the advancement of their theories. They now must deal with our theories and philosophical praxis as well. How else is cross-culturalism practised, and how else shall we truly 'dethrone' the Empire?

The Aboriginal bases for contemporary scholarship and criticism is in the process of development. As we seek to develop a "critical center" (Blaeser) we are also academics who must aspire for that "critical and relatively independent spirit of analysis and judgement," which Edward Said argues, "ought to be the intellectual's contribution." (86) In my concern for intellectual freedom and fluidity in this task, I have assiduously avoided being a mere conduit of community or political voices. Critical Aboriginal scholars present complexities in that we are "pushing margins," crossing boundaries and cultures, disciplines and genres, and we do not fit the standard patterns of both western and nativist pressures. But just because we are on the cutting edge of cultures and boundaries does not mean we are abandoning our Native-specific heritage with its substantial and particular worldview(s) and knowledge base(s). And we are bringing "the other half" of Canada into light. As I have written elsewhere, we are creating a space from which to enter the mandates of western thought and format without having to internalize its coloniality or to defy our personal and cultural selves. And just because we are not abandoning our heritage does not mean we are quagmired in confessional subjectivity. On my part, I have strived towards a personal and intellectual liberation which, among other things, has entailed both 'living' and theorizing decolonization, a 'decolonization' that would ultimately be free of rigid paradigms, ideological or cultural formulas and fads or the jargon that often comes with each of these respective methodological tools or theories. As a professor I have encouraged all my students to engage in critical thinking, reading and writing. To that end I facilitate students to study and approach Native history, identities, literatures or any other modes of cultural productions and representations from a variety of genres, eras, cultural, theoretical and critical perspectives. I do of course emphasize 'the Native experience' as is mandated by Native Studies.

Much has changed in the ideological climate within the

Empire since my youthful encounter with my Dean about the value of teaching Aboriginal Literatures in universities but much work remains to be done to facilitate even greater comprehension of pedagogical and canonical issues and challenges specific to the teaching of Aboriginal histories and literatures, cultural achievements and epistemologies.

Favorite Poem

THERE IS MY PEOPLE SLEEPING
Sarain Stump

And there is my people sleeping
Since a long time
But aren't just dreams
The old cars without engine
Parking in front of the house
Or angry words ordering peace of mind
Or who steals from you for your good
And doesn't wanna remember what he owes you
Sometimes I'd like to fall asleep too,
Close my eyes on everything
But I can't
I can't.

Notes

[1] For a detailed chronological history of Native writing, see Petrone, *Native Literature of Canada*, 1990.

[2] At the time the English department at the University of Manitoba offered no Native literature courses; I believe they offered one course for a brief time sometime in the late 1990s. As far as I know they did not consult our department about the course.

[3] Most Native writers and/or scholars have located school textbooks as significant sources in their dehumanization and alienation. For an absorbing view of the eurocentricity of

textbooks see Blaut's *The Colonizer's Model of the World.*

[4] I believe cultural differences among Aboriginal students, not to mention, between Aboriginal and non-Aboriginal, are quite profound but exquisitely and increasingly more subtle. I have noticed, for example, many northern Native students expressing confusion and alienation from pow wow or elder ceremonies which have become popularized on campuses. These practices reflect the Plains Indian tradition, if not caricature (Pakes).

[5] For further comment on the many levels of political discourse that goes on in Native Studies classrooms, see my article "From the Land To The Classroom: Broadening Aboriginal Epistemology."

[6] My generation of Native university instructors have had to deal with intellectual suspicion, classicism, patriarchy and standardized evaluation systems derived from this 'unconscious' climate. Though much has improved over the last two decades, much remains to be 'foregrounded' about the colonial discourse of 'bias' in the academic system.

[7] I first described my work as "resistance scholarship" in "The Colonization of a Native Woman Scholar."

[8] Feminist and decolonization criticism has advanced the concept and use of voice in scholarship. I introduced my use of voice in the context of literature in my "Preface" (1990). I have since developed the theoretical grounds for voice, engaged research and resistance scholarship in my dissertation *Native Writers Resisting Colonizing Practices in Canadian Historiography and Literature* (1999).

[9] See Duchemin's brilliant exposition of Alexander Mackenzie's imperial contructions of Indians cloaked as impartial science. Mackenzie typically indulges in "mind numbing" ethnography, all the while skillfully employing an "almost scientific" vocabulary which "While appearing to be neutral ... is in fact highly evaluative and judgemental" in language and imagery (1990: 61).

[10] Other minority peoples, perhaps especially for women of colour with critical approaches, are also confronted with similar situations in universities. See for example Mukherjee, 1994.

[11] There is afoot a positivist movement in our midst which views treatment of colonization as "too negative" and basically consigns

"native studies" to cultural programs, particularly spirituality, ceremonial practice or craft replications.

[12] How Native narratives, or for that matter, other cultural information, was collected and interpreted should accompany any study of Aboriginal oral literatures. Notice too how Basil Johnston adds an Indigenous dimension and texture to oral literature in his "One Generation From Extinction."

[13] I treat these co-existing themes in my dissertation (1999).

[14] Richardson employed not just the civ/sav master narrative (the effects of which are often diluted by the blanched term 'eurocentrism') but racist slander, often comparing "Indians" to "cunning" or vicious animals or reptiles. Such virulent anti-Native text qualifies as hate literature. Hate literature is associated with neo-nazism, but it in fact forms a consubstantial part of colonial records. For more on Richardson and hate literature see my dissertation.

[15] In my dissertation (1999) I devote several chapters to the fascinating, if not confusing, intersection of issues on cultural difference and criticism in light of the overwhelming history of misrepresentation.

[16] What constitutes specialization: a Ph.D. thesis? A Native-authored book? A Native-themed work?

[17] Apparently self-conscious on these matters many universities now turn to the "Native community" for input on culture and hiring. But care should be taken that Aboriginal (or any other) scholars not be evaluated as if they are cultural ambassadors elected to office. Not only are candidates being subjected to many disparate communities or "cultures" but also to ideological control and non-university review (LaRocque "From the Land to the Classroom").

[18] I am not contradicting my self here about too much ethnographication, on one hand, and my concern about the erasing of *real* cultural differences, on the other. Negotiating around and through these mercurial siamese twins is convoluted. The discussion, which I pursue at some length in my dissertation (1999) is centrally about misrepresentation.

[19] In substantially different ways of course! Needless to say, colonization benefits one at the expense of the other.

[20] As I show in "Native Identity and the Métis: *Otehpayimsuak*

Peoples" (2001), Métis identity is complex but it is grounded on Aboriginality and well-defined by Métis Nation peoples.

[21] Margery Fee in "Deploying Identity in the Face of Racism" treats Métis (métis?) identity cautiously.

[22] Janice Acoose has so faithfully used my works and so I find it puzzling that she refers to me in a broad stroke as a "Métis nationalist" (1999:229), especially since I have hardly published any works specifically on the Métis. My theoretical decolonizing positioning on 'voice' should not be confused with nationalism.

[23] In response to so much misinformation about the Métis, especially the recent emphasis on "hybridity" I feel compelled to repeat this bit of ethnographic detail in a number of works. The repeating of information also has to do with addressing different audiences that comes with interdisciplinary work now spanning more than two decades.

[24] Basil Johnston's creative and ethnographic work especially comes to mind, but as I have already explained every Native author and intellectual of my generation has tried to teach our audiences an Aboriginal "way of seeing and naming our worlds" (1990: xx).

[25] As Armstrong's collection *Looking at the Words of Our People* shows, reading Native works through the eyes of Native critics does make a difference. Native writers and scholars have long been 'looking at' Native words, it is just that it has not been recognized as (Aboriginal) criticism under western literary standards.

[26] At the risk of 'going against the grain' in the recent emphasis on "Native North America" (ie in the Hulan anthology), I argue for the foregrounding of *Canadian* Native literature because there are a number of significant cultural and national differences between Canadian and American Native intellectuals (Dissertation 1999).

[27] For a lovely read and excellent modeling on Indigenity-based literary treatment, see Renata Eigenbrod's "Reading Indigenity from a Migrant Perspective: Ruby Slipperjack's Novel *Silent Words* – 'log book' or Bildungsroman?" (2000)

[28] Works in 'traditional ecological knowledge' have established the theoretical grounds for the 'science' of Indigenous methods in the 'coding,' recovering and interpreting of data (Colorado, Ridington, Simpson, Smith). This field has much to teach those engaged in Aboriginal literature(s), not only in the validation of

Aboriginal knowledge system(s) but also about respecting Aboriginal cultural/intellectual property rights.

Works Cited

Acoose, Janice. The Problem of 'Searching' For April Raintree." *In Search of April Raintree: A Critical Edition.* Cheryl Suzack, ed. Winnipeg: Portage and Main Press, 1999.

Armstrong, Jeannette, ed. *Looking at the Words of our People: First Nations Analysis of Literature.* Penticton: Theytus Books, 1993.

- - -. *Slash.* Penticton: Theytus Books, 1987.

- - -. *Whispering in Shadows.* Theytus Books, 2000.

Ashcroft, Bill and Gareth Griffiths, Helen Tiffin. *The Empire Writes Back: Theory and Practice in Post-Colonial Literature.* New York: Routledge, 1989.

Blaeser, Kimberly. "Native Literature: Seeking a Critical Center." Armstrong, *Looking* 51-63

Blaut, J.M. *The Colonizer's Model of the World: Geographical Diffusionism and Eurocentric History.* New York:London: The Guilford Press, 1993.

Campbell, Maria. *Stories of the Road Allowance People.* Penticton: Theytus Books, 1995.

Colorado, Pam. "Bridging Native and Western Science." *Convergence* 21, 2-3 (1988): 49-67.

Connor, Ralph. *The Patrol of the Sun Dance Trail.* Toronto: The Westminster Co. Ltd., 1914.

Culleton, Beatrice. *In Search of April Raintree.* Winnipeg: Pemmican Publications, 1983.

Duchemin, Parker. "A'Parcel of Whelps': Alexander Mackenzie among the Indians." *Native Writers & Canadian Writing.* W.H.New, ed. Vancouver: UBC Press, 1990.

Dunn, Marty. *Red on White: The Biography of Duke Redbird.* Toronto: New Press, 1971.

Eigenbrod, Renate. "Reading Indigenity from a Migrant Perspective: Ruby Slipperjack's Novel *Silent Words* – 'log book' or *Bildungsroman*?" *ESC* 26 (2000): 79-93.

Fee, Margery. "Deploying Identity in the Face of Racism." *In Search of April Raintree: Critical Edition.* Cheryl Suzack, ed. Winnipeg: Portage & Main Press, 1999.

Freire, Paulo. *Pedagogy of the Oppressed.* Transl. By Myra Bergman Ramos. New York: Continuum, 1986.

Frideres, James S. *Aboriginal Peoples in Canada: Contemporary Conflicts.* Scarborough: Prentice Hall Allyn and Bacon Canada, 1998 (1st edition 1974).

George, Chief Dan. *My Heart Soars.* Saanichton: Hancock House, 1974.

Harlow, Barbara. *Resistance Literature.* New York: Methuen, 1987.

Hulan, Renee, ed. *Native North America: Critical and Cultural Perspectives.* Toronto: ECW Press, 1999.

Joe, Rita. *The Song of Eskasoni: More Poems of Rita Joe.* Charlottetown: Ragweed Press, 1988.

Johnston, Basil. *Moose Meat and Wild Rice.* Toronton: McClelland & Stewart, 1978.

- - -. "One Generation From Extinction." New 10-15.

Kane, Margo. "Moonlodge." *An Anthology of Canadian Native Literature in English.* Moses, Daniel David and Terry Goldie, eds. Toronto: Oxford University Press, 1992.

Kulchyski, Peter. "From Appropriation to Subversion: Aboriginal Cultural Production in the Age of Postmodernism." *American Indian Quarterly* 21, 4 (Fall 1997): 605-620.

LaRocque, Emma. "From the Land to the Classroom: Broadening Epistemology." *Pushing The Margins: Native and Northern Studies.* J. Oakes, R. Riewe, M. Bennett and B. Chisholm, eds. Winnipeg: Native Studies Press, 2001.

- - -. "Native Identity and the Métis: Otehpayimsuak Peoples." *A Passion for Identity.* D. Taras and B. Rasporich, eds. Scarborough: Nelson Thomson Learning, 2001.

- - -. *"Native Writers Resisting Colonizing Practices in Canadian Historiography and Literature.* Unpub. Interd. Ph.D. Dissertation, University of Manitoba, 1999.

- - -. "Preface." *Writing The Circle.* Jeanne Perreault and Sylvia Vance, eds. Edmonton: NeWest Press, 1990.

- - -. "The Colonization of a Native Woman Scholar." Christine Miller and Patricia Chuchkryk, eds. *Women of the First*

Nations. Winnipeg: University of Manitoba Press, 1997.

Maud, Ralph. *Transmission Difficulties: Franz Boas and Tsimshian Mythology*. Burnaby: Talonbooks, 2000.

McMaster, Gerald and Lee-Ann Martin, eds. *Indigena: Contemporary Native Perspectives.* Vancouver/Toronto: Douglas & McIntyre, 1992.

Mukherjee, Arun. *Oppostional Aesthetics: Readings from a Hyphenated Space*. Toronto: TSAR, 1994.

Pakes, Fraser J. "Seeing with the Stereotypic Eye: The Visual Image of the Plains Indian." *Native Studies Review* I, 2 (1985): 1-31.

Petrone, Penny. "Indian Literature." *Oxford Companion to Canadian Literature* (1983): 383-388.

- - -. *Native Literature in Canada.* Toronto: Oxford University Press, 1990.

Richardson, John. *Wacousta*. Philadelphia: Kay and Biddle, 1832.

Ridington, Robin. "Cultures in conflict: Problems in Discourse." in W.H. New, ed., 1990.

Said, Edward W. *Representations of the Intellectual*. New York: Vintage Books, 1996.

Shilling, Arthur. *The Ojibway Dream*. Montreal: Tundra Books, 1986.

Simpson, Leanne. *The Construction of Traditional Ecological Knowledge: Issues, Implications and Insights*. Unpub. Interd. Ph.D. Dissertation, University of Manitoba, 1999.

Slemon, Stephen. "The Scramble for Post-colonialism." *The Post-Colonial Studies Reader*. Ashcroft, B., G.Griffiths and H. Tiffin, eds. London/New York: Routledge, 1995.

Slipperjack, Ruby. *Honour The Sun*. Winnipeg: Pemmican Publications, 1987.

Smith, Linda. *Decolonizing Methodologies: Research and Indigenous Peoples*. London: Zed Books, 1999.

Stump, Sarain. *There Is My People Sleeping*. Sidney: Grays, 1970.

Wagamese, Richard. *Keeper'n Me*. Toronto: Doubleday Canada, 1994.

- - -. *Quality of Light*. Toronto: Doubleday Canada, 1997.

"What about you?": Approaching the Study of "Native Literature"[1]

Kristina Fagan

There is a story in every line of theory.... It seems a waste of words to dispassionately delete character from plot line, tension and conclusion. It takes a great deal of work to erase people from theoretical discussion....

No brilliance exists outside of the ability of human beings to grasp the brilliance and move with it. Thus we say what we think. No thought is understood outside of humanity's interaction. So we present thought through story, human beings doing something, real characters working out the process of thought and being.

For Native people, the ridiculousness of European academic notions of theoretical presentation lies in the inherent hierarchy retained by academics, politicians, law makers, and law keepers. Power resides with the theorists so long as they use a language no one understands. In order to gain the right to theorize, one must attend their institutions for many years, learn this other language, and unlearn our feeling for the human condition. Bizarre.

If it cannot be shown, it cannot be understood. Theory is useless outside human application.

Lee Maracle, *"Oratory, Coming to Theory" (236-239)*

A year ago, I presented a conference paper in which I complained about much of the existing criticism on literature by Native writers. I denounced the very term "Native literature," arguing that it limits critical analysis by putting the focus on a homogenized and simplified "Nativeness." After presenting the paper, however, my feelings of satisfaction were quickly challenged when several audience members approached me and asked some fundamental questions: Okay, if the usual "Native literature" approach doesn't work, what should we do? And – a much scarier question – what about you? What do you do? At the time, I answered that, as critics, we need to become aware of our own assumptions and their limitations. But, even then, that answer felt like a cop-out. Can we do anything at all as long as we are self-conscious? True, we need to think about why we do what we do. But don't we also need to think about what we *should* do?

Since then, I have been grappling with this question of what kind of work on Native literature I should do. So, when I sat down to rewrite that conference paper for this collection, I was no longer happy with simply taking aim at the approaches of other critics, a practice that kept me comfortably detached. I instead decided to describe my own experiences and impressions as I have tried to figure out how to approach the study of Native literature. I have moved back and forth on the question of whether we should focus on the "Nativeness" of literature by Native writers. I end the essay with some suggestions on how we might move the study of Native literature beyond this preoccupation with a vaguely defined "Native identity."

Writing about my own experiences has been an uncomfortable experience, but in order to shake up the field we need to move out of the realm of comfort. To move forward, I believe that we need to be willing to talk openly about the personal, cultural, theoretical, and institutional reasons that we do what we do. We need to show that the issues we deal with are concrete, personal, ordinary, and therefore very important. As critics, we usually present our ideas as fully formed, polished and apparently static, but as Lee Maracle argues so well in her essay on Native oratory,

> No brilliance exists outside of the ability of human beings to grasp the brilliance and move with it. Thus we say what we

> think. No thought is understood outside of humanity's interaction. So we present thought through story, human beings doing something, real characters working out the process of thought and being. (238)

To present this process, I begin where I began. I am a member of the Labrador Métis Nation, an Aboriginal people of Inuit and European descent who live on the south coast of Labrador. My mother grew up in Charlottetown, Labrador, but she left in order to pursue her education and so I was raised in St. John's, Newfoundland, away from my ancestral land and without a sense of being part of an Aboriginal community. Nevertheless, I was always told by my mother that we were Native, and I learned what that meant from my grandparents, who live a traditional lifestyle, living off the land by hunting, trapping, gathering berries, and growing vegetables. My grandfather is a trapper with a deep knowledge of the land, who taught me to give thanks for the food that it provides. My grandmother is a wonderful storyteller who taught me about the history of our people.

As I got older, I became more curious about that history. I was particularly drawn to the tradition of storytelling and writing among the Labrador Métis. As a people, we have a detailed memory of our history, which extends back to long before the arrival of the Europeans. Some, like my grandmother, pass on this history through stories that have been told over innumerable cups of tea in innumerable kitchens. Others have written the stories down. Some of these writings were stored away and disintegrated, some held in missionary archives, some passed around the community, and some published in local newspapers and magazines. I trace my own role as a writer, creative and academic, back through all those who have felt the need to pass on our people's stories.

When I began graduate studies in English, I wanted to write my doctoral dissertation on the literature that was most important to me, those stories of the Inuit and Métis of Labrador. I soon, however, came face to face with the constraints of graduate school. I knew that, in order to do such a study, I would have to travel, interview, visit archives, and probably work with documents not in English. Considering the lack of time and money available for me to complete my dissertation, I realized that I needed a project that could be completed entirely within the campus libraries. In addition, I quickly became aware of the professional need to establish myself within an identifiable field and to study recognized writers. Maybe I also lacked the confidence to stand up for my unusual project. In any case, I decided to take an easier path: I wrote my dissertation on a much broader topic and one in which I sensed a growing academic interest: humour in contemporary Native literature.

I tell this story not to criticize the English department within which I studied. I was not forced into changing my topic. In fact, several professors were quite supportive of my original plans. Rather, I want to point out the very real and practical institutional forces that work upon those of us studying Native literature. Many of us working in this field like to see ourselves as working against the forces of canonization and institutionalization, as freer than those who study the "dead white males." However, the reality is that those of us working within the area of "Native lit" are, like other academics, under pressure to produce work that will impress our peers while facing the constraints of time, money, and academic norms. Throughout this essay, I argue that these pressures shape the kind of work that we do — from the authors we work on, to the theories we embrace, to the research methods we employ. In order to open up new possibilities in the field and the university, we need to admit to our own self-interest and the ways in which our institutional positioning both enables and compromises our work.

The lack of awareness and open discussion of these institutional forces within the study of Native literature is not surprising. After all, Native literature has been recognized within university literature departments only over the past twenty years or less. During this time, a great deal of effort has been put into legitimizing Native literature within the university, showing that the literature exists, that it is good, that it is part of a tradition, and that it is worth studying. There has understandably been more emphasis on getting the literature within the institution than on thinking about the consequences of such institutionalization. An example of this emphasis can be seen in the introduction to Daniel David Moses and Terry Goldie's 1992 *An Anthology of Canadian*

Native Literature in English. Goldie claimed that his main concern was showing that the literature exists, "to get the material out, get people to read it" (xiii). He further claimed that the editors were not concerned, at that point, with finding "the best" of Native writing. In fact, he said, no one was yet concerned with that, since there had been no canonization of Native literature: "No community, whether it's the Native writers themselves or Native communities or the literary community, or whatever, has made the decision about what should go in." (xiii) Since the anthology appeared, however, things have changed in the study of Canadian Native literature. Today, Native writers are widely taught and are written about in reputable journals. Careers are built on the study of Native literature and tenure-track positions are appointed in the field. There is certainly a Native literature canon, recognizable by a quick look through the syllabi of Native literature courses from across the country. If it was not before, it is now time to think about how and why Native literature is situated within the academy.

The desire to legitimize the field of Native literature has led, I would argue, to two widespread and problematic assumptions about the literature. First of all, in order to have a field, one must have a large body of literature with something in common. This need, combined with a widespread lack of knowledge about tribal identities and traditions, has led to all writing by people of Native descent being commonly collapsed together into "Native literature." That term, "Native literature," implies a constant link between the category "Native" and the literature. As a result, the texts are often seen as a direct reflection of "Native" life and culture, and there is a prevailing emphasis on aspects of the work that are seen as distinctively "Native" - certain themes, traditions and social issues. A number of Native writers and scholars have complained about this approach, saying that their work has been interpreted as a transparent chronicle of "Native oppression, dispossession and suffering" or as "Native folklore." (Maria Campbell qtd. in Jannetta 63; LaRocque xvii) This assumption is, as Roy Miki points out, also widely applied to other so-called "ethnic" writers who are "not approached in terms of aesthetic form ... but for the transparency of the referential, confirming the assumption that the signs 'Joy Kogawa' and 'Sky

Lee' are products of 'groupness'." (173; see also Chow 99-100) Meanwhile, white writers are not often analyzed in terms of their "whiteness."

Second, for a body of literature to be popular within the academy, it has to fit into current critical and theoretical thinking. As a result, Native literature has been repeatedly read as a challenge to colonialism and to white society—"postcolonial," "postmodern," "transgressive"—a fashionable function in a critical climate that so values difference, subversion, and resistance. This positioning of Native literature, however, is a form of idealism, making Native people the political "good guys" who stand for all that is non-centred, non-oppressive, kind, and good. While this assumption may seem harmless, it actually posits Native people as purer, simpler, and consequently less human than non-Natives. Thomas King, whose writing has often been read in terms of such theories of resistance, recognizes such readings as reductive: "You make it sound as though the Native people spend their entire existence fighting against non-Native whatever. That just isn't true." (111)

Both of these critical assumptions also have appeal because they reduce the amount of time and effort required to approach the study of Native literature. It is much easier to generalize about the colonization of Native people than to study specific tribal histories and traditions, many of which are very complex and often not written down. It is more convenient to use familiar theoretical approaches than to explore ways of thinking and knowing within Native communities. And the attention placed on Native literature's subversion of the dominant society allows critics to continue to focus on dominant forms and values. In short, these approaches make Native literature more easily accessible for most critics, reducing the sense of the "unknown."

When I first began work on my doctoral dissertation on Native humour, I certainly felt faced with the unknown. My undergraduate university had offered no courses in Native literature and I knew very little about Native people outside Labrador. I went looking for critical approaches, and, when I encountered the assumptions that I described above, I fully accepted them. I therefore began my dissertation with a clear vision: I would show how Native humour subverts the dominant society through satirical portraits of "the whiteman." Essentially, I created a fairy tale of the struggle between the good (Native literature) and the bad (dominant and oppressive white society). Accepting the critical status quo, I put aside my own experiences, which told me that, at least among the Labrador Métis, the situation was much more complicated.

Around this time, I was also taking graduate courses in which the theoretical tone was definitely poststructural and postmodern. In these courses, I was taught to question and to break down social constructions and categories and I gradually began to doubt the accuracy of concepts such as "Native" and "Resistance." I read a number of influential works which take apart cultural categories in general or popular ideas of "Nativeness" in particular, such as Roland Barthe's *Mythologies*, Hobsbawm and Ranger's *The Invention of Tradition*, Terry Goldie's *Fear and Temptation* and Daniel Francis's *The Imaginary Indian*. My perspective was also influenced by other critics who take a postmodern approach to Native literature, such as Sheila Rabillard, Robert Nunn, and Gerald Vizenor. I began to believe, as I argued above, that the notion of a culturally and politically unified Native literature was a limiting one, created largely by forces within the academy. I therefore altered my approach to my dissertation, putting aside the idea that there is a distinctively "Native humour" that represents a single political stance. Instead, I began to explore "Nativeness" as a construction, arguing that Native writers use humour to variously create, negotiate, and challenge the notion of Native identity. This was the stage at which I had arrived when I delivered the conference paper that I mentioned earlier, entitled "'Native Literature' without 'Native Identity'?"

In that conference paper, I asked, "What aspects of the writing are we missing and which writers are we neglecting when we look *only* through the lens of 'Native literature'?" Later, however, thinking about that question, I realized that my work generally did not explore those neglected aspects and writers. Rather I was caught in a critical holding pattern, circling continually around questions of identity and authenticity. Is this "Native" or not? Is there any such thing as "Native?" How does this writer challenge or confirm concepts of "Nativeness?" I began to suspect that these issues were keeping me from engaging in myriad other critical possibilities. In fact, *American Indian Quarterly* has stopped accepting articles on identity issues for just this reason. The problem was that I was working with a group of texts classified as Canadian Native literature while at the same time challenging the relevance and accuracy of that grouping. As a result, I was stuck, hovering self-consciously rather than getting down to business.

Was it time, I wondered, to throw out the category of "Native Literature" altogether and to find new categories and new approaches? As I thought it over, I recognized several problems with such a dismissal. First of all and on the most pragmatic level, I was by this time entirely invested in the Native Literature category – studying it, writing about it, and applying for jobs in it. This institutionalization of the category is a powerful force. But there are also other, less self-serving, reasons not to dispose of this way of grouping the literature. In short, the "Native Literature" category can be both useful and descriptive. It is useful in that it provides solidarity and visibility to Native writers. In a situation where literature and literary criticism are dominated by non-Native perspectives, there is a need to gather Native voices in order to disrupt that status quo. In this sense, the term "Native literature" can be useful within a larger movement that seeks to strengthen Native nations, sometimes through a pan-Native commonality of purpose. Osage scholar Robert Warrior pushes for the careful consideration of how our critical categories can work with the goals of Native peoples, arguing that we must "go beyond merely invoking categories and engage in careful exploration of how those categories impact the process of sovereignty." (qtd. in Cook-Lynn *Why* 89) Indeed, for many scholars, especially perhaps Native scholars, we cannot separate academic work and activism.

Some may argue that we should not choose to use literary categories because of a particular political agenda, that we should be objective. But the truth is that there is no literary criticism that does not have a political agenda – it is just a matter of how well it is hidden. In particular, as Vine Deloria points out, "There has never been an objective point of view regarding Indians and there never will be." (66) Remembering this, we must give the deconstruction of the category of "Native" some careful scrutiny as well. Dismissing the notion of a coherent Native tradition can be a reactionary effort by non-Native scholars to hold onto intellectual authority in the face of challenges from Native people. (Deloria 66-68) Abenaki poet Cheryl Savageau concisely criticizes the academic deconstruction of Native traditions: "It's just now, when we are starting to tell our stories that suddenly there is no truth. It's a big cop-out as far as I'm concerned.... If everybody's story is all of a sudden equally true, then there is no guilt, no accountability, no need to change anything." (qtd in Womack 3)

But we need not look only to political agendas and strategies in order to justify or criticize the use of the Native literature category. The term also has descriptive potential. While, as I suggested earlier, the term may obscure many aspects of the literature, it reveals others. It is not appropriate to reject the category before scholars have even begun to understand the distinctive qualities of that body of literature. Most criticism of Native literature has been so focussed on issues of resistance and subversion that little attention has been paid to what might be unique in Native literature. As Agnes Grant writes, "Western culture has long paid lip service to the 'different' Native world view but little attempt has been made to understand what this might be." (113-114)

A number of scholars are now working to understand and to document this Native worldview - which has also been called "indigenous knowledge," "aboriginal metaphysics," "native philosophy," etc. For instance, Robert Warrior has traced intellectual traditions among Native writers and activists. Craig Womack has documented a long Creek literary tradition. Elizabeth Cook-Lynn has described a tradition of Native literary nationalism. Dennis McPerson and J. Douglas Rabb have worked to define a Native philosophical tradition. Marie Battiste and Sakej Henderson have worked together to bring Native ways of knowing and thinking into legal and academic institutions. As I read the careful work of these and other scholars, I came to the conclusion that it is not time to get rid of the term "Native literature." On the contrary, it is time to carefully examine the literature, not primarily in opposition to white society, but on its own terms. This means looking at the literature with an eye, not only to Western theory, but to "Native theory" as well. When scholars have looked at "Native traditions" in Native literature, they have too often looked only for easily pinpointed objects, spirits, figures, stories and ceremonies. But when we consider "Native theory," we must look at "Native traditions" as active, complex, and fully developed ways of seeing and interacting with the world. Looking at the literature on its own terms also means looking beyond a few popular books that have been published in English in the last two decades. Native people have been creating literatures for thousands of years. Surely this history offers a multitude of approaches to Native literature.

Not surprisingly, having re-thought the significance of "Native literature," I once again found myself re-envisioning my dissertation. Putting aside the questioning of Native identity, I decided to closely examine what the literature did have in common. I wrote about the use of humour in Native literature in terms of distinctively Native approaches to using language, witnessing to trauma, and reconciling to change. This research direction was exciting, offering ways into the complexity of Native literature that I had seen little discussed within the field. But I was still not satisfied, still worrying about homogenizing, idealizing, labelling, or ghettoizing the writings of Native people. As a result, my dissertation suffers from a split personality, pulled back and forth between understanding the distinctive Aboriginal quality of the literature and resisting any over-simplifying conclusions. At this point, I have resolved that the best approach to Native literature may lie in a balance between these two forces. This is a balance, not so much between construction and deconstruction, but between similarity and difference. There is a deep value in looking at the shared history and perspectives of Native people on their own terms. But this move should be balanced, not by deconstruction of Native knowledge, but by careful attention to the diversity of Native people, their particular complexities whether they be individual, tribal, regional, political, etc. Such specificity, which is often missing in criticism of Native literature, can give content and meaning to our broader work on Native people. In trying to maintain this balance, we are following what the thirty elders and spiritual leaders who collaborated on *The Sacred Tree* called one of the principles of a Native worldview:

"There are two kinds of change. The coming together of things ... and the coming apart of things ... Both of these kinds of changes are necessary." (Bopp 27)

Moving towards greater specificity in the study of Native literature means two things: first, being more specific in the scope of our research; and second, being more specific about our reasons for doing our work. I will start by suggesting five ways in which the first kind of specificity might be moved towards:

1. Critics need to extensively study individual Canadian Native writers, their styles, visions, and influences, recognizing that the writers are unique and not only products of "groupness." Too often, we try to lump together extremely different Native writers. Fortunately, there are new and upcoming book-length works on single authors, such as Cheryl Suzack's critical edition of Beatrice Culleton Mosionier's *In Search of April Raintree* and Percy Walton and Jennifer Andrews' forthcoming book on Thomas King.
2. There is, of course, a place for studies of Native literary traditions and movements, but such studies need not attempt to cover all Native people. There is a need for studies of tribal literary traditions. For example, examining Cree literature would allow a close look at how the literature is informed by the Cree language and by very specific historical circumstances, tribal norms, traditional stories, etc. Gregory Sarris's *Keeping Slug Woman Alive,* which focuses on Pomo-Miwoc traditions, and Craig Womack's *Red on Red,* which examines Creek literature, illustrate the significant insights that can arise from taking a tribal approach to Native literature. Of course, there are also other, non-tribal traditions that could be explored. For instance, there is a strong community of Native artists and writers in Toronto. What movements and traditions are they creating among themselves?
3. Moving towards the study of particular groups of Native writers logically leads to a further step: studying the language(s) of those writers. Many Native writers speak a Native language and many who do not are still influenced, aesthetically and politically, by their ancestral language. Native literature, even when written primarily in English,

persistently grapples with the usage or non-usage of Native languages. Yet, as far as I know, there are currently no literary critics who draw on knowledge of Native languages to read contemporary Native literature. Such knowledge would open up a world of literature, stories, and ways of speaking and thinking about the literature and the world that are not available in English. Furthermore, understanding Native languages would probably add greatly to our understanding and appreciation of the distinctive textures and rhythms of Native literature in English.

4. First languages are just one form of Native knowledge that can help readers to understand Native literature. As I suggested above, rather than seeing Native people as "objects of knowledge," we need to see them as producers of theories, philosophies and interpretations. A number of scholars are working to record and publish forms of Indigenous knowledge, but much of it is still not written down. So, literary critics need to be willing to talk about their work to people in various Native communities - not as "sources" but as critics, partners, and leaders.
5. Finally, work needs to be done on the reader reception of Native literature. Many critics working on Native literature are self-reflexive about their own readerly position. However, I would presume that there are differences between the reading practices of literary critics and those of non-professional readers. As Janice Radway discovered in her ethnography of readers of romance novels, the predictions of scholars on how other readers read is often very different than what the readers themselves say they are doing. Jonathan Rose calls the lack of attention to this difference the "receptive fallacy": "the critic assumes that whatever the author put into the text—or whatever the critic chooses to read into that text—is the message that the common reader receives, without studying the responses of any actual reader other than the critic himself." (49) The obvious solution to this problem, and the one suggested by Radway and Rose, is to undertake sociological or historical studies of reading practices, using such techniques as questionaires, interviews, examination of sales records, etc. No such study of readers of Native literature

> exists, but such research would help in understanding the growing popularity and appeal of this literature by answering some important questions. Who is reading Native literature? Which authors and genres are they reading? How are they reading? What do they expect and/or like in the literature? Does their reading change their views of Native people? How might reading practices, attitudes and preferences vary from one community to another?

These research directions would be time-consuming and many of them require that we move our research outside the library, a perhaps uncomfortable or inconvenient possibility. We may, for instance, feel that we do not have time to study Native languages or feel uncertain about how to access oral sources. For such reasons, it can be tempting to carry on in a more established approach to Native literature. But in order to make clear and ethical decisions about what kind of work we should do, it is important that we also move towards another kind of specificity. Scholars working on Native literature need to get specific about why we do what we do. By this, I do not mean the quick positioning of one's race and gender that has become conventional in the field. I am talking about something more revealing. I believe that critics need to be more open about their assumptions, desires, and purposes in studying Native literature.

First of all, critics need to be honest about their fundamental critical assumptions. What is our guiding theory? How are we defining our terms and categories? What do we believe is the purpose of "Native Literature?" But these questions are inevitably connected to deeper questions about the goals of our research. We all do research because of a combination of pragmatic and idealistic goals. But, when we write, we tend to cover up these goals, rendering them invisible. We often make it sound as though we do our work out of pure critical curiosity. But even this stance is not without problems; as Devon Mihesuah puts it, "Researchers should not look upon Indians as curiosities." ("Suggested" par. 25) In reality, however, our goals are often much more mundane. We may be trying to get a publication or a job, find a "hot topic," or fit a theoretical fashion. We may be trying to work within limited time or resources. As I have suggested in this essay, such goals form and often limit how we choose to work. In developing our careers, we may have to make difficult choices between prestige and integrity. For instance, the University of Saskatchewan, where I was recently hired, is very progressive in its approach to Aboriginal peoples. It has stated its objective to "build partnerships with Aboriginal communities," has a relatively large number of Native students, has Native law and education programs, and supports large interdisciplinary research projects on decolonizing the university and valuing Indigenous knowledge. According to Mohawk scholar Patricia Monture-Angus, it is the best university in Canada in which to be a Native person. And yet the University of Saskatchewan is chronically underfunded and consistently falls near the bottom of the *Maclean's* ranking of research universities. Such situations inevitably impact the career and research choices and possibilities of those of us working in the area of Native literature.

In addition to such pragmatic considerations, most of us also have critical ideals. Those of us studying Native literature may see ourselves as opening the university to wider range of voices, offering a forum for under-recognized ideas, challenging canons, understanding the Aboriginal basis of this land and country, or helping Native people. While these goals sound admirable, they also need to be fully articulated and scrutinized. For instance, do we call for the inclusion of diverse and marginalized voices, all the while writing in a language that effectively excludes those outside the academic institution? Does the inclusion of Aboriginal knowledge in the university benefit Native people or does it just give the university the appearance of diversity? In challenging canons, are we creating new ones? Can the seeking of knowledge be a kind of cultural theft? If we see ourselves as helping Native people, have we asked them what kind of help they want? Does this stance of "helping" contribute to our own sense of authority?

Only when we admit our own involvement in forces of legitimization, canonization, and institutionalization can we really begin to challenge the way that such forces can be limiting or unfair. As Len Findlay said in a recent talk, "Like turtles, we can only move when we stick our necks out." Open and public discussion is necessary because, in many cases, to change our work we must also change institutional expectations and policies.

For those people and institutions who are unwilling to change their practice with regards to Native people, I would suggest that they consider how radically Native people have had to adapt because of the European invasion. In the realm of education in particular, more and more Native people are moving through the Western education system, going to university (often moving away from their communities to do so), and dealing with unfamiliar expectations and values. Surely universities can learn something from this example of adaptability and come to value Native languages, experiences and theories.

So where has the thinking process that I have described in this essay left me? Not surprisingly, back where I started. Having completed my dissertation, I have come back to my study on the Labrador Métis that has been sitting on the shelf for several years. For my next research project, I am planning to write a history of the Labrador Métis Nation through our traditions of storytelling and autobiography. I come back to this topic with more than the personal interest with which I first devised it. I now believe that I will be able to work in a more grounded way on "Native literature" with a clearer sense of where I come from. Furthermore, this project has a concrete purpose. In recent years, the federal and provincial governments have openly refused to recognize the existence of the Labrador Métis Nation and the legitimacy of our land claim. This refusal continues despite the acknowledgement by the *Report of the Royal Commission on Aboriginal Peoples* (Vol 4.3.1) that the Labrador Métis are an "Aboriginal people" with "the social and geographic distinctiveness, the self-consciousness and the cohesiveness of a people, along with an unmistakably Aboriginal relationship to the natural environment." Because of this lack of government recognition, the Labrador Métis have no say in, for instance, the building of a highway through our people's traplines and communities or the distribution of tourist fishing and hunting licences on our land. As part of our struggle for recognition, the Labrador Métis Nation has been working to record our people's history and relationship to the land. I plan to work with the Labrador Métis people to contribute to the community's goals.

In this essay, I have tried to model the openness and self-awareness for which I am calling. It has been a difficult process, requiring that I give away a lot of authority. I have been afraid of not being taken seriously or of making people angry. And I have been worried about stating the obvious. After all, the questions that I have raised are not new ones. We all know that critical self-awareness is a good thing, that the personal is political, that critical categories are partial and exclusive, and that literary criticism is far from innocent. Nevertheless, I think that these are issues that need to be continually discussed as the study of Native literature works to establish itself. When I began graduate studies in Native literature, I needed to hear (but didn't) some open discussion of the pressures, temptations, pitfalls, and possibilities involved in working in this area. And so that is what I have tried, drawing on my admittedly limited experiences, to provide here.

Note

[1] I would like to thank all the participants in the Roundtable on Native Literature hosted by the Canadian Association for Commonwealth Literature and Language Studies at the Congress of Social Sciences and Humanities in Edmonton last year. Their openness and thoughtfulness about the study of Native literature initiated my thinking about this paper. I would also like to thank Stephanie McKenzie whose conversations with me about this essay helped me clarify my ideas and encouraged me to be brave.

Works Cited

Barthes, Roland. *Mythologies*. Trans. Annette Lavers. London: J. Cape, 1972.

Battiste, Marie, ed. *Reclaiming Indigenous Voice and Vision*. Vancouver: UBC P, 2000.

Bopp, Judic et al. *The Sacred Tree*. 3rd ed. Wilmot, WI: Lotus Light, 1989.

Chow, Rey. *Ethics After Idealism: Theory-Culture-Ethnicity-Reading*. Theories of Contemporary Culture Series. Bloomington: Indiana UP, 1998.

Cook-Lynn, Elizabeth. "American Indian Intellectualism and the New Indian Story." *Natives and Academics: Researching and Writing about American Indians.* Ed. Devon A. Mihesuah. Lincoln: U of Nebraska P, 1998. 111-138.

- - -. *Why I Can't Read Wallace Stegner and Other Essays: A Tribal Voice.* Madison: U of Wisconsin P, 1996.

Deloria, Vine. "Comfortable Fictions and the Struggle for Turf: An Essay Review of The Invented Indian: Cultural Fictions and Government Policies." *Natives and Academics: Researching and Writing about American Indians.* Ed. Devon A. Mihesuah. Lincoln: U of Nebraska P, 1998. 65-83.

Fee, Margery. "Aboriginal Writing in Canada and the Anthology as Commodity." *Native North America: Critical and Cultural Perspectives.* Ed. Renée Hulan. Toronto: ECW, 1999. 135-155.

- - -. "What Use is Ethnicity to Aboriginal Peoples in Canada?" *Canadian Review of Comparative Literature* 22.3-4 (Sept-Dec 1995): 683-691.

Findlay, Len. "Decolonizing the University." Northrop Frye Professorship Lecture, University of Toronto. 28 March 2001.

Francis, Daniel. *The Imaginary Indian: The Image of the Indian in Canadian Culture.* Vancouver: Arsenal Pulp, 1992.

Goldie, Terry. *Fear and Temptation: The Image of the Indigene in Canadian, Australian, and New Zealand Literatures.* Montreal: McGill-Queen's UP, 1993.

Goldie, Terry and Daniel David Moses. "Preface: Two Voices." *An Anthology of Canadian Native Literature in English.* Eds. Daniel David Moses and Terry Goldie. Toronto: Oxford UP, 1992. xii-xxii.

Grant, Agnes. "Native Drama: A Celebration of Native Culture." *Contemporary Issues in Canadian Drama.* Ed. Per Brask. Winnipeg: Blizzard, 1995. 103-15.

Hobsbawm, Eric and Terence Ranger, eds. *The Invention of Tradition.* Cambridge: University Press, 1983.

Jannetta, A.E. "Anecdotal Humour in Maria Campbell's *Halfbreed.*" *Journal of Canadian Studies* 31.2 (Summer 1996): 62-74.

King Thomas. Interview with Hartmut Lutz. *Contemporary Challenges: Conversations with Canadian Native Authors.* Saskatoon: Fifth House, 1991. 107-116.

Labrador Métis Nation Homepage. www.labmetis.org

LaRocque, Emma. Preface to *Writing the Circle: Native Women of Western Canada.* Eds. Jeanne Perrault and Sylvia Vance. Edmonton: NeWest, 1990.

Maracle, Lee. "Oratory: Coming to Theory." *by, for and about: Feminist Cultural Politics.* Ed. Wendy Waring. Toronto: Women's Press, 1994. 235-240.

McPherson, Dennis H. and J. Douglas Rabb. *Indian from the Inside: A Study in Ethno-Metaphysics.* Thunder Bay, Ont: Centre for Northern Studies, Lakehead University, 1993.

Mihesuah, Devon A, ed. *Natives and Academics: Researching and Writing about American Indians.* Lincoln: U of Nebraska P,1998.

- - -. "Suggested Guidelines for Institutions With Researchers Who Conduct Research on American Indians." Available: http://jan.ucc.nau.edu/~mihesuah/Research_guidelines_for_sc.html

Miki, Roy. *Broken Entries: Race, Subjectivity, Writing: Essays.* Toronto: Mercury, 1998.

Monture-Angus, Patricia. Personal communication. February 2001.

Mosionier, Beatrice Culleton. *In Search of April Raintree.* Critical Edition. Ed. Cheryl Suzack. Winnipeg: Portage and Main, 1999.

Nunn, Robert. "Hybridity and Mimicry in the Plays of Drew Hayden Taylor." *Essays on Canadian Writing* 65 (Fall 1998): 95-120.

Rabillard, Sheila. "Absorption, Elimination, and the Hybrid: Some Impure Questions of Gender and Culture in the Trickster Drama of Tomson Highway." *Essays in Theatre Etudes Theatrales* 12.1 (Nov. 993): 3-27.

Radway, Janice. *Reading the Romance: Women, Patriarchy, and Popular Literature.* 2nd ed. Chapel Hill: U of North Carolina P, 1991.

Report of the Royal Commission on Aboriginal Peoples.

Available: http://www.indigenous.bc.ca/rcap.htm

Rose, Jonathan. "Rereading the English Common Reader: A Preface to A History of Audiences." *Journal of the History of Ideas* (1992): 47-70.

Sarris, Gregory. *Keeping Slug Woman Alive: A Holistic Approach to American Indian Texts.* Berkeley: U of California P, 1993.

Smith, Linda Tuhiwai. *Decolonizing Methodologies: Research and Indigenous Peoples.* New York: Zed, 1999.

Sollor, Werner. *Beyond Ethnicity: Consent and Descent in American Culture.* New York: Oxford UP, 1986.

Taylor, Drew Hayden. *AlterNatives.* Burnaby, B.C.: Talonbooks, 2000.

Warrior, Robert and Paul Chaat Smith. *Like a Hurricane: The Indian Movement from Alcatraz to Wounded Knee.* New York: New Press, 1996.

Warrior, Robert. *Tribal Secrets: Recovering American Indian Intellectual Traditions.* Minneapolis: U of Minnesota P, 1994.

Womack, Craig. *Red on Red: Native American Literary Separatism.* Minneapolis: U of Minnesota P, 1999.

"Fringes, Imposture, and Connection: Armand Garnet Ruffo's *Grey Owl: The Mystery of Archie Belaney* and "Communitist" Literature"

Jonathan R. Dewar

Growing up, I knew two Indians, or, rather, I knew of two representations of Indians. One was my great-grandfather, Alderic Groslouis, a full-blooded Huron-Wendat, who died shortly before I was born. The other was Grey Owl, and I knew him in the same way that I knew my great-grandfather: through photographs, most notably, in Grey Owl's case, the famous Karsh photo that hung in the Chateau Laurier's Karsh collection. My family had many pictures of my great-grandfather. Newspaper articles too, for he had a somewhat public profile as Prime Minister Louis St. Laurent's personal aide, the Indian who accompanied a Prime Minister around the world. The photographs were, as my family often said, unmistakably Indian; he was, in fact, lovingly referred to as the Cigar Store Indian whenever someone attempted to describe him without the aide of those photographs. But I never saw the Cigar Store Indian in Grandpa Groslouis, and not, I hasten to add, because of any advanced sense of political correctness. It was quite simple, really. He was always wearing a three piece suit in those photos. A wholly costumed Grey Owl, on the other hand, seemed truly unmistakably Indian despite the fact that I knew he was not. He fit the stereotype, desirable though it may have been, and looked just like the museum Indians who, as Paula Gunn Allen says, "exist, frozen in time, as nostalgic accompaniments of [North] American flora and fauna." (12) Grandpa Groslouis just did not fit the bill for me as a child. I was, without knowing it, living up to Louis Owens' assessment that "In order to be recognized, to claim authenticity in the world—in order to be seen at all—the Indian must conform to an identity imposed from the outside." (12-13) So, as Gerald Vizenor said, the "real" Indian is the "absolute fake" (4), and I was, and perhaps still am, guilty of idealizing a relationship to my heritage rather than seeing what Huron-Wendat scholar Georges Sioui has called "the persistence of a particular ideological portrait" (31), that is, the "Amerindian's singular awareness of their duty to remain, essentially, Amerindian." I confused both "costumes" as definitively limiting, and did not consider how my great-grandfather saw himself, despite the three piece suit.

Without making too strong a point, I guess you could say that is when my fascination with the tenuous nature of connection to culture and heritage began. Of course, I now use terms like authenticity, imposture, and identity, and discuss the notion of the ideal Indian in much more academic terms. But there was a time when I did not know those terms even existed, a time when I naturally turned to representations of Natives in literature and pop culture to fill in the blanks. And this is precisely the point. Whose representations most accurately taught me how to reconcile the desire to connect with the heritage of my maternal family and the realization that, though a fraud, Grey Owl had made the transition I could only imagine? He was my ideal, in a sense, and I understood him as best one can a historical figure. Imagine my surprise when years later, though several years ago now, I read Robert Kroetsch's *Gone Indian* and found myself relating to Jeremy Sadness in his quest to "go Grey Owl" rather than Indian. The complexities of such a relationship began to crystalize and I recalled the many instances throughout my childhood when the white-man-adopted-by-Indians motif rang truer than what I would now describe as the sort of back-to-the-reserve story of re-connection as opposed to simple connection. And so I began to examine representations of Natives from a mixed-blood perspective and found that the above dichotomy – adopting or being adopted by a community versus a more legitimate (re)connection – was not at all unique. If anything, much of the literature and critical accompaniment that I was now engaged with as a student of Native Literature dealt with similar themes of identity, authenticity, and cultural specificity.

Native Literature is, of course, an enormous and fast-growing field of study, and this paper does not contain all the answers. What it does, though, is place itself within the much larger question of the role of Native literature, picking up on Jace Weaver's notion of "communitism ... a combination of the words 'community' and 'activism'" because literature "is communitist to the extent that it has a proactive commitment to Native community" (xiii). Weaver's notion is useful here because, as a person of mixed-blood heritage, I have often turned to literature for answers as much as for entertainment. Part of this may indeed be akin to non-Natives' inexhaustible fascination with all things Native (or at least the comfortable stereotypes). But when that fascination is also a part of one's legitimate attempts to learn as much about one's heritage as possible, the fascination ceases to be simply voyeuristic, paternalistic, or appropriative. Instead, texts become utilitarian in the sense that they provide a way in, a way to explore the boundaries of community. This is not to say that all Native literature serves this purpose, but rather that many readers do approach certain texts with an eye to explore connection. As such, I will narrow my focus considerably within to discuss a text that serves just such a purpose, Ojibway poet Armand Garnet Ruffo's *Grey Owl: The Mystery of Archie Belaney,* which just happens to have as its cover image the same famous Karsh photo of a solemn looking Archie Belaney that I mentioned above.

The 90's saw a proliferation of critical and popular texts and other representations dealing with Grey Owl, Canada's most famous Indian impostor. We could add to that the fact that Archibald Stansfeld Belaney's Grey Owl was also, for a time, Canada's most famous Indian. That he was a fraud is not at all in question. It is the fraud, however, that gets most, if not all, the attention, as if, once unmasked, his Native "identity" could become secondary to the telling of his story as an impostor. In a recent article called "Too Good to be True," Christine Sismondo asks "Do Grey Owl's books and films deserve re-evaluation in light of his literary deception and appropriation of Native culture?" and alludes to the merits of his work despite his imposture. Similarly, the 1999 biopic *Grey Owl,* directed by Richard Attenborough, concentrates almost entirely on his fraud (when it isn't preoccupied with the love story) and his conservation work. However, that is, in many ways, the story. But the critical work being done on the "Grey Owl Syndrome" (35) as Margaret Atwood has termed it is mostly guilty of devaluing the Native aspect to his story. Carrie Dawson's "Never Cry Fraud: Remembering Grey Owl, Rethinking Imposture" actually goes so far as to say "The purpose of this paper is not to consider why Grey Owl represented himself as indigenous" (120) but, rather, to (re-)examine the imposture itself, and Dawson argues against further psychoanalyzing Belaney. But we should examine why he sought to represent himself as Native, and, more importantly, why others, particularly those with a tangible connection to the heritage, do so as well. Sismondo overlooks, despite a short discussion of Ruffo's *Grey Owl,* an important viewpoint: a Native viewpoint. Dawson claims that the "schematized image of the North [*in Grey Owl: The Mystery of Archie Belaney*] places Ruffo within a tradition of Canadian artists who reserve the Arctic as a stage for personal transformation." (130) But, the tradition to which Ruffo most importantly belongs is the tradition of literature written in English by Native and mixed-blood Native Canadian writers, a tradition within which Grey Owl's much acclaimed writing resided until his unmasking; though debunked as Native literature, that writing now resides within the larger canon of Canadian literature. This connection deserves more exploration as well, and, to date, only Ruffo's polyphonous long poem does this.

While this is a further blurring of an already formidable "grey" area, Ruffo's hint at possibilities is a worthwhile avenue for Native and non-Native scholars alike, but, most importantly, for those readers who turn to literature by Native and mixed-blood Native Canadians for insight into so-called Nativeness, to find a deeper connection to a culture they may be only tenuously connected to, wherein feelings of imposture are truly valid. This paper will explore the important role Grey Owl plays for readers looking to understand their own feelings of imposture when attempting to connect to some aspect of Native culture. Was Grey Owl the ideal Indian, or was it his ability to "go Native" that is the ideal for contemporary Native and mixed-blood Native Canadians? Or, is the message more akin to the repeated offer of kinship proffered by Natives in Ruffo's *Grey Owl*: "Dance with us as you can?"

It is appropriate that Ruffo's *Grey Owl: The Mystery of Archie Belaney* begins with two epigraphs, the first attributed to Grey Owl himself and the second to N. Scott Momaday, the influential Native American author and poet who was the first Native American to win the Pulitzer Prize for fiction. The Grey Owl epigraph from *Men of the Last Frontier* reads:

> The trail then is not merely a connecting link between widely distant points, it becomes an idea, a symbol of self sacrifice and deathless determination, an ideal to be lived up to, a creed from which none may falter.

The Momaday epigraph from *The Man Made of Words* reads:

> ... an Indian is an idea which a given man has of himself. And

> it is a moral idea, for it accounts for the way in which he reacts to other men and to the world in general. And that idea, in order to be realized completely, has to be expressed.

The epigraphs are an extra-textual hint of the influence the tradition of Native literature has had on Ruffo's writing. Using a narrative style similar to fellow Canadians Margaret Atwood, with *The Journals of Susanna Moodie,* and Michael Ondaatje, with *The Collected Works of Billy the Kid,* Ruffo reconstructs the story of Archie Belaney and asks what it means to be Indian. Ruffo's use of these two distinct influences combines successfully, albeit subtly, with the unique quality of his chosen subject matter. The prefacing poem that follows the two epigraphs forces the reader to consider exactly whose need to connect we are dealing with. Essentially, we must ask, why is Archie Belaney's need to recreate himself as an Indian made so important to both the narrator of that prefacing poem and the "you" it addresses, by its placement, and the placement of quotes from Grey Owl and Momaday, before the actual narrative of Belaney's need to connect?

Working with both archival record and the oral history of his own family's connection to Belaney, Ruffo re-constructs a historical figure in a text that is part fact, part fiction. Ruffo is a well educated writer of Ojibway heritage and his knowledge of the inherent schism between the oft overlooked Native perspective and the white, academic canons and methodologies of literature and historiography plays an important role in his choice of both his subject matter—the non-Native who passes himself off as Native—and the form it takes. Aware that a "harmony of perspectives exists within the cultural pluralism of Native America" (Wiget 2), Ruffo has taken a step outside of the Canadian literary tradition of Atwood's and Ondaatje's abovementioned texts as well as a step outside of the literary traditions of Native writers past and present to create a narrative that is unique in its perspective.

Grey Owl differs significantly from *The Journals of Susanna Moodie* and *The Collected Works of Billy the Kid* due to Ruffo's subtle subversion of a historically problematic genre: the Indian autobiography or biography. While clearly not autobiography, *Grey Owl* contains elements that resonate in a manner that

Atwood's and Ondaatje's autobiographical-izations cannot because this tradition is unique to the larger forum of Native literature, and precludes *Journals* and *Works* from being examined in the same context. Atwood's and Ondaatje's books are pure fiction (with the odd exception in *Works*) with each respective author giving the Moodie and Billy the Kid stories a fictionally autobiographical thrust. The autobiographical or first-person sections of *Grey Owl* are not all fictionalized in the manner of Atwood's Moodie and Ondaatje's Billy – some are in fact direct reproductions of archival material. Both *Journals* and *Works* purport to be creations by their "authors," making the texts objects unto themselves. Ruffo sets up no such writerly conceit. While he readily employs the actual writings of Belaney/Grey Owl and others, we are not meant to confuse *Grey Owl*, the object, as writing by Grey Owl or any other of the first person voices within the narrative. However, the prominence given to Grey Owl's writing in the first of the book's two epigraphs is meant to serve as a validation of his role as text-producer and rightfully places him "in the pantheon of nature writers ... with Henry David Thoreau, John Muir, Aldo Leopold, and Rachel Carson." (Brower 74) So while writings attributed to Belaney/Grey Owl play an important role, we should not treat the text in the same manner that the title of Atwood's *Journals* implies, and Ondaatje's *Works* to a lesser degree (by this I mean that the "Works" of the title are deliberately ambiguous and need not be read with the narrow focus of "Journals" to solely mean written works).

Ruffo's subversion of the Indian autobiography, while not necessarily overt to those unfamiliar with the history of Native literature as a distinct category, is evident on one basic level even before an engagement with the actual text. A quick glance at the author's bio and photo immediately following the narrative's close allows one to pick up on the fact that in this case the author is Native and his subject is non-Native. While Louis Owens has been critical of this extra-textual departure with regard to reviews of his own novels, saying "Do we really need to go beyond 'END' and consider photograph and bio blurb to decide the authenticity of a fiction" (14), I argue that in this case it is a worthy exercise and one that adds, deliberately, to the flavour of the "mystery." The Native writing the story of the non-Native is an immediate send-up of the conventional early Indian biography, and, although Ruffo did not actually converse with Belaney for the book, he does employ excerpts from his journals and gives fictional voice to other undocumented events and so approximates what Arnold Krupat termed the "bi-cultural composite authorship" (262) or co-authoring of the Indian autobiography. While both Atwood's Moodie and Ondaatje's Billy were inhabitants of literary ages in which biography and autobiography were popular genres they were not subjected to the same kind of undeniable re-versioning that first-or second-hand Indian stories were subjected to as both Moodie and Billy existed within the margins of white culture and were not excluded from a literary tradition for this reason alone. While Moodie may have been marginalized due to gender and Billy may have opted for a life outside of lawful society, they were still part of the dominant culture. It is important to remember that the revisionist feminist movements that brought Moodie and other women writers to the canon have only very recently begun to similarly re-examine early biographical writings about and autobiographical writings "by" Native women. As well, Indianness was often seen as inherently lawless and immoral and was rarely mythologized as heroic—even outlaw hero—in the manner of Billy the Kid. More often than not, Indians served as fodder and were portrayed as a wooden cultural stereotype (literally in the case of the Cigar Store Indian), a situation that was revitalized by a movement from the page to the screen. While it is true that the Indian was in some ways romanticized as the noble savage, Native peoples did not have their own voice with which to create their own image. We need only look to the still prevalent *Dances With Wolves* motif of white protagonist adopted as Indian to serve as Native voice.

The Indian autobiography has essentially been ignored by literary scholars because, as Krupat notes, "[they] have been presented by the whites who have written them as more nearly 'scientific' documents of the historical or ethnographic type than as 'literary' works" (261) and do not conform to the accepted definition of autobiography as a narrative of a person's life written by that person. Krupat correctly notes that the Indian autobiography is a contradiction in terms. They are "collaborative efforts, jointly produced by some white who translates, transcribes, compiles, edits, interprets, polishes, and ultimately determines the 'form' of the text in writing, and by an Indian who is its 'subject' and whose 'life' becomes the 'content' of the 'autobiography' whose title may bear his 'name'." (262) On a very simple level, since the methodology of autobiography and even biography is limited to the telling of a story, so to speak, the distance between the white culture's definition of history and a Native definition of history in so far as it applies to these genres should not be too great. After all, the exchange of personal "histories" is an integral part of Native cultural interaction. For example, a traditional greeting ceremony between the Mohawk and Ojibway nations would necessarily involve the exchange of stories that make up each respective group's history. However, because Native cultures do not see history as necessarily progressive and linear or "evolutionary, teleological, or progressive" (261) and did not traditionally engage in a written tradition of recording stories as empirical data, the Indian "autobiography" is flawed at its roots because it cannot convey the necessary sense of mutability of story and even personal history. Krupat's essay concerns itself with the importance of treating the traditional Indian autobiography as literature rather than science and it is an important point. His principle of bi-cultural composite authorship at least acknowledges that there was a Native voice despite its diminishment through translation and transcription and the culturally biased notion that the story of one's life as told by oneself (whether independently or in conjunction with another) can be used as historical fact. Whether white or Native, though, the voice can only approximate a perspective.

This issue of voice is an important one to Ruffo's *Grey Owl* because Archie Belaney as Grey Owl was the Native voice, at least to the White world on whose fringes Indians remained. His was an accepted point of view. And he was not truly Native. He was essentially the embodiment of Krupat's bi-cultural composite authorship except that he did not work in conjunction with someone who actually belonged to the culture he spoke of – unless we count his relationship with Ruffo's family at Biscotasing and his numerous relationships with women of Native heritage. His life as Grey Owl had no ethnographical or anthropological significance because it was a fiction. As history, too, it is flawed because it necessarily demands that one choose a perspective. In this way, Belaney/Grey Owl, despite the openness with which his fraud is treated by Ruffo, is treated historically in much the same way as many famous Native North Americans. Consider the stories of Geronimo, Sitting Bull, or Cochise, whose words Belaney memorized as a child. ("Influences" 2) Only until recently with the advent of revisionist history movements, the kind that would see the influential Canadian poet Duncan Campbell Scott as a racist assimilationist and necessitate a re-examination of his poetry (specifically his "Indian" poems) in this light, have these stories been told from a Native perspective.

As revisionist history can be employed irresponsibly and the messages these revisions send can be contradictory, confusing, or misleading, a situation exists in many cases in which different, sometimes opposing, camps are formed with one side adamantly defending its position and deriding its opponents'. Even Atwood's *Journals* and Ondaatje's *Works*, those two canonical precursors to the form of Ruffo's narrative, can be seen to operate within the parameters of revisionism. While there was considerable scandal concerning Belaney's unmasking ("Since the death of Grey Owl a remarkable conflict of opinion has arisen over his parentage, particularly regarding his Indian blood" ("London Times, April 21, 1938" Ruffo 207)), he has been treated relatively kindly by history, even by those who insist on concentrating on his ruse. Consider the excerpts from news reports that Ruffo closes with: "The chances are that Archie Belaney could not have done nearly such effective work for conservation of wildlife under his own name. It is an odd commentary, but true enough" (*Ottawa Citizen*, April 20, 1938); "What, after all does his ancestry matter? The essential facts about his life are not in dispute, for as a conservation officer under the Canadian Government, and as a lecturer and broadcaster in Great Britain, he worked unceasingly for the protection of wildlife" (*Liverpool Daily Post*, April 21, 1938); "His attainments as a writer and naturalist will survive and when in later years our children's children are told of the strange masquerade—if it was a masquerade—their wonder and their appreciation will grow." (*Winnipeg Tribune*, April 23, 1938) This last passage is particularly telling and no surprise that Ruffo ends with it. It is surprising, however, that the conservative *Winnipeg Tribune*, like the *Ottawa Citizen* and *London Times*, should justify his fraud at all, but not surprising that they do so in that manner. His deception is acceptable, they imply, because it was for a good cause. Only the *Winnipeg Tribune* alludes to what Ruffo has similarly been alluding to all along: "if it was a masquerade," or, more succinctly put, if it was simply a masquerade. Now, of course, this passage has been taken out of context and the original did not have the benefit of some sixty years of hindsight, but the reference to "children's children" is important. Ruffo is one of these children as it was his grandparents' families that "adopted" Belaney. However, the newspaper article's reference to children was likely to those of its white readership and not inclusive of Natives. Throughout, Ruffo has subverted this and has made the last line a link to the Grey Owl epigraph that opens the book. Within the context of its original, this reference to "the Trail" is a concrete one, although it is certainly mystified by Grey Owl. Here, though, as the textual introduction to Ruffo's narrative, it must be read in a different light. The fact that the word connection appears here is immediately significant, and the trail as symbol of the need to find one's way between two points—places, states of being—resonates heavily within the text where this subject matter is more overtly verbalized. Even the use of the word "distant" carries weight. It echoes the distance Krupat notes exists between the white and Native cultures.

Andrew Wiget has said that before Momaday's Pulitzer Prize "called attention to literature written in English by Native Americans, the interest of scholars had been directed primarily to the traditional tribal oral literatures and had been carried on under the rubric of anthropology, linguistics or folklore" (1), which is essentially the same thing Krupat said with regard to the Indian autobiography. The two epigraphs are an embodiment of the movement from what Krupat and Wiget have both categorized as the marginalization of Native "literature" as something other than literature (although, as Weaver points out, "For too many non-Native scholars like Arnold Krupat and John Bierhorst, the only 'genuine' Indian literature consists of oral myths" and it "ceases to be Indian when it employs Western forms such as the short story or the novel (x)). Like Krupat's definition of the Indian autobiography, Grey Owl's life and writing live up to the notion that, as Bill Ashcroft et al write, "the text creates the reality of the Other in the guise of describing it [and] although [it] cannot operate as ethnography ... the literary text ... is not the site of shared mental experience and should not be seen as such." (59) However, Ruffo's narrative, despite spending little time on Belaney's life within the Native community at Biscotasing (in fact, the nearly three years that Belaney spends living with the Espaniels comprises only nine pages of the narrative) subtly works to show the kinship between Belaney's perception of the Indian and Ruffo's own. This is accomplished by Ruffo's piecing together of authentic Belaney/Grey Owl writings and fictionalizing others. Except in Belaney's own mind, the severity of his fraud is never truly played out within the narrative. One would assume that his fraud would elicit a much stronger response from both the Native and non-Native camps. Certainly, Great Britain should be embarrassed for permitting its Royal Family to entertain an impostor and Canada for its role in proffering Grey Owl as both a representative of Canada and its Native peoples. And one might expect Native groups to have voiced concern as it is made clear by Ruffo that "an Indian can tell who's Indian" ("John Tootoosis, 1936" 128).

The non-Native posing as Native is another tradition of sorts that spans many different media. From James Fenimore Cooper's *The Last of the Mohicans* to the film *Dances with Wolves,* the motif of the white man adopted by the Indians is a common one. Outside of this purely fictional arena there are historical accounts of this as well. Similarly, Belaney is not the only white man to have gained prominence after recreating himself as Native. In his introduction to *Coyote Country,* Arnold E. Davidson opens with the story of the young "colored" man from Winston-Salem, North Carolina, who went west to Southern Alberta and created the persona of Buffalo Child Long Lance, a chief of the Blackfoot. Long Lance went on to produce and star in films in the U.S. and, like Grey Owl, wrote and spoke of Native issues. Davidson makes the interesting point that his "achievement is undeniable but so is his fraud. His fraud is also understandable." (1) The reasons for an understanding are significantly different, though, from those offered in *Grey Owl*. Despite denying a "Negro" heritage, Long Lance's family was officially deemed "colored" and so, to escape one form of prejudice, he "falsely inscribed himself as a Native, as simply another (although preferred) 'Other.'" There was no such movement from one form of Other to an-Other for Belaney. Davidson also notes, however, that "Natives early recognized that Long Lance could not act or speak for them, for he simply did not know their ways." Ruffo takes a distinctly different direction with *Grey Owl* in two sections, both titled "John Tootoosis, 1936": "An Indian can tell who's Indian. / Grey Owl can't sing or dance. / But he's doing good / and when we meet / I call him brother" (128) and, later:

> We know Wa-Sha-Quon-Asin is not born of us, and we say nothing. For us it is of no importance. We do not waste our words but save them, because we know in this struggle of generations they are our strongest medicine. The man flies for us true and sharp, and we are thankful he has chosen our side. While we cheer, and the elders nod in approval, we can see the light shine in his face. We can see he feels better about himself than before. This is good. This is how it should be, to feel good about yourself and your duty in the honourable way. Wa-Sha-Quon-Asin, we say, dance with us, as you can. (145-6)

Many of the photographs that accompany Ruffo's narrative serve to fuel the debate over how Belaney managed to pass himself off as an Indian. In this sense, the book, with its famous Karsh photograph front cover, acts as object despite my earlier insistence that it not be treated as such. In this case, the front cover has a concrete, hands-on role to go with its more philosophical one. The photo appears remarkably "Indian." Even Belaney's famous blue eyes are obscured somewhat. The photo is genuine but its subject is not. To the photographer's eye and to the general public as well, however, Grey Owl was a genuine Indian and a return to this cover photograph reveals much after reading Ruffo's narrative. Consider the following lines from "The Thing About Photographs": "The thing is / everybody looks / the moment / as if that's all there is / or was / but there's more, he knows / only too well ... there is a click / and life goes on / in another direction. / the thing is / to get at that." (153) A good place to start and to return is that first photograph that seems so unmistakably Indian but is not. It was how the world once saw him, though, and how Ruffo would have us see him even before we engage with the text. Once inside, it is a different Belaney we see. The first photograph that accompanies the opening section is of a twelve year old Archie "posing stiffly in his dark woolen Sunday suit, / beside his Aunt's collie" ("An Imagined Country" 6). This photograph, too, has captured a moment that defines him and the poem; the voice of an unspecified narrator continues with "(Never does he suspect / that one day / you will catch him / like this.)" This idea of capture is important. A photograph such as this is one of the many ways in which he could be caught in his lie, but that does not seem to be quite what the narrator is getting at. The narrator asks us to do essentially the same thing I have suggested doing with the cover photograph: "look into the boy's eyes and ask yourself what you detect. / For this is the same boy who has the ability to see himself / (as you see him) clear across the ocean, all the way, into the heart of an imagined country called Canada."

The cover photograph also helps kick start the "Mystery" of the title. The meaning of "Mystery," like the meaning of Ondaatje's "Works," is deliberately ambiguous and in both cases a full and careful reading is needed to flush out any symbolic reading. It immediately refers to the historical scandal over the identity of Grey Owl but, when taken in the context of the narrative as Ruffo constructs it, it also alludes to that unsolved question of connection. Grey Owl's identity is never presented as a mystery to the reader. But what it meant to be known as Grey Owl is a mystery as Belaney died without having explicitly answered that question. So, the "autobiographical" answer to why Archie Belaney felt the need to become Grey Owl can only be speculated upon by both historians and writers such as Ruffo, or invented.

There is a third extra-textual section to *Grey Owl* as well. It is the untitled poem that follows Momaday's epigraph and contains the first example of Ruffo's use of the second-person, "you," which here seems not to be an address to the implied reader as within the text but rather to a writer, historian, storyteller who may or may not be Ruffo. It begins:

Archival memory.
Paper brittle as autumn, unearthed
across the desk, files scattered.
Words floating like smoke
smell of moccasins you are wearing
warming of the bright neon,
carrying you on
to the beginning
It is past midnight, everyone
is gone, except uniformed security
and you – What is it you are digging for
exactly? (iv)

This an interesting decision by Ruffo, who is otherwise absent in the tradition of the biographer or Krupat's autobiographer. Clearly, though, we are meant to see that there is a connection between author and subject. When that unspecified narrator I mentioned earlier says, "one day / you will catch him," the "you" could apply to anyone who has been introduced to the Archie Belaney/Grey Owl mystery and who has seen the photograph of Archie as a child, or to this persona in charge of putting together the story. Similarly, when Grey Owl says, "You in the audience who sit in expectation cannot know. / This fear, this inexorable fear, I take with me" ("Grey Owl, 1935" 104), the address could be to the implied reader of his journals or could be seen to be working on another level, with Ruffo, or the narrator of that prefacing poem, again addressing his implied reader.

The real, historical connection between Ruffo and Belaney and a story about Belaney's need to connect with the culture of Ruffo's heritage is a complicated and cleverly disguised examination of his own or any connection to cultural heritage. His ambiguous address to an unspecified "you" allows other like-minded readers to explore the troubling issue of connection to Native heritage. A truly cultural component exists, then, to Krupat's bi-cultural composite authorship. Ruffo has made the making of Belaney's story his story. As such, this narrative line can be seen as an example of Sioui's "autohistory," what Weaver defines as "the struggle to be self-defining" (44) in that Ruffo's use of Belaney's "history" as an exploration of a theme—connection to culture—speaks directly to a Native experience. The two epigraphs work to show the tradition of Native writer that Ruffo has ultimately become a part of and the prefacing poem essentially sets up everything after it as a justification of this journey of self discovery. Momaday again plays a significant role here. As part of that influential movement that brought the study of literature in English by writers of Native heritage to the acceptance of scholars and canon-makers, Momaday has continued to influence young writers like Ruffo. Momaday's 1976 *The Names*, a narrative that traces his mixed heritage roots, is a true Indian autobiography, not in the archaic sense that Krupat deconstructed, but in the sense we would expect: an autobiography by a writer of Native heritage. *The Names* encompasses so many of the movements still at work within contemporary Native literature and can be seen as one of the important building blocks to more experimental writings by new writers.

To many young people of Native heritage, Grey Owl was more successful as an authentic Indian than they could ever imagine themselves to be. And Grey Owl is part of Ruffo's heritage. It was his family that "adopted" Belaney. Why should he, or we, not look to Grey Owl as both professional and cultural example? The answer for both may be because Belaney was an impostor. But it is this notion of impostor that Ruffo deconstructs. That feeling of not belonging or being an impostor is a real and valid emotion that contemporary Native writers deal with regularly, particularly with regard to the mixing of white and Native cultures and the issue of mixed cultural backgrounds. Belaney himself is literally responsible for this mixing of heritages by siring numerous children with Native women. Ojibway playwright Drew Hayden Taylor's "Pretty Like a White Boy," a non-traditional "short story," deals with the difficulty of growing up as a status Indian who looked white:

> In this big, huge world, with all its billions and billions of people, it's safe to say that everybody will eventually come across personalities and individuals that will touch them in some peculiar yet poignant way. Individuals that in some way represent and help define who you are. I'm no different, mine

> was Kermit the Frog. Not just because Natives have a long tradition of savouring frogs' legs, but because of his music. If you all may remember, Kermit is quite famous for his rendition of 'It's Not Easy Being Green.' I can relate. If I could sing, my song would be 'It's Not Easy Having Blue Eyes in a Brown Eyed Village.' (436)

This should remind the reader of Belaney's own eyes and the ambiguity of the cover photograph. It reminds us of the tricks of perception.

We can look to Grey Owl as something more, if not noble then complex, than a man who simply passed himself off as something he was not because Ruffo deliberately includes sections that do so overtly. It is no coincidence that most of these justifications are Native voices, like the John Tootoosis sections mentioned earlier. By the end of Ruffo's narrative, Belaney's transformation is so much more than the simple addition of a name and costume. Belaney's own justifications for his actions are made understandable, perhaps even acceptable, because of Ruffo's early foreshadowing of the fact that the trail that leads to one's cultural heritage may not be as clear cut as historians and ethnographers of Grey Owl's day would make it. This "Trail" is an idea, the way "an Indian is an idea." in the words of both Grey Owl and Momaday, and in the way Ruffo's narrator finds a connection between his past and the story of a man who feels the need to create an Indian heritage. If Drew Hayden Taylor can look to Kermit the Frog to help understand why he feels like an outsider, then Grey Owl would seem to be a logical choice to fill that role for those people who feel a connection but cannot reconcile the feeling of being an outsider looking in. Here, at least, was a man who made these feelings into actions and the fact that he cannot truly claim a Native heritage is of less importance. The point seems to be that we are to find inspiration where we may and Ruffo has suggested we at least look to Archie Belaney/Grey Owl philosophically if not literally as an example of the accepting nature of Native culture. To return to Jace Weaver's notion of communitism, Native literature is a tool that teaches as much as it is an area of study to be taught, with both avenues deserving of equal weight within the academy. *Grey Owl* exists then as a tool as well, insofar as it allows for a complex issue to be approached on new terms.

Work Cited

Allen, Paula Gunn. *Off the Reservation: Reflections on Boundary-Busting, Border-Crossing Loose Canons*. Boston: Beacon Press, 1998.

Ashcroft, Bill, Gareth Griffiths, and Helen Tiffin. *The Empire Writes Back: Theory and Practice in Post-Colonial Literatures*. London: Routledge, 1989.

Atwood, Margaret. "The Grey Owl Syndrome." *Strange Things: The Malevolent North in Canadian Literature*. Oxford: Clarendon Press, 1995.

- - -. *The Journals of Susanna Moodie*. Toronto: Oxford UP, 1970.

Brower, Kenneth. "Grey Owl." *Atlantic Monthly*. Jan. 1990. 74-80.

Davidson, Arnold E. *Coyote Country: Fictions of the Canadian West*. Durham, NC: Duke UP, 1994.

Dawson, Carrie. "Never Cry Fraud: Remembering Grey Owl, Rethinking Imposture."*Essays on Canadian Writing*. 65 (Fall 1998).

Kroetsch, Robert. *Gone Indian*. Toronto: New Press, 1973.

Krupat, Arnold. "The Indian Autobiography: Origins, Type, and Function." *Smoothing the Ground: Essays on Native American Oral Literature*. Ed. Brian Swann. Berkeley: U California P, 1983. 261-282.

Momaday, N. Scott. *The Names*. New York: Harper & Row, 1976.

- - -. "The Man Made of Words." *The Remembered Earth: An Anthology of Contemporary Native American Literature*. Ed. Geary Hobson. Albuquerque: U New Mexico P, 1979. 162-173.

Moodie, Susanna. *Roughing it in the Bush*. London: Bentley, 1852.

Ondaatje, Michael. *The Collected Works of Billy the Kid*. Toronto: Anansi, 1970.

Owens, Louis. *Mixedblood Messages: Literature, Film, Family, Place*. Norman, OK: U Oklahoma P, 1998.

Ruffo, Armand Garnet. *Grey Owl: The Mystery of Archie Belaney*. Regina: Coteau Books, 1996.

Sioui, Georges. *For An Amerindian Autohistory*. Montreal: McGill-Queen's UP, 1992.

Sismondo, Christine. "Too Good To Be True." *The Literary Review of Canada.* 8:1 (February 2000).

Taylor, Drew Hayden. "Pretty Like a White Boy: The Adventures of a Blue Eyed Ojibway." *An Anthology of Canadian Literature in English.* Ed. Daniel David Moses and Terry Goldie. Toronto: Oxford UP, 1998. 436-439.

Vizenor, Gerald. *Manifest Manners: Postindian Warriors of Survivance.* Hanover, NH: Wesleyan UP/UP New England, 1991.

Weaver, Jace. *That the People Might Live: Native American Literatures and Native American Community.* New York: Oxford UP, 1997.

Wiget, Andrew. "The Study of Native American Literature: An Introduction." *Critical Essays on Native American Literature.* Boston: G.K. Hall & Co., 1985. 1-20.

Stories of Destruction and Renewal: Images of Fireweed in Autobiographical Fiction by Shirley Sterling and Tomson Highway

Deanna Reder

fire weed *n: a hardy perennial so called because it is the first growth to reappear in fire-scarred areas; a troublesome weed which spreads like wildfire invading clearings, bomb-sites, waste land and other disturbed areas.* (Silvera 2)

It is curious that Canadian First Nations autobiography has drawn little critical attention; there is no Canadian equivalent to David Brumble's *Native American Autobiography* or Arnold Krupat's *For Those Who Come After*. In works such as these it is generally conceded that in Native American studies, autobiography is a European invention that is adopted and modified by First Nations authors. (Brumble131; Krupat 10-15) Krupat argues that Indian autobiography ought to be seen "as a ground on which two cultures meet ... the textual equivalent of the frontier." (33) This metaphor is inadequate to describe Canadian First Nation's autobiographical texts (although, to be fair, Krupat looks primarily at texts that are at least fifty years old and in a different historical context). The image he suggests, however, is of two opposing forces, the dominant on one side, always advancing and the dominated on the other, barring the occasional uprising, in steady bloody retreat or tragic defeat. It is the familiar binary of the "Dominant", this time in covered wagons and cowboy clothes, and the "Other", with face paint and feathers. And like other binaries, these images alienate even further the "Other" as the hopelessly conquered against the unassailable conquerors, always defined in defeat by its opposite's success. It is difficult to use Krupat's metaphor without embedding within it all our associations of the frontier, many of them constructed around "cowboy and Indian" movies.

An adequate metaphor is required, especially as autobiography dominates Canadian Native literature. From seminal texts like Maria Campbell's *Halfbreed* (1973) and Lee Maracle's *Bobbi Lee: Indian Rebel* (1975), to more recent publications such as George Littlechild's *This Land is my Land* (1993) and Emma Minde's *Their Example Showed Me the Way* (1997), autobiography has continued to be a central genre in First Nations Literature in Canada. Works like Drew Hayden Taylor's *Funny You Don't Look Like One* (1998) – a collection of newspaper columns and occasional writing – and Rudy Wiebe and Yvonne Johnson's *Stolen Life. The Journey of a Cree Woman* (1998), a collaborative life story, are highly influenced by the genre.

Another variation of this are those works that contain large amounts of autobiographical detail but are published as fiction, works that could be called "autobiographical fiction."

These works inhabit an odd and blurred space where we recognize the author's life story in the narrative but do not recognize the main character's name. The most famous example is Beatrice Culleton's *In Search of April Raintree*. Kateri Damm, as one example, compares Maria Campbell's autobiographical *Halfbreed,* with Culleton's novel and declares that they both speak "from a personal, First Person, autobiographical perspective." (96) Helen Hoy probes further, discussing the problematic shift of Culleton from the function of author to that of "source of authentic life experience." (288)

I'd like to propose a metaphor to describe Native autobiography (including autobiographical fiction) in Canada, one without reference to the frontier, one without opposites; the First Nations autobiography ought to be seen as fireweed, the textual equivalent of the relentlessly enduring perennial that is first to reappear in earth, scarred by fire, ironically spreading "like wildfire". It is a striking, scrappy and troublesome weed that invades "clearings, bombsites, waste land and other disturbed areas." (Silvera 2) The fact that fireweed, as a metaphor, alludes to destruction, is fitting. Linda Tuhiwai Smith states, in *Decolonizing Methodologies: Research and Indigenous Peoples* (1999), that "Imperialism frames the indigenous experience. It is part of our story, our version of modernity. Writing about our experiences under imperialism and its more specific expressions of colonialism has become a significant project of the indigenous world." (19)

While Canadian Native autobiography grows out of many different, disturbed landscapes, beautiful and relentlessly enduring, its beauty does not celebrate the destruction of the fire but is undeniably the result of it. Think of Maria Campbell's *Halfbreed*. She writes in her introduction:

> Going home after so long a time, I thought that I might find again the happiness and beauty I had known as a child. But as I walked down the rough dirt road, poked through the broken old buildings and thought back over the years, I realized that I could never find that here. Like me the land had changed, my people were gone, and if I was to know peace I would have to search within myself. That is when I decided to write about my life. I am not very old, so perhaps

> one day, when I too am a granny, I will write more. I write this for all of you, to tell you what it is to be a Halfbreed woman in our country. I want to tell you about the joys and sorrows, the oppressing poverty, the frustrations and the dreams. (2)

The text itself then, is the fireweed, growing over the rough dirt roads, the once familiar but now estranged landscape. No longer does she need to return to the geographical sites of her childhood because she can make sense of her life to find peace and express it through her writing. Key to her healing is her need to articulate her memories publicly, to provide a testimonial to her own life.

Yet Campbell's sense of her "self" and her story is not static. When she states that "like me the land had changed", the passage above encapsulates the shifting versions of Campbell as a child, a woman returning to a home no longer there, an author searching within, a Halfbreed woman. She suggests that she will have more to say as she ages, that this isn't her final word on her own story.

I'd like to suggest that fireweed works as a metaphor for First Nations autobiography because it can be compared to current ideas about the "self." Fireweed is not only beautiful after times of ordeal but also can be used in many forms: as a fresh or cooked vegetable, a tobacco substitute, a medicinal tea; the stem of the fireweed, in the spring, is full of syrup that can be eaten or used by bees to make fireweed honey, while the stem peeling can be dried and used as twine. Also, fireweed contains a potent anti-inflammatory agent that traditionally has been used to treat infection. (Marles et al 211-212)

Linda Marie Brooks, editor of *Alternative Identities: The Self in Literature, History, Theory,* describes the current "multicultural project of replacing the static, unified self of traditional views with a notion of personal identity as evolving and multifaceted." (4)

It is in autobiographical writings, then, that First Nations authors can accomplish these three objectives: 1. to write out experiences under imperialism and colonialism, 2. to author testimonies of survival, and 3. to articulate the existence of an ever-changing self. Fighting against stereotypes of Indians in Canada, Indigenous authors write about the anxiety over identity that has become a marker of Canadian Native Literature.

I've chosen the metaphor of fireweed also because it quite serendipitously appears in two works of autobiographical fiction that illustrate this anxiety. Shirley Sterling's *My Name is Seepeetza* and Tomson Highway's *Kiss of the Fur Queen* both use fireweed to signify the complex, evolving state of flux their characters must live in, both beautiful and horrifying, with resonance to Sterling and Highway's own childhoods. For example, Sterling, now a professor at UBC, calls herself Seepeetza, the name given to her by her father, with students and colleagues. Yet in Sterling's novel, the fictional main character, Martha Stone has an Indian name, Seepeetza, which she is also called by her family. On the book cover, there is a picture of Sterling with two other Native girls, dressed up in Irish costume presumably after they danced, as the fictional Martha Stone does, at various provincial competitions. On the back there is another one of her, looking a little older with a suitcase in one hand, her eyes shyly closed. Is it Martha Stone, disguised as Shirley Sterling, or Sterling posing as Martha Stone?

Tomson Highway also bears a striking resemblance to his main character, Champion-Jeremiah Okimasis. Both are accomplished pianists and subsequently successful playwrights. Highway has a brother, Rene, who like Jeremiah's brother, Gabriel, was an accomplished dancer before his death to AIDS. The hardcover first edition of Highway's book is a stunning photo of a man and a dogsled team, dwarfed by the expanse of tundra, with a picture of Rene Highway, posed as Gabriel Okimasis might be, mid-air, mid-dance, mid-flight. There's something intimate yet strangely distancing about this gesture, of sharing personal portraits under the guise of fiction. We look at the pictures and think we recognize the characters, yet really, how can we know who they are?

As autobiographical fiction Sterling and Highway's works are the fireweed flowers growing in the burned dirt. The two characters, Seepeetza-Martha and Champion-Jeremiah, are fireweed, too, in its many forms, as they cover the ground between one world and the other, at times cut down and always full of possibilities.

The state of flux in which Seepeetza-Martha and Champion-Jeremiah have to exist is the result of their being defined as "Other." While cataloguing a "brief contemporary history of the binary", Timothy B. Powell discusses how in the mid 1980's scholars began to revolt against Eurocentrism and consequently felt the restrictions of the Self/Other binary:

> The critical penchant for identifying cultures as "Other" blurred meaningful historical and social distinctions between these unique forms of ethnic identity and, even more importantly, this binary critical framework implicitly relied on the very Eurocentric model that it was attacking - reducing these complex forms of cultural identity to being simply an "odd metaphorical negation of the European." (3)

In other words, there is nowhere to go when you are identified as "Other". You are defined, not in your own terms but as the opposite of what you are not. According to Powell, "a new generation of scholarship focused on exploring cultural identity in isolation ... searching to recover 'authentic' historical voices that would reveal a racial past that had been 'lost,'..create[ing] bitter academic battles about who would occupy the newly formed centre or even who had the right to speak" (4). While the identity politics of the 1990's simmered, scholars eventually turned their attention to a more multicultural framework that implied that one could

> reconstruct cultural identity in the midst of a *multiplicity* of cultures, in a theoretical matrix where there are no centres and no margins - a critical paradigm that will allow scholars to study the polyvalent nature of lived cultural identity. (5)

It would be possible to argue credibly that Seepeetza-Martha and Champion-Jeremiah are, because of their ethnic identity, oppressed by the dominant culture. In other words, they are red and the culture is white and therefore they are subjected to strange and elaborate systems of education to strip them of their Native culture and assimilate them into white society. But this binary form of analysis is inadequate to reveal the contradictions Martha and Jeremiah must live with, the "polyvalent nature" of their "lived cultural identity."

I compare these two works because both are in that blurred category I call autobiographical fiction; also they are united by many themes, not coincidentally because both deal with

Native children enduring lives mostly separated from parents, forced to grow up at residential schools. There is the inevitable recount of the first day of school, with the trauma of the haircut and the rejection of their early childhood names. And in both texts, there is the image of fireweed.

In the last chapter of *My Name is Seepeetza,* Martha and her family go on one last day trip before another school year begins. They go straight up the side of the mountain and find "thousands of purply-pink flowers all together in the tall grass along the creek. We stopped and looked at it for awhile because it was so pretty. 'Fireweed,' said Dad." (124) As Seepeetza decides to complete her year-long journal, she decides to store the diary in her father's old violin case and ask her maternal grandmother, Yay-yah, to make a buckskin cover for it "and bead fireweed flowers on it." (126) It is a satisfying image of beauty, although a deceiving one. Having read the heartbreaks and secret thoughts of a lyrical child, on the verge of womanhood, we the readers want to carefully bind and preserve these words. We want to decorate them with something not from her school yard but from the mountains, that reminds her (and us) not of her teachers but of her people and her own beauty. In fact, I found that I was lulled by the narrator's honest and charming young voice, and almost overlooked the darker themes. So much of the novel is about Seepeetza's fears, her impulse for self-destruction, her alienation and loneliness.

The novel is a chilling indictment of the residential school system, with a seemingly simple binary division of BAD SCHOOL versus GOOD HOME. But Seepeetza's relationship to her community and her family is complicated. For instance, Seepeetza is her "Indian name", given to her by her father, after "an old lady who died a long time ago." (77) At the Kalamak Indian Residential School, she is forbidden to use it, "never to say that word again" (18) and forced to use her white name, Martha Stone, a name so unfamiliar to her that she has to hunt down her older sister, Dorothy, to find out what it is: "I said it over and over. Then I ran back and told Sister Maura. After that she gave me a number, which was 43 ... we had to chain stitch our numbers on all our school clothes." (19)

But it is a mistake to look at the title of the novel, *My Name is Seepeetza,* and read it as a rejection of her "White" name and an affirmation of her First Nation's identity; after all, Seepeetza means White Skin or Scared Hide. She considers it "a good name for me because I get scared of things, like devils." (77) She doesn't link this name with the fact that she looks white, although clearly this is significant to her identity. For example, while she is accepted in her immediate community, she still looks white enough that other Interior Salish children, most notably her childhood nemesis, Edna, can label her "Shamah" or "white." (29) And it gets more complicated. To state it simply, *My Name is Seepeetza* is about a red girl, who looks like she might be white, who because her status is Indian and therefore "officially red", is removed from her family (also officially red) to be educated, in effect, to be turned white. Added to this, her parents, also victimized by this process, are complicit in it. They refuse to teach Seepeetza or her siblings any of the six Indian languages that her father uses as a court interpreter. Of course, Seepeetza's parents are trying in earnest to ensure a happier future for their children. Seepeetza's mother had welts on her hands and arms throughout the few years she went to the residential school herself:

> That's why she didn't want us to learn Indian. When Mum and Dad want to talk without us understanding them, they speak Indian. It sounds soft and gentle, like the wind in the pines. (89)

Because of this, Seepeetza is robbed of the language of her mother, of her mother tongue, and the "Indian" her parents speak is a language of secrecy.

It was Seepeetza's great-grandmother, Quaslametko, who told Seepeetza's mother that she didn't want her grandchildren to go to school "because school would turn them into white people. They wouldn't be able to hunt or fish or make baskets or anything useful anymore." (30) And it is after the year-long testament to the meager rations, small praise, corporal punishment, and constant fear that Frank Stone, after admiring the fireweed and eating lunch, tells his children that their valley is getting crowded:

> People will be building houses all around the ranch. Ranching won't pay much any-more. You kids want to get

> yourselves an education. Get a job. That way you'll be okay. (125)

At the close of the novel Seepeetza is to be sent back to school, perhaps with a few more skills that maturity and respite might give her but also with similar problems of years' past. Instead of Sister Theo, who would clobber Martha when she misstepped during dance class, Sister Kerr awaits, as she did for Dorothy:

> "You Stones think you're so smart ... But I'm going to take you down a peg or two." (42)

It is not comforting that Seepeetza is securing her future by returning to the Kalamak Indian Residential School - K.I.R.S. for short (or Curse, as her brother Jimmy aptly refers to it). Nor is there consolation in her visits from Saint Joseph, who tells her that she needs to learn humility (as if her compliance to humiliation, punches and insults from the nuns and teachers isn't enough). But it is in her dream of St. Joseph that she realizes her deepest hope and simultaneously her deepest fear:

> I guess what I want most in the world is for someone to like me, to be my best friend. Nobody wants to be friends with someone who looks like a shamah. Even Cookie avoids me most of the time. I miss my mum. I miss her all the time. (85)

Seepeetza-Martha wants unconditional love and acceptance; she yearns for her mother and home. However it is "home," in the person of her cousin, Cookie, and the other Interior Salish girls, that rejects her. By definition, as "white" or "shamah," at home she is an outsider.

David T. Mitchell, in *Beyond the Binary*, provides a helpful definition of postcolonial writing, even if his article is about emigre works:

> The central tension is informed by a desire to look back on what has been "lost" in order to restore or regain one's place of origin. The impossibility of such a repossession, imaginative or otherwise, produces profound uncertainties about cultural belongingness and the artistic pursuit of "authentic expression".... The critique of culturally produced binaries that separate enunciative positions such as home/exile ... serves as

> the guiding impetus of the postcolonial writer's narrative explorations and calls into question those divisions as flawed and unnatural categories of contemporary cultures and identities that are always already hybrid cultural products. (165)

For Martha, what has been lost is her home, in the figure of her mother, whom she misses all the time. Knowing she cannot return permanently there, produces her anxiety about her cousin, Cookie, who "avoids her most of the time" (85), and about her sense of belonging. Seepeetza-Martha's plans to wrap her year-long journal in buckskin, beaded with fireweed flowers, is an attempt to affirm her authentic place in her community, first, by binding it with something from home, made from her grandmother's own hands and second, to decorate it in order to mediate the horror of the words of her father, who tells her that she needs to get an education, and therefore needs to accept the abuse and alienation meted out at school.

Fireweed plays a similarly ambiguous role in Tomson Highway's *Kiss of the Fur Queen*. It first appears in Gabriel's hand just as he is about to leave his parents and community for another year of residential school. He is almost fifteen and about to go to Winnipeg to join his older brother Jeremiah. His mother, Mariesis, knowing he is now old enough to legally quit school, does not want him to go:

> Wasn't that the drone of the airplane coming to take him away? Again? Hearing footsteps, she turned. Framed in a wash of golden light, Gabriel stood, twirling in one hand – pink, mauve, purple – a bloom of fireweed. How handsome he was! (110)

The image of Gabriel as a young man in flower is symbolized by the blooms in his hand. It is a pleasant image of a mother, recognizing the beauty of her almost grown son, the poetic prettiness of the fireweed:

> She pleads to him, "Quit school, my son," Mariesis said, trying her best to sound matter-of-fact. "Stay home with us." ... "I have to be with Jeremiah," replied Gabriel. "You have

> been away since you were five. You'll be fifteen next January. For Jeremiah, It's too late. But you, you're our youngest." (111)

Yet the reason why Gabriel feels more loyalty to Jeremiah than to his parents is not only because they sent him away to a place where he was sexually used by the priests. It is made clear in chapter ten where their parents' loyalties lie. Then the Okimasis brothers travel during summer holidays with their parents and two sisters over Mistik Lake when Gabriel sees a flicker of light:

> "Look, a fire!" he exclaimed softly.
>
> "Where?" asked Jeremiah, turning drowsily to look at Gabriel...
>
> The brothers looked with wonder at the distant glow ... Mariesis had seen such fires before. She had known this lake like an intimate friend, a relation, an enemy, a lover for nearly fifty years – such occurrences were not new to her. She merely kept her gaze straight ahead, as if nothing had happened. Abraham, too, was looking straight ahead ... "That's the island where Father Thibodeau's men caught Chachagathoo." It was their mother's voice, though as if someone else was giving expression to the words. "Don't look at it." (89, 90)

Told since childhood not to mention the name of Chachagathoo, this is the first time that the boys learn anything about her. Mariesis finally tells them that Chachagathoo had *machipoowamoowin*, or bad dream power. The instruction from their parents is clear. They are not to look at the light of that flame, they are not to mention Chachagathoo, they are to believe in the priest who in this case is Father Thibodeau.

When the boys speak to each other in English, a secret language from their parents, Gabriel asks if it is '*machipoowamoowin*' that Father Lafleur does to the boys at the residential school (91). Jeremiah's answer is chilling because it is accurate: "Even if we told them, [meaning their parents] they would side with Father Lafleur." (92) What hope do they have if their own mother, who knows the lake "like an intimate friend", never questions the truth of the things the priests have told her? Even at almost age fifteen, when Gabriel flies away to be at school with Jeremiah, Mariesis' last words are: "Tell Jeremiah if he misses

Holy Communion on Sundays, I'll never cook caribou *arababoo* for him again. Do you hear me?" (112)

In chapter fourteen, the Okimasis brothers, in Winnipeg, enter a large shopping mall that stands like a large Weetigo, the Cree cannibal, consuming people who eat and shop and are then shat out. When Gabriel goes alone to the bathroom he finds there a man:

> Standing there, transported by Gabriel Okimasis's cool beauty, holding in his hand a stalk of fireweed so pink, so mauve that Gabriel could not help but look and seeing, desire. For Ulysses' sirens had begun to sing "Love Me Tender" and the Cree Adonis could taste, upon the buds that lined his tongue, warm honey.

Just as the syrup of the fireweed can be sucked upon, so can the penis of the anonymous man. The semen is sweet on his tongue like "warm honey" but the image is arresting. This fourteen-year-old boy, the same who the day before was holding a fireweed flower in his hand while talking to his mother, is engaged in a random sex act in a public toilet in a shopping mall.

A few months later, mid-November, tired of his brother's constant piano practice, Gabriel, still fourteen until January, heads out late at night and ends up at "The Hell Hotel", on North Main. After a few beers he goes with another stranger to a dark passageway, where at the end a group of young men are raping a Cree woman. Seemingly undeterred, he and the stranger turn the corner where they begin to have sex:

> The cold November air was like a spike rammed through the hand – his feet floated above the earth – and he saw mauve and pink and purple of fireweed and he tasted, on the buds that lined his tongue, the essence of warm honey. (132)

There is a clear connection between this sexual experience and the games he used to play with the other children at the residential school, when they acted out the Stations of the Cross. Gabriel often played Jesus as the boys chanted around him: "Kill him! Kill Him! Nail the savage to the cross, hang him high, hang him dead!" (83) In one instance "Jeremiah and his nine-year-old soldiers hurriedly 'nailed' Gabriel to the cross, swung it up, and banged its base into a groundhog hole." (86) During his sexual encounter in the alleyway behind the Hell Hotel, it is the cold wind that "nails" his hand and orgasm that floats his feet "above the ground" and again there is the vision of the fireweed and the taste of "warm honey."

Of course the re-enactment of the Stations of the Cross is a game sanctioned by the priests, and one that has clear connection to the sexual abuse Gabriel endures as a small child at residential school:

> Gradually, Father Lafleur bent, closer and closer, until the crucifix that dangled from his neck came to rest on Gabriel's face. The subtly throbbing motion of the priest's upper body made the naked Jesus Christ - the silver of silver light, this fleshly Son of God so achingly beautiful - rub his body against the child's lips, over and over and over again. The pleasure in his centre welled so deep that he was about to open his mouth and swallow whole the living flesh - in his half-dream state, this man nailed to the cross was a living, breathing man, tasting like Gabriel's most favourite food, warm honey." (78-9)

The sacred act of communion, the eating of the flesh of Christ, mixed in with the act of oral sex, the unholy sexual abuse of the child, and the child's own attempt to make sense of the experience and the religion is horrifyingly blended in all its obscene multiplicities. Here it is the penis of Father Lafleur, whose name is French for flower, whose semen the young child, Gabriel, can only understand as honey.

Some chapters later, Jeremiah is in the most important piano competition of his life and Gabriel, now a professional dancer, misses Jeremiah's concert because he is flying off with his lover, Gregory. There is one last image of fireweed in the novel when Jeremiah plays his piece for the judges and imagines the airplane taking off and his brother leaving him. Then:

> Jeremiah played a northern Manitoba shorn of its Gabriel Okimasis, he played the loon cry, the wolves at nightfall, the aurora borealis in Mistik Lake; he played the wind through the pines, the purple of sunsets, the zigzag flight of a thousand white arctic terns, the fields of mauve-hued fireweed rising and falling like an exposed heart. (213)

Fireweed, here, is not a profane symbol but an achingly beautiful one of his love for and his sense of loss of his brother, mixed with the magnificence of the land they came from. The allusion is not diminished by its association with exploitative sexuality although, unlike its first mention in the text, when Gabriel, at fourteen, is with his mother, we cannot forget the other forms it takes in further passages.

Winning the competition but feeling alone, Jeremiah goes himself to the Hell Hotel on Main:

> Try as he might to will Gabriel into its smoke-obscured universe, [his image in the mirror] remained infuriatingly alone. Beyond it, across the room, drunken Indians as far as the eye could see. He had tried. Tried to change the meaning of his past, the roots of his hair, the colour of his skin, but he was one of them. What was he to do with Chopin? Open a conservatory on Eemanapiteepitat hill? (215)

Again David T. Mitchell's definition of postcolonial writing, fits the text and Jeremiah's experience. In the music competition, Jeremiah plays his and his brother's story, as Gabriel leaves him for Gregory and the world. Jeremiah's piano then soars over northern Manitoba, over Mistik Lake and across the same finish line that their father, Abraham Okimasis had crossed twenty years before; Abraham's race begins the novel, a race that culminates with the winning silver cup, a kiss from the Fur Queen, and a few days later, Jeremiah's conception. That attempt to "restore or regain one's place of origin", that Mitchell identifies, creates Jeremiah's "profound uncertainties about cultural belongingness." (165) Champion-Jeremiah knows he cannot become white but it seems to him, at this point in the narrative, that he cannot be both Indian and a classical pianist. Yet we, the readers, know that his identity, like the identity of author Tomson Highway, is in fact this "hybrid cultural product" that Mitchell describes. (165) It is only later on in the narrative that Jeremiah can allow different facets of himself to co-exist. In the words of Amanda Clear Sky: "'You are born an artist ... It's a responsibility, a duty; you can't run away from it.'" (259)

While Seepeetza is sometimes mistakenly identified as white, Jeremiah never has this problem. Yet even though he spends his early childhood with his people, living on the land, speaking his Aboriginal language fluently, all the time looking "Native," he feels distanced from traditional Aboriginal spirituality. It is not accurate to say that he is distanced from his own culture because his own culture is infused with Catholicism, that is itself distanced from traditional practices. Jeremiah has been taught by his parents to be suspicious and frightened of what existed before colonialism. When Amanda, as a teenager, slips a picture of a Pow Wow dancer into his locker at school, "Jeremiah recoil(s). There was something so ... pagan about the image, primitive - the word made his eyes sting - Satanic." (162) Later on, Amanda's grandmother Ann-Adele Ghostrider, talks to Jeremiah about the culture his northern people have lost. Jeremiah is skeptical:

> And what the hell was this tired old bag yattering on about anyway? What dances? What songs? "Kimoosoom Chimasoo"? [a profane nonsensical rhyme] "The Waldstein Sonata"? [a work by Beethoven]. (175)

Even in adulthood, when he works as a social worker, "after ten years of southern Manitoba Pow Wows ... they still made him feel like a German tourist." (242)

In an attempt to help Jeremiah, Gabriel invites him to dance at the Pow Wow but:

> Against all reason, Jeremiah was still frightened of this dance, this song, this drum, 'the heartbeat of our Mother, the Earth' as he had heard it said on more than one occasion. Like the door to a room off-limits to children, it still made his blood run cold. (243)

Soon after, Ann-Adele talks about Chachagathoo, describing her as the "last shaman in that part of the world, the last medicine woman, the last woman priest!" (247) As Ann-Adele talks about Chachagathoo's attempt to cure a man from the Weetigo and the interference of the priest that caused the sick man's death, a sound grew larger:

> Where was it coming from? The forest? Across the channel? The bowels of the earth? And what was it? More drumming?

> Or someone pounding at some great steel door, demanding it be opened? Gabriel was perplexed but Jeremiah knew. (246)

Jeremiah knows that the room "off-limits to children", the subject of which his parents would never speak, was about to be opened.

But it is not only the knowledge of Chachagathoo's power that Jeremiah needs but also the opening of another door. He begins to play piano again and eventually collaborates with Jeremiah and Amanda on plays, blending his education and his sense of being Cree:

> "Well," said Jeremiah [to Gabriel] cavalierly, "if James Joyce can do 'one day in the life of an Irishman in Dublin, 1903,' why can't I do 'one day in the life of a Cree man in Toronto, 1984'?" (277)

It is not until the review of the first play where a reviewer is confused by the image of the Weetigo dressed in a priest's cassock, that Gabriel tells Jeremiah that he "didn't say it loud enough" (285). At first Jeremiah does not understand. "Jeremiah tried to ask again. But, finally, his memory opened the padlocked doors" (285). Whereas Gabriel is fully conscious of the abuse he suffered, Jeremiah has locked it away in his memory. After this revelation, he begins to write plays full of Cree mythology, that as a child he never knew.

Finally, at the end of the book, both brothers and even their very Catholic mother are able to participate in Aboriginal traditions, unknown to them in childhood and shared with them by Ann-Adele Ghostrider. Gabriel is on his deathbed in hospital, sick with an AIDS-related illness, nearly devoured by the Weetigo. He is surrounded by his lover, as well as his mother, his brother and friends. Ann-Adele takes Mariesis' rosary out of her hands and substitutes an eagle feather. She burns the four sacred herbs, triggering the fire alarms; Jeremiah, fearless, stands up to the fire-fighters and hospital staff. Upon the last wishes of his brother and against the pleas of Mariesis, he ensures that there is no priest present. In the end the Fur Queen comes to escort him away.

This is the power of fireweed: first, to survive the ordeal; next, as you flourish in burnt soil not to forget the fire but inscribe within your own beauty the colours of the fire that testify to your survival and finally, to constantly assume further incarnations.

Both Shirley Sterling and Tomson Highway have had difficult childhoods because they are First Nations. Their Indian status made them legal wards of the state and they were compelled to attend residential school, where abuse was commonplace, not permitted to speak their Aboriginal language, and separated from their families. Instead of autobiography, Sterling and Highway write fiction infused by their own experiences, perhaps because they are able, as authors, to reconcile their own disparate experiences into an understandable fiction. Still, we are grateful to them because their autobiographical fiction, like other First Nations autobiography, is the beauty after destruction, the fireweed and the articulation of the colonization that was not only the agenda of their education but also woven through their home life. In both works Sterling and Highway are able to construct themselves as Native and simultaneously hybrid mixes of all the influences about them, internalizing the paradoxes that surround them: Seepeetza and Jeremiah carry about with them two names as well as the knowledge that their parents love them yet are complicit in sending them away; their teachers are supposed to guide them and yet hurt them; and the very things they choose to express their artistic selves, Seepeetza through her journal and Jeremiah through his piano, provoke keen discomfort. When Brother Reilly praises Martha's writing, "A golden feeling kept washing over [her]" (61). Yet she denies this when classmates ask what the teacher has told her: "I didn't want Edna finding out what he said to me about my writing. She'd twist my arm and ask me if I thought I was smart" (62). And in *Kiss of the Fur Queen*, in the middle of a riotous kitchen party in Wasaychigan Hills, Jeremiah asks Amanda:

> "Ever thought you were born on the wrong planet?" Jeremiah asked Amanda… "Into the wrong … era? The wrong … ," he laughed pathetically, "race? " … "I just couldn't figure it out. I mean, what the fuck are Indians doing playing … Chopin? " (257)

By stating that Seepeetza-Martha or Champion-Jeremiah have anxieties about their identity doesn't for one minute free them from the racism that oppresses them. They can not cross the colour line to become white. Even if Seepeetza is lighter skinned than her peers, it does not open the doors of the residential school to let her out. And even if Jeremiah can't understand how he can be a classical pianist and an Indian, he can't readily deny these two aspects of his identity (although he tries by quitting piano for many years).

Both characters, and many First Nations people in Canada can not easily regain their place of origin, because, as with Maria Campbell, home no longer exists or they have found another place to reside for a while. Both novels question what it means to be an Aboriginal person. For Jeremiah the question is "Can I be a classical pianist and still be an Indian?"; For Seepeetza, if she looks white, does that make her a shamah? In the last vignette at the school, before Seepeetza returns home for the summer, she has the chance to defend herself from girls, who accuse her of picking on Edna: "I curled my fists again and said, "She's the one who calls me shamah. I'm not. I'm a halfbreed." (100) It is her chance to lay claim to her First Nations identity, despite the seeming conflicts.

I know that as a Métis woman, with a Cree speaking mother from northern Saskatchewan and a German speaking father from Manitoba, growing up on Army and Air Force bases across Western Canada, I had little interest in searching out any Aboriginal or European aspects of my cultural identity; I just wanted to get as far away from home as possible. In university I reflected the assumptions that were around me, that if I wanted to read Great Books (I even attended a Great Books program), by definition these would be European. (Besides Maria Campbell and Pauline Johnson, I didn't know of any Native authors out there.)

I did feel a profound sense of alienation, never seeing any reflection or reference to my community in my education, but this reinforced my fear that Indians hadn't done anything worth studying and that Native people didn't go to university. If it weren't for my looks, which causes people to ask me my ethnicity, I wouldn't ever have mentioned my Cree roots. I majored in English and Liberal Arts, at Concordia University in Montreal, and decided, as I sat in my Feminist Literary Criticism class, that I was as far away from home as I could get. It was years before I recognized that my understanding of the world as stories, linked together, to read closely or mull over, as well as my love for literature, is the result of my mother's continual story-telling that infused my childhood and, I think, wired my brain.

In the last year of my B.A., in Montreal in the late 1980's, I attended an international women's conference at the University of Montreal. Participants had to use earphones to listen to translations of the scholarly papers, work that was already densely theoretical, and I almost fainted from the alienation. The anxiety I felt was palpable as I tried to understand why I was there. At that point I stumbled into a session of about a dozen poets, all First Nations women from across North America, who were giving readings of their work. Not only did I feel elation and relief, as though I was being rescued from suffocation by an oxygen tent, but I also felt a sense that I was "at home". For the first time ever in a university setting did I think, "yes, my mother would be comfortable here." I am still grateful to those poets and to the organizers of that session. It seemed to me then that I could be both an academic and a Métis woman, without contradiction.

Works Cited

Brooks, Linda Marie. "Alternative Identities: Stating the Problem." *Alternative Identities: The Self in Literature, History, Theory*. Ed. Linda Marie Brooks. New York, NY: Garland, 1995.

Brumble, H. David III. *American Indian Autobiography*. Berkeley, CA: of California, 1988.

Campbell, Maria. *Halfbreed*. 1973. Toronto, ON: McClelland and Stewart-Bantam, 1979.

Damm, Kateri. "Dispelling and Telling: Speaking Native Realities in Maria Campbell's *Halfbreed* and Beatrice Culleton's *In Search of April Raintree*." *Looking at the Words of our People: First Nations Analysis of Literature*. Ed. Jeannette Armstrong. Penticton: Theytus Books, 1993.

Krupat, Arnold. *For Those Who Come After: A Study of Native American Autobiography*. Berkeley, CA: of California, 1985.

Hoy, Helen. "Nothing but the Truth": Discursive Transparency in Beatrice Culleton" in *In Search of April Raintree, Critical Edition.* Ed. Cheryl Suzack. Winnipeg: Portage & Main, 1999. Littlechild, George. *This Land is my Land.* San Francisco, CA: Children's Book, 1993

Maracle, Lee. *Bobbi Lee: Indian Rebel.* Richmond, BC: LSM, 1975

Marles, Robin J. and Christina Clavells, Leslie Monteleone, Natalie Tays, Donna Burns. *Aboriginal Plant Use in Canada's Northwest Boreal Forest.* Vancouver: UBC Press, 2000.

Minde, Emma. *Their Example Showed Me the Way: A Cree Woman's Life Shaped by Two Cultures.* Eds. Freda Ahenekew & H.C. Wolfart. Edmonton, AB: of Alberta, 1997.

Mitchell, David T. "The Accent of 'Loss': Cultural Crossings as Context in Julia Alvarez's *How the Garcia Girls Lost Their Accents.*" *Beyond the Binary: Reconstructing Cultural Identity in a Multicultural Context.* Ed. Timothy B. Powell. New Jersey: Rutgers, 1999.

Powell, Timothy B. "Introduction: Re-Thinking Cultural Identity." *Beyond the Binary: Reconstructing Cultural Identity in a Multicultural Context.* Ed. Timothy B. Powell. New Jersey: Rutgers, 1999.

Silvera, Makeda, ed. *Fireworks: The Best of Fireweed.* Toronto, ON: Women's, 1986

Smith, Linda Tuhiwai. *Decolonizing Methodologies: Research and Indigenous Peoples.* New York, NY: St. Martin's, 1999

Sterling, Shirley. *My Name is Seepeetza.* 1992. Toronto, ON: Douglas & McIntyre, 2000.

Taylor, Drew Hayden. *Funny, You Don't Look Like One: Observations from a Blue-Eyed Ojibway.* Penticton, BC: Theytus,1998

Wiebe, Rudy and Yvonne Johnson. *Stolen Life: The Journey of a Cree Woman.*Toronto, ON: Alfred A. Knopf Canada, 1998.

Contributors

Anna Marie Sewell, Polish, Anishnaabe and Mi'gmaq by heritage, has a BA in Drama from the University of Alberta. After her participation in the Japan Exchange and Teaching Program in 1994, she studies Creative Writing at the En'owkin Centre, an Aboriginal arts college in Penticton, BC, in 1995. In 1998, she founded Big Sky Theatre, and after three years of lively adventures is looking forward to graduate studies and more new horizons. In 1999, Anna was honoured with the Prince and Princess Edward Prize in Aboriginal Literature.

David Brundage teaches at Athabasca University but also has a career as a creative writer. Nine of his plays have been produced in Edmonton and Vancouver, he has also published poetry in various journals including The *Fiddlehead*. Appearing with James Kwong and other musicians as the group *Confluence*, Brundage has performed at Edmonton's Myer Horowitz Theatre and other local venues. *Confluence* will be releasing their first CD of songs and poetry, *City of Champions*, in 2002. Recently, Brundage received an Alberta Playwright's Network grant to complete a script about a Cree woman and her fascination with William Shakespeare.

Jo-Ann Episkenew is the Academic Dean at the Saskatchewan Indian Federated College, University of Regina Campus.

Renate Eigenbrod has been teaching Canadian Aboriginal literatures at Lakehead University, Thunder Bay, since 1986, and will continue at Acadia in the fall of 2001. She gratefully acknowledges the support for her teaching and research on Aboriginal writing (which eventually led to a Ph.D. in this field) by the Aboriginal communities she became acquainted with - the Aboriginal students in her class, the Anishnaabe friends, writers, artists and community workers from Thunder Bay, and the adult students in the small communities of Northwest Ontario, particularly the Sandy Lake reserve.

Debra Dudek received her Ph.D. from the University of Saskatchewan and her MA from the University of Manitoba. Her main areas of interest are Canadian literature, Writing by Women, and feminist and postcolonial theory with particular emphasis on the body. Currently, she teaches in both the English Department and the Women's Studies Program at the University of Winnipeg.

Karen MacFarlane is an Assistant Professor in the Department of English at Mount Saint Vincent University in Halifax, Nova Scotia. She holds a Ph.D. in English from McGill University. Her areas of interest include Canadian literature, post-colonial literatures and theory, feminist literary theory and the popular adventure novel. She has published on Margaret Atwood, Margaret Laurence and imperialist adventure fiction; her current research projects include work on Lee Maracle, L.M. Montgomery and the idea of the "heterotopia" in Margaret Laurence.

Renée Hulan teaches Canadian literature at Saint Mary's University in Halifax, Nova Scotia. She is the editor of *Native North America: Critical and Cultural Perspectives* (ECW 1999) and the author of *Northern Experience and the Myths of Canadian Culture* (McGill-Queen's UP 2001).

Linda Warley teaches Canadian literature at the University of Waterloo, Ontario. Her research and teaching interests include autobiography and Native literature.

Jennifer Kelly lives with her partner and their two small children in Pincher Creek, Alberta. She teaches part-time at Red Crow Community College of the Kainai Nation, has developed a community based project to record Kainai stories of Residential School, is involved in cross-cultural/anti-racist activism with the communities of Pincher Creek and the Peigan Nation, and is revising her thesis for publication in 2002.

Sharron Proulx – Métis professor

Aruna Srivastava is an associate Professor of English at the University of Calgary. She teaches in the fields of postcolonial, minority and Aboriginal literatures and has a deep interest in and commitment to anti-racism in her community and academic work.

Emma LaRocque, a Plains Cree Métis originally from northeastern Alberta, is a writer, poet, historian, social and literary critic, and a professor in the Department of Native Studies, University of Manitoba. She is the author of *Defeathering the Indian* (1975), and she recently completed her doctoral dissertation which focuses on colonial misrepresentation in historiography and Aboriginal resistance literature.

Kristina Fagan is a member of the Labrador Métis Nation. She recently completed her Ph.D. in English at the University of Toronto, writing her dissertation on humour in Canadian Native literature. She is now an assistant professor of English at the University of Saskatchewan.

Jonathan Dewar is a SSHRC Doctoral Fellow in literature at the University of New Brunswick in Fredericton. His dissertation is an exploration of themes of connection to culture, authenticity, positionality, and imposture in contemporary Canadian Aboriginal literature and criticism, specifically the role of literature as a site of (re)connection for persons of mixed-blood heritage. He writes from his position as Heron-Wendat/Scottish/French Canadian.

Deanna Reder is working on her Ph.D. at the University of British Columbia (in English). Her research interests include First Nations autobiography and theories of the self and she has had extensive experience in community education and literacy. She is a Métis woman and is the mother of three sons.

Krista Ferguson is a Métis artist from Brandon, Manitoba, and a student in Fine Arts at Brandon University. Her main interests are painting and drawing human figures, although a good science background enables her to produce botanical drawings as well. She has exhibited in group shows in Brandon, and will soon exhibit in Winnipeg. She won first place in the annual Brandon University student exhibition of 2001. Krista did all the black and white fireweeds in the test of the book, as well as the colour front cover. The original, titled *Fireweed,* was done in chalk pastels and is 22″ x 18″.